ALSO BY ANNETTE INSDORF

François Truffaut

INDELIBLE SHADOWS

VINTAGE BOOKS
A DIVISION OF RANDOM HOUSE NEW YORK

ANNETTE INSDORF
INDELIBLE SHADOWS
FILM AND THE HOLOCAUST

FIRST VINTAGE BOOKS EDITION, June 1983
Copyright © 1983 by Annette Insdorf
All rights reserved under International and Pan-American
Copyright Conventions. Published in the United States by
Random House, Inc., New York, and simultaneously in
Canada by Random House of Canada Limited, Toronto.

Library of Congress Cataloging in Publication Data
Insdorf, Annette.
Indelible shadows.
Filmography: p.
Includes index.
1. Holocaust, Jewish (1939–1945), in motion pictures.
I. Title.
PN1995.9.H53157   1983   791.43′09′09358   82–48892
ISBN 0–394–71464–4 (pbk.)

Typography by J.K. Lambert
Manufactured in the United States of America

DEDICATED TO ANDRZEJ KORNHAUSER (1915–1981),
   hero of the Holocaust

AND TO THE MEMORY OF MY GRANDPARENTS,
   Juda Insdorf
   Rachel Insdorf
   Anna Weindling
   Emil Weindling

CONTENTS

PREFACE

Ever since I was a little girl, I have heard about "the camp," "Auschwitz," "*Lager,*" "Belsen"—words mysteriously connected with the number tattooed on my mother's arm. Throughout my adolescence, I never tried to know more: it embarrassed me when my mother got visibly emotional about painful memories of her experiences. When I was a graduate student at Yale, however, I saw the film *Night and Fog,* and, for the first time, I had an inkling of what my parents—among others—had endured. The film provided a shape for, and a handle on, abstract fears. It occurred to me that if I, the only child of Holocaust survivors, needed a film to frame the horror and thus give it meaning, what about others? How great a role are films playing in determining contemporary awareness of the Final Solution?

As my involvement with the cinema grew, I began writing a screenplay in 1979, based on my father's escape from a labor camp, and his hiding in the woods with Polish peasants. The more I struggled to reshape the true stories, the more I realized how difficult it is to make a film about this era. How do you show people being butchered? How much emotion is too much? How will viewers respond to light-hearted moments in the midst of suffering? I was caught between the conflicting demands of historical accuracy and artistic quality. As I sat in Paris movie houses and observed how other filmmakers had yielded to or had overcome such obstacles, I put the screenplay away, and decided to wait until I had more distance from the stories of my father and his heroic cousin—and until I had learned from what others had done on screen.

Perhaps Elie Wiesel's comments about Holocaust literature are applicable to film. In *A Jew Today,* he declares,

> there is no such thing as Holocaust literature—there cannot be. Auschwitz negates all literature as it negates all theories and doctrines; to lock it into a philosophy is to restrict it. To substitute words, any words, for it is to distort it. A Holocaust literature? The very term is a contradiction.[1]

And to substitute images? Can the camera succeed where the pen falters? These questions gave rise to the following pages, where the reader will find a descriptive voice yielding to a prescriptive one, and film scholarship tinged with moral concerns. I have decided to respect both tones, for the tension between them is inherent in the cinematic experience; surely the goal of the film critic (like that of the filmmaker) is to move as well as observe, to challenge as well as record, and to transform as well as perceive. Moreover, as Terrence Des Pres articulated at a "Teaching Holocaust Literature" session of the 1981 Modern Language Association conference, there is a moral imperative implicit in this subject, and a natural connection between consciousness and conscience.

I wish to acknowledge the inspiration and encouragement of Terrence Des Pres, as well as the kind assistance of my agent Georges Borchardt, Robert Bender, Harold Bloom, Norman Briski, Karen Cooper, Florence Favre Le Bret, Renee Furst, Claude Gauteur, Miriam Hansen, Bernard Henri-Lévy, John Hollander, John Hughes, Michael Insdorf, Stanley Kauffmann, Howard Lamar, Robert Liebman, Arnost Lustig, Peter Morley, Marcel Ophuls, Alan Parker, Alain Resnais, Jeannie Reynolds, Robert Seaver, Charles Silver, Francois Truffaut, Claude Vajda, Michael Webb, Elie Wiesel, Ken Wlaschin, John Wright, Dan Yakir.

I am grateful to the following for helping with photographs: Rick Bannerot, Carlos Clarens, Mary Corliss, Ira Deutchman, Francine Davidoff, Suzanne Fedak, Sally Fischer, Hamilton Fish, Robert Harris, Volker Hinz, Curt Kaufman, Donald Krim, Tom Luddy, Ruth Robbins, Alicia Springer, Elliot Tiber. And I thank my editors at the following publications, where some of the material in *Indelible Shadows* first appeared: *American Film, Cineaste,* the *International Journal of Political Education,* the Los Angeles *Times,* the New York *Times* (Arts and Leisure—Lawrence Van Gelder), *Newsday.*

I was able to write the book thanks to a Rockefeller Foundation Fellowship, supplemented by a grant from the A. Whitney Griswold Fund at Yale; the research was facilitated by Yale University's Summer Language Institute, which permitted me to develop and teach two courses on film and the Holocaust. Finally, I owe thanks to my students, and deepest gratitude to those who criticized and strengthened the manuscript—Cecile Insdorf, David Lapin, Edward Baron Turk, and my splendid editor Erroll McDonald.

INTRODUCTION

ilmmakers and film critics confronting the Holocaust face a basic task —finding an appropriate language for that which is mute or defies visualization. How do we lead a camera or pen to penetrate history and create art, as opposed to merely recording events? What are the formal as well as moral responsibilities if we are to understand and communicate the complexities of the Holocaust through its filmic representations? Such questions seem increasingly pressing, for the number of postwar films dealing with the Nazi era is steadily growing. I had seen at least sixty such films from around the world by 1980; since then, at least twenty more have been produced.

My point of departure is therefore the growing body of cinematic work— primarily fiction—that illuminates, distorts, confronts, or reduces the Holocaust. Rather than prove a thesis, I wish to explore the degree to which these films manifest artistic as well as moral integrity. The focus is on the cinema of the United States, France, Poland, Italy, and Germany,[2] because these countries have released the most significant, accessible, and available films about the Holocaust. Throughout Eastern Europe, fine films have treated the effects of World War II, but they are difficult to see in the United States. (Titles are included in the filmography.)

While it might have been easier to structure the book by chronology or nation, I have chosen a thematic approach because a number of central issues emerged from the films themselves:

1) the development of a suitable cinematic language for a unique and staggering subject. I contrast Hollywood's realism and melodramatic conventions with the tense styles and dialectical montage of many European films, as well as present notable American exceptions. This section includes discussion of the savage satire in black comedies about the Holocaust;

2) narrative strategies such as the Jew as child; the Jew as wealthy, attractive, and assimilated; characters in hiding whose survival depends on performance; families doomed by legacies of guilt;

3) responses to Nazi atrocity, from political resistance to individual transformations of identity, and to the guilt-ridden questions posed by contemporary German films;

4) a new form—neither documentary nor fiction—that shapes documentary material through a personal voice. Here, attention is paid to the films made by survivors, their children, and especially to the works of Marcel Ophuls.

A major question throughout *Indelible Shadows* is how certain cinematic devices express or evade the moral issues inherent in the subject. For example, how is Alain Resnais's tracking camera in *Night and Fog* involved in moral investigation? In what ways does editing not only shape but embody the very

The Vilner Troupe from *Image Before My Eyes,* **directed by Josh Waletzky.** CINEMA 5

content of *The Pawnbroker* or *The Memory of Justice?* And to what degree can montage be manipulative? On a national scale, what change in attitude, if any, is implied by the sudden surge in the early seventies of French films dealing with deportation and collaboration? What about the increasing number of German films that are finally turning their lenses onto the Nazi era? Whether the film is a dark comedy like Ernst Lubitsch's *To Be or Not to Be* or an enlightening drama like Andrzej Munk's *Passenger,* these works suggest both the possibilities and limitations of non-documentary approaches to World War II, especially the ghetto and concentration camp experience.

The term "Holocaust" requires definition, for popular usage has particularized it from a general idea of disaster to the brutal and massive devastation practiced by the Nazis during World War II. I have chosen to use the word in this latter sense, and more precisely to refer to the genocide of European Jewry. For unlike their fellow victims of the Nazis—such as political opponents, Gypsies, and homosexuals—Jews were stripped not only of life and freedom, but of an entire culture that flourished throughout Eastern Europe in the early thirties. As chronicled in Josh Waletzky's superb documentary, *Image Before My Eyes* (1980), Polish-Jewish civilization was highly developed between the wars and included experimental education (a Montessori school in Vilna), progressive politics (the *Bund,* a Jewish Socialist party), and ripe artistic movements (Yiddish writers' groups like *Di Khalyastre*). The Nazis' avowed intention was not merely to annihilate the Jews, but to wipe their traces from history, and to destroy the very notion that a Jew was a human being. Even within the concentration camps, the Nazis developed a hierarchy among inmates: political prisoners were enemies, but Jews were insects. As Hitler declared, "anti-Semitism is a form of de-lousing . . . a matter of sanitation." Among the female inmates in Auschwitz, for instance, only the Jewish women's heads were shaved.

One of the dangers inherent in my argument, however, is the assumption that the Holocaust "belongs" to—or is the domain of—one set of victims more than another. Does the Holocaust belong to the survivors? To those who were killed during World War II? To those who died primarily in concentration camps or ghettos? To the Jews who were the main targets of the Nazis? To all Jews today? Some individuals claim the Holocaust as a personal tragedy. Many Jews claim it as a religious one. And then there are those who had no direct experience with the Holocaust but feel transformed by learning of its cruelty and mass indifference—as well as of resistance and survival.

And to whom do the dead "belong"? The ending of *Just a Gigolo* (1979), an otherwise negligible British film, presents a chilling image of appropriation: a bumbling young man (David Bowie) with no interest in politics is accidentally killed in a street fight between a Nazi group and its adversaries. The Nazi leader (David Hemmings, who also directed the film) takes the corpse, dresses it in the brown-shirted uniform of the SA, and has the young "hero" displayed and buried as a Nazi. How many of the dead are likewise unable to defend themselves from the post-factum appropriation of groups who claim the Holocaust as theirs?

The Holocaust is often exploited by those who simply have access to the media. The only versions of Nazi persecution that we see in film are the few that have made it to the screen, and often this is less a question of choice, quality, or logic than of chance: the commercial exigencies of film make it a dubious form for communicating the truth of World War II, given box-office dependence on sex, violence, a simple plot, easy laughs, and so on. Nevertheless, it is primarily through motion pictures that the mass audience knows—and will continue to learn—about the Nazi era and its victims. Whenever I show *Night and Fog* in my courses, students are shocked and profoundly moved, for it is generally their first encounter with the palpable images of Auschwitz.

The cinema thus fulfills the function articulated by film theorist Siegfried Kracauer more than twenty years ago. In his *Theory of Film: The Redemption of Physical Reality,* the morally vigorous German critic recounted the myth of the Gorgon Medusa,

whose face, with its huge teeth and protruding tongue, was so horrible that the sheer sight of it turned men and beasts into stone. When Athena instigated Perseus to slay the monster, she therefore warned him never to look at the face itself but only at its mirror reflection in the polished shield she had given him. Following her advice, Perseus cut off Medusa's head with the sickle which Hermes had contributed to his equipment.

The moral of the myth is, of course, that we do not, and cannot, see actual horrors because they paralyze us with blinding fear; and that we shall know what they look like only by watching images of them which reproduce their true appearance . . . the reflection of happenings which would petrify us were we to encounter them in real life. The film screen is Athena's polished shield.[3]

Kracauer's analogy is particularly apt for films that show or reconstruct scenes of ghettos, deportation, and extermination. However, his argument includes the belief that "these images have nothing in common with the artist's imagina-

tive rendering of an unseen dread but are in the nature of mirror reflections."
To merely show the savage surfaces of Auschwitz might not lead to much
beyond a numbing of response. One of the purposes of this book is to see how
filmmakers apply their art in shaping history into a heightened form of communication.

Kracauer understood "that the images on the shield or screen are a means
to an end; they are to enable—or by extension, induce—the spectator to
behead the horror they mirror." But we are bound to raise the same question
as Kracauer: Do such films serve the purpose? His conclusion was that the
mirror reflections of horror are an end in themselves, beckoning the spectator

to take them in and thus incorporate into his memory the real face of things too dreadful
to be beheld in reality. In experiencing . . . the litter of tortured human bodies in the
films made of the Nazi concentration camps, we redeem horror from its invisibility
behind the veils of panic and imagination.

In fifty years, the average person will probably not be drawn to source
material like archival footage from the camps, or the Warsaw Ghetto diaries
of Emanuel Ringelblum or Janusz Korczak. Knowledge of the Holocaust
might be filtered through the fictions of the television program *Holocaust* and
William Styron's *Sophie's Choice*. This places a special burden on the
filmmaker who is trying to illuminate rather than exploit the Holocaust—and
on the film critic with a stake in historical truth. As Arthur Schlesinger, Jr.,
warned, "fiction films do live as much by cumulative dramatic convention as
they do by fidelity to fact, and addiction to stereotypes dilutes their value as
historical evidence."[4] Does this mean that more first-person accounts by survivors must be filmed before they die? Certainly, but even survivors' accounts
can provide only a segment of the truth: many of the most courageous victims
perished. Each individual story is a sorely needed (and often dramatically rich)
piece of the puzzle. Other pieces might never be found. For example, how
many of the six million Jews died not as passive victims but as active opponents
of the Third Reich?

Some of these questions require historical and theoretical analysis which
falls outside the scope of this book. The issue of anti-Semitism is a case in point:
it was not born with the Holocaust. As Bernard Henri-Lévy demonstrates in
The Testament of God, Jews have always constituted a threat to national
authority. Throughout history, they have embodied perpetual resistance to
oppression, from ancient Egypt to contemporary Russia. As thinkers ready to
transform governments and structures of life, many Jews represent subversion
—in the most resilient and constructive sense of the word. It is not hard to
understand why some ideologues of the Argentine military dictatorship singled
out three Jews in their verbal assault on Jacobo Timerman:

One of the most elaborate definitions went as follows: "Argentina has three main
enemies: Karl Marx, because he tried to destroy the Christian concept of society;
Sigmund Freud, because he tried to destroy the Christian concept of the family; and
Albert Einstein, because he tried to destroy the Christian concept of time and space."[5]

It is significant that this scene comes not from a German concentration camp but an Argentine prison in the 1970s.

It might appear facile and cheap to compare the destruction of European Jewry with other attempts at genocide; after all, there is no comparison for the rabid persecution of individuals who were a respected and assimilated part of European life, especially after it became strategically unsound for trains to transport concentration camp inmates rather than the soldiers and ammunition needed for battle. Nevertheless, the impulse behind Nazism—if not the massive scale of its realization—has been shared by other peoples and nations. This can take the form of synagogue bombings in Paris, marches in Skokie, or witch hunts in Argentina.

Consequently, the avowed purpose of this book is not merely an exercise in film criticism, but a grappling with the legacy of the Holocaust. As long as there are people like Professor Faurisson in France who proclaim in print that the gas chambers did not exist, there must be active resistance by those who know they did exist. The luxury of forgetfulness is not possible because the Holocaust is neither a closed chapter nor an isolated event. As Alain Resnais explained to me about his film *Night and Fog,* "the constant idea was to not make a monument to the dead, turned to the past. If this existed, it could happen again; it exists now in another form." I hope that the following pages result in insight and incitement, reflecting the conviction that films not only commemorate the dead but illuminate the price to be paid for unquestioned obedience to governmental authority. In recognizing our ability to identify with characters, whether Jewish, German, Kapo, or Communist, we move one step closer to guarding against that which permitted the Holocaust to develop —indifference. Perhaps the beam cast by film projectors can pierce the continuing willed blindness.

New York City
January 1983

PART I
FINDING AN APPROPRIATE LANGUAGE

The immensity of events calls
for restraint, even dryness, and this
is only fitting where words
do not suffice.
— Czeslaw Milosz, *Native Realm*

CHAPTER 1

THE HOLLYWOOD VERSION
OF THE HOLOCAUST

Few American films have confronted the darker realities of World War II—ghettos, occupation, deportation, concentration camps, collaboration, extermination. The Holocaust has been only touched upon in such Hollywood studio productions as *Exodus, Cabaret, Ship of Fools, Marathon Man, Julia, The Boys from Brazil,* and *Victory,* and brought to the fore in only a handful of postwar films like *Judgment at Nuremberg, The Diary of Anne Frank, Voyage of the Damned,* and—increasingly—movies made for television. When "Judgment at Nuremberg" was first presented as a teleplay on *Playhouse 90* in 1959, however, commerce clearly got in the way of authenticity: the sponsor of the show, the American Gas Association, objected to the use of the word "gas" in reference to the concentration camp death chambers. According to the producer Herbert Brodkin, the sponsor wanted it deleted; he refused; they got their way behind his back: "Although the program was televised live, CBS delayed its transmission for a few seconds, long enough for an engineer to bleep out the word gas each time it was mentioned."[1] The major difference between "telefilms" like *Holocaust* and *Playing for Time* and theatrically distributed features is the commercial interruptions to which the former is subject. In conception, style, and appeal to a mass audience, nevertheless, these *are* "Hollywood" films, simply made for a smaller screen. Moreover, in the cynically realistic appraisal of screenwriter Paddy Chayefsky,

NBC wanted to do *The War Against the Jews.* That's before they did *Holocaust.* I said the subject was simply too painful for me to write about. But if I had agreed to do it for television, I'd have had to make a soap opera of the whole thing. You'd have to get high emotional moments, regularly, because you have these damn ten-minute intervals all the time. You can never really accumulate the power; you have to capsulize a lot of emotion, and you have to overdramatize things. In fact, the word critics used on *Holocaust* was "trivialize," and in a sense that was an unfair criticism, even though accurate. Trivialization *is* television.[2]

Whether on a small or silver screen, there is perhaps nothing inherently wrong in an entertaining film set against the backdrop of World War II, like *Victory,* for example. But as we move further in time from the realities of Nazism and closer to comforting myths, many people shrug off the complexity of history to embrace the simplifications offered by films. It is consequently a premise of this study that filmmakers confronting the Holocaust must assume a special responsibility, commensurate with its gravity and enormity. Elie Wiesel told an interviewer, "Before I say the words, Auschwitz or Treblinka, there must be a space, a breathing space, a kind of zone of silence."[3] His fear that the Holocaust is becoming "a phenomenon of superficiality" is applicable to films.

The television program *Holocaust* (1978) heightened awareness of both the historical facts and the problems of how to dramatize them on film. This mini-series took Nazi atrocities out of the province of specialized study and made them a "prime-time" phenomenon—with both the benefits of exposure and the drawbacks of distortion. Its case illustrates the rewards and tendencies inherent in films made for mass audiences—from the power of sensitizing, to the danger of romanticizing and trivializing. Indeed, *Holocaust* must be appreciated for its stimulation of concern, both in America and Europe, but questioned for its manner of presentation—including commercials (for example, it packaged devastating gas chamber scenes into neat 15-minute segments separated by commercials for an air deodorizer and panty shields).

Deborah Norton (Marta)
and Michael Moriarty (Erik)
in *Holocaust.* LEARNING
CORPORATION OF AMERICA

Meryl Streep (Inga) and James Woods (Karl) in *Holocaust.*
LEARNING CORPORATION OF AMERICA

Holocaust was saddled with the dubious term, "docu-drama," which co-producer Herbert Brodkin now repudiates: "In my mind, what are called 'docu-dramas' don't exist. We like to take a real situation, then create a drama out of it."⁴ The introductory voice-over says, "It is only a story. But it really happened." *What* really happened? Not the story of the Weiss family, but the backdrop of events. The second "it" blurs the distinction between fact and fiction, as does the rest of the film. Directed by Marvin Chomsky from a teleplay by Gerald Green, *Holocaust* traces the victimization of the Weiss family—cultured Berlin Jews—by the Nazis, incarnated especially by Erik Dorf (Michael Moriarty). The Weiss family is uprooted, deported, and killed (with the exception of the youngest son Rudi) in scenes that depict the growth of Nazism, the Warsaw Ghetto Uprising, the "efficiency" of Nazi planning, Auschwitz, the partisans in the forest, the "model" camp Theresienstadt, and the departure of Rudi (Joseph Bottoms) for Palestine.

The ground-breaking telecast sparked a great deal of controversy in the United States; some critics and viewers praised the fine acting of Moriarty, Rosemary Harris, Fritz Weaver, Meryl Streep, James Woods, Tovah Feld-shuh, among a uniformly good cast, and the sensitizing effect it could have on mass audiences, while others decried the program for its lack of accuracy (a Jew keeping his suitcase in Auschwitz?!) and melodramatic contrivances. Rabbi Wolfe Kelman, for example, faulted *Holocaust* for distorting the image of the victims: most of those who perished were not cultured Berlin doctors, but ordinary Jews—shopkeepers, housewives, and day laborers as well as

Yiddish poets and Talmud scholars—he claimed in an "NBC Reports" program that followed the rebroadcast of *Holocaust* in September 1979. The program came up with some astounding statistics: 220 million people had seen *Holocaust,* and in West Germany alone, 15 million. The broadcast in West Germany on January 22, 23, 25, and 26, 1979, provoked passionate public response. Television station switchboards and newspapers were flooded with reactions attesting to the failure of general education and historians regarding Auschwitz. Many writers credited the program with destroying a taboo and creating a climate favorable to discussing the Holocaust at home, work, and school:

From now on German has been enriched by a new American word "Holocaust," which simultaneously covers the Jewish genocide, the tv movie and its personalized tragedy, and the emotional and political reactions it provoked. These five days of collective emotion seem to have permitted the younger generation to perceive the Auschwitz trauma and the Jews from a totally new perspective, which could be called "the pedagogy of the Holocaust."[5]

Nevertheless, critics of the telecast presented forceful arguments against its aesthetic—and by implication, ethical—shortcomings. Like Elie Wiesel in the New York *Times,* West German critics denounced the "soap opera" and its "kitschy music," inaccuracies, and sensationalism. As an article in *Der Spiegel* put it, "*Holocaust* as docu-drama blurs fact, trivializes events, and neither illuminates nor forces one to think about them."[6] Critics ultimately acknowledged—albeit grudgingly—that drama could have more emotional power than documentary, that trivialized information was better than none, and that the history of the Final Solution could be made accessible only through dramatic presentation: "The death of six million is beyond human comprehension, hence empathy, the death of six is not. . . . Finally, critics maintained that Germans had to experience the Holocaust emotionally, even if it was portrayed in Hollywood terms."[7]

More than three years later, the effects of the program are less palpable. Although an article in a 1979 issue of *Cahiers du Cinéma* claimed "that the fiction of *Holocaust* has more effect, *today* . . . than all the documentary material ever accumulated on the genocide of the Jews,"[8] time has taken its toll. In the opinion of German filmmaker Peter Lilienthal, "*Holocaust* was like a thriller, and the level of the reaction was on the level of the film: how long did it last?"[9] For the New York *Times* television critic John J. O'Connor, "the event demands intensity and a searing vision. NBC's 'Holocaust' can claim neither."[10]

Intensity does not necessarily mean sweeping drama: given the emotion inherent in the subject matter, perhaps the Holocaust requires restraint and a hushed voice—a whisper rather than a shout—as evidenced by the effective understatement of films like Lilienthal's *David* or Markus Imhoof's *The Boat Is Full.* Simplistic and emotionally manipulative, *Holocaust* is characteristic of American feature films on the subject. For example, *The Diary of Anne*

Frank and *Judgment at Nuremberg*—the former originally a hit play and the latter a television drama—depend on a confined theatrical setting, superfluous dialogue, star turns, classical editing (mainly with close-ups), and musical scores whose violins swell at dramatic moments. These studio productions essentially fit the bristling new material of the Holocaust into an old narrative form, thus allowing the viewer to leave the theater feeling complacent instead of concerned or disturbed. The fact that both films are in black and white gives them a stark quality—which is, however, undercut by their lush scores.

The *Diary of Anne Frank* (1959) was adapted by Frances Goodrich and Albert Hackett from their 1956 Pulitzer Prize–winning play, based on the published diary of a young victim of the death camps, and some brief location footage was shot of the Amsterdam house where she wrote it. Reality also enters by way of documentary footage of camp life. Nevertheless, the authenticity of the tale is compromised by Hollywood conventions of casting and scoring. The thirteen-year-old Anne is played by Millie Perkins who is clearly much older; when she dresses up, the thin, dark-haired actress bears a striking resemblance to Audrey Hepburn, one of the most popular female stars of the fifties. Peter, the boy on whom she has a crush, is played by Richard Beymer, a teen idol who later played the All-American lead in *West Side Story.* From the very start of the film—a postwar present tense that introduces a long flashback—the soundtrack plays an overly prominent role. Upon returning to

Millie Perkins (Anne) in *The Diary of Anne Frank.*
THE MUSEUM OF MODERN ART/FILM STILLS ARCHIVE

his home after the war, Mr. Frank (Joseph Schildkraut) finds and puts on a scarf, and the lush Alfred Newman musical score signals that this is *significant.* (The scarf will subsequently be revealed as a gift from Anne.) The same thing occurs when he is handed Anne's diary; and when Anne and Peter are about to kiss, the music again rises—a redundancy, considering the image. The soundtrack also dominates by means of Anne's voice-over narration, as well as through the punctuation of sirens and Allied bombings that symbolize the continuous danger outside the attic. The only real "cinematic" element added to the play is superimposition, such as the sequence with the sneak thief at the safe on the second floor while at the same time the Jews remain immobile in the attic above. This spatial layering within a fixed frame is an effective device for stressing their claustrophobic life.

Judgment at Nuremberg, directed by Stanley Kramer in 1961, begins with more cinematic élan: an iris shot of a swastika opens up to reveal that the symbol is on a monument. During the credits, we hear a Nazi marching song; the swastika suddenly blows up; and a hand-held camera leads us through a hazy dissolve into ruins. We read "Nuremberg, Germany, 1948" before meeting the crusty American judge Dan Haywood (Spencer Tracy) who has come out of retirement in Maine to pass judgment on four Nazi war criminals. Most of the film is devoted to the tense trials, which are orchestrated mainly by the raging American prosecutor Colonel Tad Lawson (Richard Widmark) and the equally excitable German defense lawyer Hans Rolfe (Maximilian Schell). Their key witnesses are Rudolf Petersen (Montgomery Clift), a nervous young man who was sterilized by the Nazis for political reasons (Rolfe tries to justify the sterilization on the grounds that Petersen is feeble-minded), and Irene Hoffman (Judy Garland), who must be coaxed to testify about a case of "racial pollution." Finally, the most important defendant—the German scholar and jurist Ernst Janning (Burt Lancaster)—breaks his silence. Respected by Judge Dan Haywood for his earlier writings on jurisprudence, Janning now bitterly explains that in a period of indignity, fear, and hunger, Hitler had returned to Germans their pride. "I am aware!" he yells. "Were we deaf? Blind? If we didn't know, it's because we didn't want to know."

Rolfe's trenchant rejoinder is that if Janning is guilty, as he himself insists, then everyone is guilty: the Vatican, Churchill who indirectly praised Hitler in 1938, American industrialists who helped Hitler rebuild his armaments, and so on. The American judge finally indicts the men in the dock because even if many more people are guilty, these four individuals *were* responsible for their actions. "If these murderers were monsters, this event would have no more moral significance than an earthquake"; on the contrary, he warns the court, "How easily it can happen." After the four men receive sentences of life imprisonment, Rolfe wagers with Judge Haywood (who refuses to accept the bet) that the sentenced men will be free in five years. The prescient cynic's prediction is fulfilled, for the closing title informs us that not one of the 99 defendants sentenced in Nuremberg is still serving time.

This film raises central issues of responsibility—individual, national, and universal—but almost exclusively through dialogue. The self-conscious opening and frequent visual flourishes do not seem anchored in any conception of a unified cinematic style. Perhaps Stanley Kramer thought he was making the

Maximilian Schell (Rolfe) and Richard Widmark (Lawson) in *Judgment at Nuremberg*.
MUSEUM OF MODERN ART/FILM STILLS ARCHIVE

film less theatrical by panning 360 degrees around a speaker like Lawson, or zooming into a tight close-up for emphasis; however, both of these techniques seem gratuitous and manipulative. For example, when Lawson takes the stand as commander of the American troops who liberated the camps, he shows harrowing archival footage of the camps and inmates, of children tattooed for extermination. Rather than letting the images imprint themselves upon us, Lawson (and Kramer) hammer them in: Lawson's voice-over is a harangue, and Kramer intercuts reaction shots which force audience identification with the surrogates in the courtroom rather than a personal response. Here, much of the same footage that is used in *Night and Fog* is material for prosecution rather than illumination. And as in Fritz Lang's *Fury* (1936), projecting a film in the courtroom carries the self-conscious suggestion that film is equivalent to truth.

Judgment at Nuremberg is more successful in the scenes dramatizing personal relations, relying as it does on the casting of recognizable stars. Some are used for their suggestion of integrity (Tracy, Lancaster, Garland), and the relationship between Haywood and Janning resembles that of Rauffenstein and Boeldieu in *Grand Illusion,* Jean Renoir's classic film about World War I. These men are bound by a code that cuts across national boundaries; their commitment to justice leads to a parallel situation in which the man in charge (Rauffenstein/Haywood) must destroy the other (Boeldieu/Janning), who understands and accepts his fate. On the other hand, Montgomery Clift and Marlene Dietrich connote the dubious psychological or moral states of their own film personas: for example, when the song "Lili Marleen" accompanies Haywood's walk with this German woman, her identity resonates beyond the frame. Dietrich's German accent rings true, whereas Hollywood's traditional neglect of language differences mars other parts of the film. At the beginning of *Judgment at Nuremberg,* there is a realistic quality when Rolfe speaks German and we hear a simultaneous translation. But after a zoom-in to a close-up, he suddenly breaks into English. Subsequently, he and Janning—two Germans—speak English between themselves! It is an accepted convention that an American film should be in English, but a strained one when we initially hear a major character speaking in his native language.

The histrionics of both Rolfe and Lawson are in keeping with their characters.[11] However, a voice of rage is not necessarily the best way to reach an audience; not unlike the violins that enter when Lawson convinces Irene Hoffman to testify, the sentimental tone betrays a fear that the material itself might not be sufficiently compelling. Some might argue that our numbed cinematic and moral senses demand a shout just to shake us out of lethargy. Nevertheless, the danger is that one could get so caught up in the emotion as to be incapable of reflecting on the message.

Otto Preminger's *Exodus* (1960) avoids this danger by presenting Auschwitz through a dispassionate verbal recollection, in the scene where the Irgun (Israeli Underground) members interrogate Dov Landau (Sal Mineo) before initiating him. The question-and-answer session about the gas chambers and ovens is powerful not because Dov shouts but because he finally remains silent: he cannot reveal "who dug the graves." His questioner (David Opatoshu) divines that Dov—who entered Auschwitz at the age of twelve—learned about dynamite as a *Sonderkommando,* digging mass graves. With these credentials, he is accepted. Auschwitz thus exists as a prelude to the Israeli struggle, and *Exodus* insists on the connection between Nazi and Arab anti-Semitism: the Grand Mufti's urbane emissary tells Taha (John Derek), the Arab friend of Ari (Paul Newman), that they must destroy the Jews. This emissary is a former Nazi, ready to train new storm troopers.

The Boys from Brazil (1978) is an entertaining thriller that raises some important questions of Nazi continuity, but never really explores them. Adapted from Ira Levin's novel, the film is directed by Franklin J. Schaffner for maximum suspense at the expense of verisimilitude. The rather contrived plot revolves around the attempts of Dr. Josef Mengele (Gregory Peck) and his Nazi network in South America to clone Adolf Hitler, and the efforts of Nazi-hunter Ezra Liebermann (Sir Laurence Olivier) to discover their scheme and stop them. Liebermann learns that Mengele managed to create and deposit around the world 94 little Adolf Hitlers (we see at least four incarnations, all played by Jeremy Black) through reproduction of the Führer's blood and skin samples. Mengele's group is to assassinate each of the 94 fathers, thus replicating Hitler's lack of a father during his adolescence. These two obsessive dreamers—the Chief Doctor of Auschwitz and the Jewish survivor clearly modeled after Simon Wiesenthal—finally confront each other at the home of one of

Mengele's victims. The sinister physician is killed by a pack of black dogs, and Liebermann subsequently destroys the list of thirteen-year-old Hitler clones still at large.

To its credit, *The Boys from Brazil* calls attention to contemporary indifference—an imprisoned Nazi guard (Uta Hagen) yells at Liebermann, "Thirty years: the world has forgotten. Nobody cares!"—and to the relatively untroubled existence led by Nazis in Paraguay and other countries equally hospitable to war criminals. We see the local military leaders bowing and scraping before Mengele at a party dotted with swastikas. The film also conveys a chilling sense of the impersonality of Nazi death-dealing: young "Bobby," one of the Hitler clones, sets the dogs onto or off visitors by calling out "Action!" and "Cut!" as if he were directing a film. And when he tells them to kill Mengele, the order is "Print"—appropriate terminology for the clone of a man who murdered by the "remote control" of barked orders.[12] There is also a striking shot that functions as a visual foreshadowing of the plot: when Liebermann visits the home of the first man murdered by Mengele's organization, he is greeted by a surly, dark-haired, blue-eyed boy. A mirror in the hall reflects—and multiplies—the boy's image, endlessly repeating itself into the heart of the frame (like the famous extended mirror image toward the end of *Citizen Kane*). When the plot reveals that there are dozens of little boys with exactly the same appearance, one is reminded of this shot's expressive construction.

Gregory Peck (Mengele), Jeremy Black (Bobby), and Sir Laurence Olivier (Liebermann) in *The Boys from Brazil.* MUSEUM OF MODERN ART/FILM STILLS ARCHIVE

Nevertheless, *The Boys from Brazil* is saddled with typical Hollywood conventions, including recognizable stars like James Mason playing Nazis. (And can we really believe that upstanding Gregory Peck with his Lincolnesque gravity is the man responsible for killing two and a half million prisoners in Auschwitz?) Moreover, for anyone who saw *Marathon Man,* in which Laurence Olivier portrayed a Nazi dentist on the rampage in New York City, his fine performance here as Liebermann suggests *too* great a versatility. Instead of delving into the suggestive Freudian theme of patricide as a prerequisite for Nazi control (as Visconti's *The Damned* had done), *The Boys from Brazil* opts for a rather evasive explanation: the threat is simply genetic implantation rather than a psychological potential for evil. At the end, Mengele is killed— a historical distortion that allows people to leave the theater with the complacent assumption that justice has been done. The fact remains that Mengele is probably still alive in South America. *The Boys from Brazil* substitutes a hokey plot—the clones are waiting to take over—for the real danger of legally untouchable Nazis. As Pauline Kael warned in her review of the film,

Nazism has become comic-book mythology, a consumer product. Movies like this aren't making the subject more important, they're making it a joke. They're cloning Hitler to death.[13]

The menace of Nazism is similarly reduced by the taut action entertainment values of *Victory* (1981). Crisply directed by John Huston, the film takes place in a World War II where Nazis are gentlemen and a POW camp is a soccer training school. With such popular figures as Sylvester Stallone and Brazilian champion Pelé in the leading roles, *Victory* seems closer to "Rocky Plays Ball with the Nazis" than to a realistic assessment of the relationship between the SS and captured Allies. As the film opens, Major von Steiner (Max von Sydow) notices that one of the officer prisoners is Colby (Michael Caine), an English athlete of former glory. They strike up a match between Colby's team and the Wehrmacht. Using his influence, the English officer manages to get more food and better clothing for his men and, as the idea snowballs into a propaganda stunt staged by the Nazis, to protect more prisoners. The single note of reality oc· ·s when Colby requests that the best East European players be transferred from labor camps to his barracks. The arrival of these athletes—now skeletal and stony figures—is sobering.

Stallone as Robert Hatch, the quintessential American bad-boy show-off, escapes (thanks to the efforts of the "escape committee" that the Nazis wink knowingly about). But his character, derived from the Bogart hero of the forties ("I ain't sticking my neck out for nobody" finally yielding to noble sacrifices), allows himself to be recaptured in order to help the French Resistance's escape plan for the entire team. Disbelief is truly suspended when the Nazis, instead of shooting Stallone, permit him to play goalkeeper in the big game. With some fancy footwork, the Allies win the match in Paris: the French crowd throbs "La Marseillaise" and storms the field—knocking down armed Nazi guards—to squire the players to safety. With this rosy last image of the mass overcoming (by sheer number and enthusiasm) its oppressors, *Victory*

Above, Soccer star Pelé (Luis) and below, Sylvester Stallone (Robert) and Michael Caine (Colby) in *Victory*. PARAMOUNT PICTURES

presents an ultimately pernicious illusion about Nazis, their prisoners, and the bravery of the average Frenchman.

Part of the problem is that the large budgets of American studio-made films permit a realistic reconstruction of period décor and costume, whether it be a stadium filled with thousands of people or the proper pleat on love-interest Carole Laure's skirt. Particularly for those who know little about the Holocaust, the apparent reality disguises the fairy-tale aspects of *Victory*. Furthermore, the film's opening image prepares the audience for a gritty reconstruction of suffering, rather than war reduced to a soccer game: a prisoner trying to escape at night through a barbed-wire fence is gunned down by the Nazis. This pre-credit sequence will quickly be forgotten by the film's makers, but only after having served its misleading purpose: to establish the authenticity of wartime imprisonment, German vigilance, omnipresent danger and pain . . . into which a contrived story will be inserted.

Ultimately, the benign Nazi—in a film that contains no contrasting image of a German soldier—is a distortion.[14] After all, this is not World War I about

Max von Sydow (Von Steiner) and Michael Caine (Colby) in *Victory*.
PARAMOUNT PICTURES

which *Grand Illusion* presented a comparable situation, the German aristocrat Rauffenstein and the French aristocrat Boeldieu who are gentlemen officers above and beyond national boundaries. In World War II, the Nazi officer was *not* simply defending his country on the battlefield; he was part of a machine that savagely persecuted and executed millions of innocent civilians. The most courageous thing Colby does in *Victory* is to ask Von Steiner for East European players. The German is somewhat embarrassed because the Reich does not recognize their countries; nevertheless, he agrees. One wonders what might have happened had Colby asked for a *Jewish* athlete.

Max von Sydow plays a similarly virtuous German in *Voyage of the Damned* (1976), which at least presents a range of German behavior. Directed by Stuart Rosenberg, this film is based on a wartime incident illustrating international indifference to the plight of 937 Jews who were permitted to leave Hamburg on May 13, 1939. Representing a broad sampling of class, profession, and situation, they board the SS *St. Louis* bound for Havana; Cuban officials refuse to accept the refugees; the good captain (Von Sydow) then assumes the burden of protecting his unwanted passengers. In a last-minute reprieve, the Jewish Agency arranges for Belgium, Holland, France, and England to take in these Jews. This ostensibly happy ending is qualified by end titles that recount the fate of the characters: "Over 600 of the 937 died in Nazi concentration camps."

Voyage of the Damned contrasts the noble German captain (who does *not* belong to the Nazi party) with the vicious purser (Helmut Griem); it also confronts the reality of concentration camps (from which two of the passengers were released, with shaved heads), corrupt bartering in which Jews were treated as a commodity, and crass blindness to their plight—even by the American government. As a Cuban official (Fernando Rey) puts it, "With elections coming up, Roosevelt will do what is politically expedient." Among the Jews as well, the casting is balanced so that some look more identifiably or aggressively Jewish (Sam Wanamaker, Ben Gazzara) and some less so (Faye Dunaway, Wendy Hiller, Julie Harris). But this very casting is problematic in the sense that *Voyage of the Damned* is primarily an "all-star" movie: everything takes place on the level of star turns and plot twists, rather than through cinematic expressiveness. Because there are so many noted actors playing virtually cameo roles, they emerge as types rather than as fully realized characters: there is the Whore With the Heart of Gold (Katharine Ross), the Jewish Aristocrat (Oskar Werner), the Slimy Cuban Official (Jose Ferrer), the Naïve Young Steward (Malcolm McDowell), the Cynical Businessman (Orson Welles), and so on. Thus the film has the same narrative strategy as *Judgment at Nuremberg* and *The Diary of Anne Frank:* a dramatic situation with stars shown in huge close-ups, nonstop dialogue, and a surging musical score. *Voyage of the Damned* is polished and suspenseful but lacks complexity, for while effectively presenting the material, it does little with it.[15]

More successful in this regard is *Playing for Time,* the controversial CBS-TV film starring Vanessa Redgrave as a Jewish musician in the orchestra of Auschwitz; it does not flinch from presenting the demeaning circumstances of

Auschwitz prisoners in *Playing for Time*.
STIGWOOD/YELLEN PRODUCTIONS

concentration camp life. *Playing for Time* was adapted by playwright Arthur Miller from Fania Fenelon's magnificent autobiographical account, and directed by Daniel Mann. By September 30, 1980, when the telefilm was first aired, CBS had learned from NBC's mistakes with *Holocaust:* "Because of the special nature of this presentation," announced a title, "CBS will only interrupt this drama four times." Within its first few minutes, *Playing for Time* re-creates unsavory conditions in the freight cars carrying prisoners to Auschwitz as Fania's young fan Marianne (Melanie Mayron) relieves herself into a pail, which then falls and causes those around her to cry out for air.

The women's arrival at Auschwitz is a signal for the hair-cutting and scalp-shaving reserved for Jewish prisoners. A finely edited scene conveys the situation with poetic compression: a close-up of Fania being shorn is crosscut with one of Marianne, both silent amid the excessively loud sound of scissors and faraway screams. Numbers are tattooed onto arms in close-up, while a long shot of smoke emerging from a building is explained by the brutal phrase, "They're cooking." The coexistence of debasement and transcendence at Auschwitz is presented through a montage of fire, smoke, and shoveling, accompanied by the voice-over of Fania comforting Marianne with a story about a princess. The authentic source of these scenes is heightened by tinted archival footage that punctuates the film throughout. Fact and fictional reconstruction are yoked when, for example, documentary images of Auschwitz are inserted into a scene of Fania's labor.

As a singer, Fania is taken into the women's orchestra, a relatively privileged domain where the women can hide inside their music. The Conductor, Alma Rosé (Jane Alexander), is a complex character because, although Jewish, she is also Gustav Mahler's niece. She feels superior to the players (and closer to the Nazis) because she is "an artist." Indeed, her harsh enforcement of discipline with the musicians—including slapping them—smacks of SS behavior. That Alma is a "special Jew" is evident since her hair has not been shorn. She plays their game and her music submissively, trying to ignore the reality of the camp; "I refuse to see!" she screams once at Fania. Moreover, when Alma is finally poisoned by the jealous Frau Schmidt (Viveca Lindfors), the monstrous Dr. Josef Mengele kisses her violin before placing it in the casket, and salutes her conductor's baton! There is equal complexity in the characterization of Frau Lagerführerin Mandel (Shirley Knight), who is attractive, prone to humane gestures (she puts boots on Fania), and clearly affectionate with a little Polish boy that she takes from a transport (and from his mother). Fania's deepest tears seem to flow when she sings for this woman after she has sacrificed the boy.

Fania specifies that Frau Mandel is "human" and "that's the problem." A figure of extreme integrity, Fania resists all the ideologies that are represented by various members of the orchestra. Whether the foil be Alma's artistic superiority, the Zionist's hyperbolic patriotism, or the Communist's barely articulated socialism, Fania transcends her fellow prisoners' beliefs. She is a defiant risk-taker: a half-Jew, she nevertheless challenges the Commandant (after her superb concert) with the statement that her father's name—and therefore her own—is really Goldstein. She refuses to join the orchestra unless they take Marianne too—an act of generosity for which her weak friend will hardly prove grateful when she becomes a Kapo. Fania's integrity is placed in relief when she spies Marianne obtaining food through giving sexual favors. There is a long pause after Marianne hands her a piece of sausage: will the hungry woman, who has been orchestrating a score all night, be able to swallow such food? The camera remains on Fania's face as she hesitates, smelling and licking the meat, and then slowly begins to chew it, her clouded eyes expressing the price she is paying. (Redgrave here conveys a poignant struggle of physical need and moral repugnance solely through the tension between the lower and upper regions of her face.)

Fania incarnates the spirit that holds the orchestra together, the spirit that Terrence Des Pres describes so accurately in his book, *The Survivor: An Anatomy of Life in the Death Camps:*

The survivor's experience is evidence that the need *to* help is as basic as the need *for* help, a fact which points to the radically social nature of life in extremity and explains an unexpected but very widespread activity among survivors.[16]

Fania warns Marianne that she must share at least a little of what she "earns" with the others, so that she won't become an animal. Refusing to judge anyone,

Fania insists on a standard of human dignity that abhors stealing or self-debasement. A similarly generous character is Elzbieta (Marisa Berenson), a Catholic Pole whose first act upon seeing the ravaged Fania is to wipe her filthy face clean with her own saliva. And Fania's "double" on a larger scale, inspiring and binding the inmates together, is the chief interpreter Mala (Maud Adams) who carries on resistance activities within Auschwitz. The scene in which she and her lover Edek are hanged after escaping and being captured is effective in its silence: as the women of Auschwitz pass the pathetically dangling bodies, they remove their scarves in speechless respect.

For the most part, *Playing for Time* succeeds courageously and admirably, with details that are corroborated in Wanda Jakubowska's definitive film about Auschwitz, *The Last Stop* (Poland, 1948). But the real Fania was five feet tall, and fresh out of her teens at the time she was taken to Auschwitz; her stamina and ability to tower over the others were thus even more remarkable when set alongside the sheer physical presence of an exceptionally tall, forty-three-year-old mature actress. One might therefore ask whether CBS was looking for some free publicity through controversy when it insisted on casting an outspoken supporter of the terrorist PLO as a Jewish concentration camp inmate —especially when she was physically a far cry from the real heroine, and when Fenelon publicly opposed the choice:

Playing for Time production photo. STIGWOOD/YELLEN PRODUCTIONS

Vanessa Redgrave is a very great actress . . . but casting her is for me a moral wrong because she is a fanatic. . . . I wanted Jane Fonda for the role. She has her political views, but she's not a fanatic. Or Liza Minnelli. She's small, she's full of life, she sings. Vanessa doesn't sing and dance, she doesn't have a sense of humor, and that is the one thing that saved me from death in the camp.[17]

Arthur Miller defended the casting by explaining that several actresses turned down the part because they were unwilling to shave their heads, "yet Miss Redgrave was so dedicated that she lost weight, inflicted needle scars on her scalp and tore at her flesh in the quest for dramatic verisimilitude."[18] Nevertheless, many viewers boycotted the telefilm.

CBS's presentation of John Hersey's *The Wall* on February 16, 1982, was riddled by more frequent commercial interruptions than *Playing for Time,* but *The Wall* (directed by Robert Markowitz) remains a compelling, well-acted, and reasonably accurate piece of TV drama. Like *Holocaust,* it focuses on a few individuals who personalize the extraordinary tale of the Warsaw Ghetto Uprising. Shot primarily in Poland (with the cooperation of Polish television in Warsaw and with a local crew), *The Wall* conveys an authenticity of place —despite the staginess of the freeze frames that end each episode—and also roots the events in history by printing the date as each segment begins.

The Wall opens with crowds of Polish Jews being deported, under the watchful eye of a Nazi film crew. Things are not yet hopeless in the Warsaw of October 1940: a prosperous and accommodating Jew like Mauritzi Apt (Eli Wallach) can still live normally with his family and entertain the prospects of buying their way out of the Ghetto. His daughter Rachel (Lisa Eichhorn) realizes that the time has come to organize the inhabitants when a Nazi soldier abruptly shoots an old Jew in the street. Others in the Ghetto, like the enterprising Berson (Tom Conti), merely try to survive, smuggle, and share their booty on a day-to-day basis. A month later, Apt buys false papers—but only for himself, thus abandoning his children, including Mordechai (Griffin Dunne) who is about to marry his fiancée (Christine Estabrook). By March 1941, "resettlement" of the Jews to the East is announced to the Jüdenrat (the Jewish leadership in the Warsaw Ghetto);[19] as Berson and Rachel learn, the trains being packed with thousands of people daily are bound for Treblinka, the death camp (actually shot on location at Auschwitz). Through a kind of visual shorthand that might not have worked before *Holocaust* and *Playing for Time,* shots of chimneys and smoke are used to suggest the burning of Jewish bodies.

By September 1942, things have worsened: a montage sequence moves briskly from roundup to gunshots, to trains filling with bodies, to arrival at Treblinka, to smoke. As mechanical cinematically as the events it portrays, this sequence acknowledges the impersonal horror in the background of the protagonists' actions. After Berson and Rachel build a new hiding place next to the oven of a bakery for the ever-diminishing group, Berson moves in and out of the Aryan sector to acquire arms. The Polish Underground makes excuses rather than offers of assistance, participating in the revolt only toward the end. The Jews launch their attack on German soldiers, using home-made bombs and the limited ammunition Berson has managed to buy. They succeed in temporarily driving the Nazi tanks out of the Ghetto. *The Wall* crosscuts these action scenes with a shot of a Nazi teletype machine constantly revising the date of the Ghetto's ultimate liquidation. Berson and Rachel finally acknowledge their love, as the group is forced into the sewers where they must hide while waiting for the Underground. Only a few manage to escape to join the partisans in the forest: Mordechai, his wife, Yitzhak (an excitable fighter who had earlier killed the couple's baby when it wouldn't stop crying as they hid in the sewer), and Rachel. In the struggle, Berson has been killed, but *The Wall* asks us to end on a more celebratory note of resistance: "The Uprising began April 19, 1943. A year later there were still Jews fighting."

The three-hour film traces Berson's crucial movement from a "close-up" to "long-shot" perspective: after acting only on an immediate level, he grows to understand the larger struggle and the need for organization. Primarily through this engaging character, we see a spectrum of characterizations: there are "bad" Poles (the hotel concierge who lets Berson escape only for a large sum) and "good" ones (Rachel Roberts as Berson's landlady), "bad" Jews (Apt and Stefan, the Jewish policeman who asks his father to volunteer for deportation to save his own skin), and simply weak ones (Rachel's vain sister and Berson's sickly wife). The larger question that remains inheres in the "docu-drama" format itself: the Nazis stage a restaurant scene for their propaganda cameras, forcing a few Jews to look as if they eat well in the Ghetto. A cut to the soup line where each inhabitant receives his meager cup provides a harsh contrast. This leaves us with the illusion that what the Nazis stage is "false," whereas what has been staged for us by director Markowitz is "real." Such reconstructions, however, are more real in terms of melodramatic convention than in historical fact.

John Toland, author of *Adolf Hitler*, called attention to distortions in the film:

Because the Polish government provided the principal settings, along with thousands of extras and some vintage World War II tanks, the producers of *The Wall* had to make certain compromises with the facts: the number of Nazi casualties in the battle scenes, for instance, is exaggerated, while the fact that few Poles at the time of the Warsaw uprising actively resisted Nazi persecution of the Jews has been conspicuously deleted. What's important, though, is that *The Wall* has managed to retain the surge and spirit of the novel by adhering to its own compellingly drawn approximation of the truth.[20]

That the Americans were careful with Polish interests should come as no surprise: the cautiousness of the American film and television industry is also reflected by the fact that almost all its movies dealing with the Holocaust are adapted from another medium: successful plays *(The Diary of Anne Frank, Cabaret)* or novels *(Exodus, Ship of Fools, Marathon Man, Julia, The Boys from Brazil, Sophie's Choice)*. *The Wall* was a celebrated novel by John Hersey before it became a Broadway play by Millard Lampell—who then went on to write the television movie. It seems, therefore, that Hollywood will take a chance on films about the Holocaust only after the material has proven its commercial potential in another medium. And even then, the films merely touch upon the historical horror rather than grasp it. The American cinema often uses Nazi images to evoke instant terror or tears, whereas many European films use the cinematic medium as an instrument to probe responsibility. Perhaps the cinema of a country that has never experienced occupation cannot plumb the depths of the Holocaust experience. Or—more likely—perhaps the commercial imperatives of Hollywood and the networks tend to pre-empt the possibilities for truthful representation.

Although *Sophie's Choice* (1982) was released after this book was completed, the film merits mention for its admirable treatment of the Holocaust material. Neither the film—intelligently directed and scripted by Alan J. Pakula—nor William Styron's verbally lush novel purport to be about the Holocaust; indeed, the story of Sophie is told—and mediated—by the obtrusive narration of Stingo, an aspiring Southern writer played by Peter MacNicol (with the voice-over of Josef Sommer as the older Stingo). Nevertheless, this tale of the love affair between a Polish-Catholic survivor of Auschwitz (Meryl Streep) and Nathan, a volatile New York Jew (Kevin Kline), contains flashbacks to World War II that are gripping in their authenticity. Three major reasons for their quality are visual texture, respect for language, and restraint of camera and music. The harrowing sequences in Auschwitz and the ghetto are presented in a distancing sepia tone whose lack of vivid color graphically conveys life drained of vitality. Unlike the characters in most Hollywood films, these speak Polish or German in those scenes where such languages would have been spoken, and this dialogue is subtitled. Also, the camera and music are models of restraint or invisible narration. Each extended flashback is preceded and punctuated by an extreme close-up of Sophie—tremulous and slightly inebriated—reminding the viewer that it is her subjective version of the past that is being reenacted. Nestor Almendros's cinematography is smooth and unselfconscious, permitting Streep's face to become an exquisitely expressive landscape. Similarly, Marvin Hamlisch's score is used with subtlety: for example, in the climactic final scene of Stingo's return to the Brooklyn rooming house where he will say farewell to the lovers, a gentle melody on a flute counterpoints the dramatic tension.

One can, of course, raise questions about the premise of *Sophie's Choice:* the survivor for whom sympathy is elicited in fact helped her father type anti-Semitic speeches, is a seasoned liar, and happened to be beautiful and multilingual enough to live through Auschwitz—as opposed to a heroine who might have been Jewish or in the Resistance. And others have asked whether it is proper to use the Holocaust in the service of Stingo's coming of age. But to the degree that people who never had direct contact with the Holocaust *should* know about Nazi brutality as they grow into civilized beings, the flashbacks of *Sophie's Choice* succeed in suggesting some of Auschwitz's horror—for those who were there and those who were not.

CHAPTER 2

MEANINGFUL MONTAGE

F ilms that depict a character's memory of a horrific past—and that character's enslavement by it—can have more consistency and integrity than a movie that purports to show *the* past in an objective way. A fictional reconstruction of a concentration camp is not quite as "truthful" as one person's subjective memory of it, for the latter acknowledges the partiality of the recollection. Most effective are films like *The Pawnbroker,* which move us by alternating the present—marked by indifference to the Holocaust—with the past. This is a cinema of flashbacks: a filmic device that permits the visible, palpable past to surface into the present. Editing in this cinema is not merely continuity, or the smooth linear transition from one shot to the next; the rhythms and juxtapositions of the cutting can create varied effects upon the viewer, from heightened suspense to an awareness of contraries. The montage of such films as *The Pawnbroker, High Street, Night and Fog,* and *Les Violons du Bal* expresses the degree to which the relatively calm present is informed by the turbulent Holocaust.

The Pawnbroker is one of the rare "Hollywood" films (shot entirely in New York!) to take on the Holocaust and its legacy with both thematic and formal vigor. Directed in 1965 by Sidney Lumet, this chiseled black-and-white portrait of a survivor living in New York City is structured through sophisticated editing. Lumet and editor Ralph Rosenblum use montage as a complex visual analogue for mental processes. Although the story takes place in the present, it is punctuated by shots of memory—flash cuts that surface momentarily into the protagonist's thoughts, searing the present with the ineradicable brand of his concentration camp past.

The film begins with a fragment whose meaning will be revealed only midway through the story: in dreamlike slow motion, a young couple, their children, and grandparents relax in a pastoral scene that ends abruptly, yield-

Rod Steiger (Nazerman) in *The Pawnbroker.* THE LANDAU COMPANY

ing to a present tense of vulgar suburban life. The same man, Sol Nazerman (Rod Steiger), now much older, is being pestered by his sister-in-law and her teenage children. He drives back to his pawnshop on 116th Street, as subjective hand-held shots of lower Harlem identify the camera with his point of view. Nazerman's behavior with various desperate customers—ranging from fatigue to contempt—suggests power, until it becomes clear that Nazerman is as helpless vis-à-vis his black boss Rodriguez (Brock Peters) as his poor clients are before him.

Nazerman's assistant Jesús (Jaime Sanchez) is the opposite of his employer: an energetic young Hispanic, he wants to move up quickly in the world—as the exhilarating tracking shots of Jesús on ladders or sprinting through crowded streets embody—while Nazerman wants only to be left in peace. When the bitter Jew rejects Jesús' offers of interest and companionship, the offended youth succumbs to his buddies' plans to rob the store. Nazerman also refuses the friendly advances of a social worker, Miss Birchfield (Geraldine Fitzgerald), and spurns Tessie (Marketa Kimbrell), the woman with whom he has been living, especially when her father dies. This cruel indifference is rendered comprehensible only in flashbacks that show Nazerman's earlier brutalization at the hands of the Nazis. Through subliminal flash cuts that gradually lengthen into painful scenes, the linear narrative is thickened with the weight of the past.

The first return to World War II occurs when Nazerman walks away from his shop in the Harlem night. The sound of dogs barking triggers a bleached-out flash cut of dogs chasing a Jewish prisoner who is trying to scale a fence. Like a cinematic poem, the film alternates quick shots of the Harlem scene (a gang of kids beating up a black boy) with the camp locale, creating visual rhymes. With a shaved head and a Star of David on his uniform, Nazerman watches his friend die on the fence; his inability to take action extends into the present. The first flashback thus establishes Nazerman's essential relationship to his surroundings: a spectator who cannot relieve suffering, only observe, register, and perhaps absorb it.

The fact that the "prisoner" in the present is black sets up a second level of oppression in *The Pawnbroker*. While it is admittedly a facile distortion to posit a one-to-one analogy between the Harlem ghetto in 1965 and the camps of the early forties, Nazerman treats his predominantly black customers with the same disdain that characterized the Nazis' attitude toward Jews. He calls them "creatures," "scum," "rejects"—and his job is ultimately one of dis-possession. Indeed, the pawnbroker can be seen as a contemporary Kapo, controlling the poor clients who barter with him, but also controlled—and imprisoned—by his superiors. He must remain unmoved by the suffering of these "creatures" in order to survive, even as they relinquish their most personal possessions to him.

Furthermore, the shop with its bars and fences replicates the storerooms of the concentration camp. The second flashback fleshes out this connection as a pregnant young woman tries to pawn her ring. This touches off a close-up of hands against wire that grows into a slow tracking shot of rings being removed by SS men from a long line of trembling hands. Once again, Nazerman is powerless before a victim. This is also the case a few sequences later

Rod Steiger as Sol Nazerman in *The Pawnbroker.* Lighting externalizes Nazerman's imprisonment. THE LANDAU COMPANY

when a desperate hooker offers the pawnbroker her body along with her jewelry. "Look!" she repeats as she bares her breasts. "Look!" says the Nazi to the same man twenty-five years earlier, pointing to the young female prisoners. As the flash cuts lengthen, we see that one of the women being pointed at is Nazerman's wife Ruth (Linda Geiser), for the film's first pastoral shot suddenly reappears within the flashback. When Nazerman refuses to look, a soldier pushes his bald head through the glass, forcing him to see. In this film, one pays a price for vision: images are wounds that will not heal.

The violation Nazerman witnesses leads him not only to refuse the hooker, but then to declare to his boss that he won't accept money if it comes from a whorehouse. Rodriguez counters with the challenge, "Where do you think the money you're living on has been coming from?" Nazerman is verbally beaten into submission when the overbearing boss pushes him to accept his demands. The cinematic technique eloquently expresses Nazerman's fractured state of mind, for flash cuts are once again employed—but within the scene itself. That these men exist in different and unreconcilable worlds is shown by their inability to share the same frame: each taunting "Yes?" of Rodriguez results in a violent cut that assaults our eyes as well as Nazerman's ears. Moreover, the use of the flash cut, already associated with the Nazis, implies that Rodriguez is but a new incarnation of an old demon.

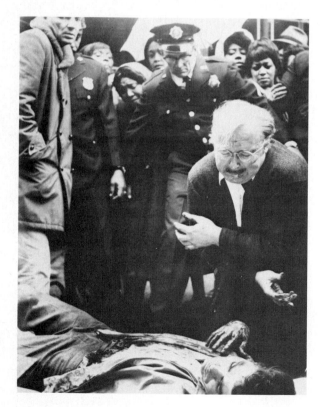

Nazerman over Jesús' dead body in *The Pawnbroker.*
MUSEUM OF MODERN ART/
FILM STILLS ARCHIVE

The film's predilection for quick cutting over pans or long takes underlines Nazerman's dissociation from people in general. His inability to touch or even see those around him is then developed in a flashback that begins in a subway car. From Nazerman's point of view, individuals stare at him blankly, until the crowded train becomes transformed into a freight car crammed with Jewish bodies on their way to misery and death. Once again, the memory sneaks up on Nazerman and is then unleashed. This residual image blinds Nazerman to the actual people in the subway train, encapsulating him within a world where he could still feel something, even if only pain. Nazerman is increasingly unhinged by these vivid ghosts, to the point that he vainly challenges Rodriguez to kill him. The next best thing is a return to the past through what is essentially the only *willed* flashback in the film. A pawned butterfly collection engenders the slow-motion scene with which *The Pawnbroker* opened, a flowing recollection of an idyllic moment. This tranquillity is shattered by the arrival of three German soldiers—just as, in the film's abrupt return to the present, the daydream is brutally interrupted by the entrance of three thieves. This parallel foreshadows that Nazerman will once again be forced to observe the murder of someone close to him: in this case, Jesús is accidentally shot while trying to save his employer. Numb and impotent, Nazerman can only open his mouth in a scream. No sound emerges.

The mute scream can be seen as the emblem of the Holocaust survivor, the witness of a horror so devastating that it cannot be told. The silent scream might also be the helpless reaction to continued anti-Semitism, as illustrated by the client who calls him a "money-grubbing kike." The intercuts of black neighbors staring indifferently from windows heighten the dissociation between Nazerman and a world that remains ignorant of his tale. Earlier in the film, one of the hooligans had asked him where he got the tattoo on his arm, but the pawnbroker could give no answer. How could he ever explain that this number was carved into his flesh to establish that he is no longer a human being but merely a statistic on its way to extermination? Subsequently, Jesús asks him if the number means he belongs to a secret society, and if so, what does one have to do to join. "Learn to walk on water," Nazerman cryptically replies.

Furthermore, Nazerman's soundless grimace expresses his essential isolation, as if acknowledging that a scream would not reach human ears anyway. *The Pawnbroker* supports this notion by presenting New York City as an urban jungle where people look at one another without seeing. Nazerman is not the only passerby who simply walks past the group of kids beating up a black boy; in the subway car, there is no communication among the passengers; and when he walks through the empty city at dawn, the pawnbroker is dwarfed by large, gray, impersonal structures.

In this dehumanized context, Nazerman's attempt to express his pain ultimately shows his inheritance of a Nazi concept: he wounds himself, rendering flesh a mere object. With his hand slowly descending onto the spike that holds pawn tickets, Nazerman turns his body into a receipt. Religious overtones aside, this excruciating shot conveys how Nazerman's need to feel can be realized only through physical pain. Here, the soundtrack insists on dissociation once more, for instead of a scream, we hear Quincy Jones's jazz score.

Nazerman's self-inflicted wound makes concrete one of the film's central themes: survivor guilt. As another survivor points out, he identifies with those who died; when Miss Birchfield asks Nazerman what happened twenty-five years ago, he answers, "I didn't die. Everything I loved was taken away from me and I did not die. There was nothing I could do. Nothing." Nazerman is caught not only between heartless exploiters and oppressed neighbors, but between the dead and the living, between exterminated Jews and manipulative blacks. As a Holocaust survivor, he carries the memory of his murdered family inside him, a living corpse unable to create a new life. By the end of the film, he is a broken pawn.

The narrative structure of *The Pawnbroker* is shared by *High Street* ("Rue Haute"), directed in 1976 by André Ernotte from a screenplay by Ernotte and Elliot Tiber. This Belgian film takes its tone from the continual utterance of its central character Mimi (Annie Cordy)—a scream of pain that never really coheres into meaning. Like Nazerman, Mimi is internally disfigured by an ineradicable memory: one night during World War II, her Jewish husband David (Claude Batelle) was taken away by the Nazis, and when she ran after him to the departing bus, their only child was accidentally killed. This information is conveyed in brief flashbacks that give form to Mimi's involuntary recollections. The camera thus becomes an interpreter of her cry, communicating visually that which she cannot articulate. Unlike Nazerman, however, Mimi is less a "survivor" than a "witness"—a non-Jew who was not personally victimized: Mimi's testimony does not indict Nazi cruelty as much as Belgian indifference.

Unlike the sweetly aggressive Jesús, who is sacrificed at the end of *The Pawnbroker,* the relatively innocent outsider in *High Street* is an arrogant, womanizing, overweight painter whose sole redeeming quality seems to be his compulsion to help Mimi. This American-Jewish expatriate, David Reinhardt, is played by singer-composer Mort Shuman (best known for his performance in *Jacques Brel Is Alive and Well*) with alternating stupor and frenzy. He arrives in contemporary Brussels for a gallery exhibition of his abstract art. When he continually notices Mimi shouting at every bus and verbally assaulting innocent bystanders, he becomes increasingly obsessed with her suffering. He tries to penetrate the solipsistic existence which she shares with a protective and sullen man (Burt Struys), but they resist his overtures. Haunted by her enormous eyes that have clearly seen too much, David paints this impenetrable woman until his exhibition consists solely of her image. The gallery opening —with its chic patrons who are simply curious to divine the model's identity —points to a chilling and perhaps self-referential problem: even "honest" art that conveys the horror born of the Holocaust can become merely a titillating diversion for bored, amoral consumers.

Their ultimate indifference to the source of Mimi's searing expression is consistent with responses in other scenes. Mimi tries to stop people from going into a church, screaming, "There's no God in there!" Embarrassed but nonplused, the good Christians enter. Mimi consequently sneaks into the church, climbs to a pulpit, and yells at the assemblage, "They did nothing!" The final

Burt Struys (The Man), Annie Cordy (Mimi), and Mort Shuman (David Reinhardt) in *High Street*. ELLIOT TIBER

flashback reveals that her cry refers to the neighbors—and the priest—who did not lift a hand against the Nazis who rounded up the Jews. Once David understands the root of Mimi's torment, he undergoes a transformation of identity and assumes her burden. Instead of painting on canvas, he finally pounds on glass, shouting obscenities at strangers in a bus. As he smacks the window of the vehicle, the screen becomes this window. It is therefore the audience that is meant to receive his blows on the other side of the glass. David —and the film—ultimately point an accusing finger at all of us, at our capacity for indifference.

Like the relatively sane characters in Ingmar Bergman films such as *Persona* and *Hour of the Wolf,* David succumbs to the "mad" figure: he is overtaken by the stronger personality that has recognized evil. The subjective hand-held shots at the end of *High Street* externalize his skewed perception, inherited from Mimi. Why should this egotistical American artist be subject to her influence? Perhaps the answer—and one of the keys to the film—can be found in her companion's claim that David wants to purge his *own* guilt by helping Mimi. What guilt? we may ask. That of being an affluent, assimilated, arrogant American Jew, spared by the accident of geography? Survivor guilt is indeed one of the central (if unstated) themes of *High Street,* beginning with this mysterious companion whom Mimi reviles even as he protects her. The last flashback, accompanied by the man's explanatory voice-over to David, contains numerous close-ups of a young German soldier who watched without

David tries to help Mimi in *High Street*.
ELLIOT TIBER

expression as Mimi's husband was led away by the armed men in black leather. "I couldn't forget her screams," he says to David—revealing that he is this German who returned after the war to make it up to her. It is clear enough that he has spent the past twenty years paying for his Nazi allegiance; less clear are David's reasons for such frenzied compassion—as well as Mimi's for never mentioning her child. The blocked memory of the boy being knocked down by the butt of a gun while she was blindly pummeling a soldier is revealed only through the companion's tale. The name Mimi cannot utter is the child's, and the pivotal relationship of the film substitutes David the son for David the husband. This also shifts the impulse of the film from victimization to guilt, and from being enslaved by a brutal past to struggling within and against an indifferent present.

Nevertheless, *High Street* is not as successful as *The Pawnbroker* in establishing a troubling actuality. Its secondary characters, such as the marginal types at the local bar, are predominantly benign, and there is little concrete arena for indictment. Whereas the flashbacks in *The Pawnbroker* connect Nazi behavior with its potential manifestations in New York City, Ernotte's montage simply expresses Mimi's inner hell. For her, a group of harmless children barging into the apartment touches off a disproportionately frightening replay of the Nazis in black leather coats bursting into her home thirty years earlier. Each passing bus becomes the vehicle that never brought her husband back. This is not to say that *High Street* is not effective in moving the viewer with

Mimi's harrowing tale; the flashbacks are indeed central to a film in which the heroine incarnates the persistence of memory. But the final image of the film reflects—and elicits—helpless anger, with an abrasive madman on one side, and not-altogether-guilty spectators on the other. Must the viewer extend the closing rhythm with a breast-beating *mea culpa?* After all, those buying tickets to see *High Street* are probably not the indifferent masses that the film attacks.

A more effective prodding of the conscience or warning against indifference is offered by *Night and Fog* ("Nuit et Brouillard"), still the most powerful film on the concentration camp experience. Directed by Alain Resnais in 1955, *Night and Fog* is a film whose very shape challenges existing visual language, mainly through an editing style that both reflects and elicits tension. Whether the counterpoint is between image and sound, past and present, stasis and movement, despair and hope, black-and-white and color, or oblivion and memory, Resnais's film addresses the audience's intelligence—and moves beyond a facile stimulation of helpless tears. As François Truffaut pointed out,

It is almost impossible to speak about this film in the vocabulary of cinematic criticism. It is not a documentary, or an indictment, or a poem, but a meditation on the most important phenomenon of the twentieth century.... The power of this film ... is rooted in its tone, the *terrible gentleness*.... When we have looked at these strange, seventy-pound slave laborers, we understand that we're not going to "feel better" after seeing *Nuit et Brouillard;* quite the opposite.[1]

Night and Fog begins with a long tracking shot of a peaceful landscape in color. As the camera glides across the grass, the narration, written by survivor Jean Cayrol, introduces the locale—Auschwitz—a façade whose present calm seems to deny its ineradicable ghosts. Simultaneously, the music of Hanns Eisler (a German composer who was himself driven from his country by Hitler's rise to power) laces the scene with a certain delicacy that will become increasingly contrapuntal as the images cut into the horrific past. Our auditory guides carry us into newsreel footage and documentary stills whose black-and-white graininess contrasts with the scenes in color. Moreover, the serene landscape gives way to harsh images of sealed freight cars and barbed wire that signify the arrival of Auschwitz's victims. The camera moving inside the abandoned structures of the concentration camp often stops, acknowledging its own limitations with a cut to a black-and-white still; while confronting and investigating, this fluid camera suggests transience, or the license of smooth mobility that can exist only after the fact. Opposing itself to the rigidity of death captured by the newsreels, Resnais's camera glides past the now-empty barracks and crematoria until it can go no further, arrested by haunting photographs.

At these moments, the voice (of actor Michel Bouquet) quietly recalls, probes, offers statistics, and bears witness—all with an admirable lack of emotionalism. (Contrast this with Richard Widmark's histrionic verbal accompaniment to some of the same archival footage in *Judgment at Nuremberg*'s courtroom.) The voice lets the images speak for themselves, illustrating the crucial lesson of restraint that Resnais might have learned from cinema master

Jean Renoir: "The more emotional the material, the less emotional the treatment." Likewise, the music invites a more complex response because, according to Resnais, "the more violent the images, the gentler the music." Unlike the pounding dramatic orchestral scores exemplified by Carlo Rustichelli's music for Gillo Pontecorvo's *Kapo* (1960), "Eisler wanted to show that hope always existed in the background," claimed Resnais.

Among other things, the soundtrack enables us to look at unbearable newsreels, such as living skeletons being prepared for hospital experiments. Cayrol's commentary takes into account the audience's predictable difficulty at seeing such horror. For example, it breaks off from its presentation of the gas chamber ceiling clawed by the victims' fingernails, insisting, "but you have to know." The stuttering montage is similarly appropriate to sentences that can be completed only with difficulty:

These are the storehouses of the Nazis at war,
nothing but women's hair . . .
At fifteen pennies per kilo . . .
It is used for cloth.

With the bones . . .
fertilizer. At least they try.

With the bodies . . . but no more can be said . . .
With the bodies, they try to make . . .
soap.

As for the skin . . .[2]

The accompanying images render further narration superfluous.

Resnais's revelatory camera is restricted to surfaces, requiring testimony from the past to complete the picture. The vacant images of the ovens are brutally defined by black-and-white photos, and montage activates the silent railroad tracks covered with green grass into sputtering newsreels of transports. The "picture postcard" becomes a stark nightmare, as *Night and Fog* assumes the function of an X-ray: through the spine of documentary footage and Cayrol's calmly vigilant meditation, we are forced to see the deformities hidden from the unaided eye (and camera), and to struggle against the imperturbability of surfaces. "Who is responsible?" asks the narrator, after a wordless presentation of soap and lampshades made from human skin.

The alternation of history and immediacy insists upon responsibility, whether for those during World War II who were responsible *for* the Holocaust, or those today who are responsible *to* it. The quiet landscape of postwar Auschwitz is deceptive, as the narrator insists:

War slumbers, with one eye always open. . . . Who among us watches over this strange observatory to warn of the new executioners' arrival? Are their faces really different from ours? . . . We look at these ruins as if the old concentration camp monster were dead under the debris . . . we who pretend to believe that all this happened in one time and one place, and who do not think to look around us, or hear the endless cry.

Night and Fog fulfills what the critic and filmmaker Eric Rohmer once said about Resnais—that he is a cubist because he reconstitutes reality after fragmenting it. The effect is not only opposition, but a deeper unity in which past and present blend into each other.

Les Violons du Bal (literally "The Violins of the Ball" but released in the United States under its French title) reverses part of the visual premise of *Night and Fog* by shooting present-day scenes in black-and-white, and the past in color. This is a revealing decision on the part of filmmaker Michel Drach, suggesting that his memories are more vibrantly compelling than his contemporary existence. In this 1973 movie, Drach plays himself, a forty-four-year-old French director attempting to make an autobiographical film about his family's struggle for survival during the Occupation. He screen-tests and casts his nine-year-old son David as himself in 1939, and his wife (Marie-José Nat) as his mother. When he tries to sell the idea to a weighty producer, the commercially minded moneyman dismisses the project: "Nobody's interested in the past." The bearded and leather-jacketed Drach obsessively continues seeking actors and locations. For instance, he stops an old woman (Gabrielle Doulcet) emerging from the metro at the Cirque d'Hiver; a few sequences later, in the film's past tense, this woman will play his grandmother.

David Drach (Michel) and Marie-José Nat (Mother) in *Les Violons du Bal*. LEVITT-PICKMAN FILM CORPORATION

The degree to which the director's imagination colors and overtakes the present is shown in the circus itself. As his wife does her spinning act, black-and-white occasionally yields to color, reflecting Drach's subjective vision. The color persists as we then see the little boy Michel in the circus. Similarly, while Drach rides a motorcycle through contemporary Paris, he passes a big old car and stares at it intently: suddenly the car is in a color scene during the war, driven by his wife/mother. The fluidity of his mental shifts in time is expressed by color fading gently in and out as his wife tries on a wig for her role. Drach's enthusiasm, however, does not infect the producer, who continues to shrug at his material and insists, "No stars, no film." A deft piece of editing solves the problem: Drach momentarily bows his head in frustration under his notebook, and the face that reappears is that of Jean-Louis Trintignant, a famous French actor. The transfer of identity between Drach and Trintignant is cleverly literalized when the actor gets on a moving escalator, walking backward on a forward track (like the movement of the film's action). On a parallel escalator, Drach hands Trintignant the key to his apartment. Multiple mirrors give the impression that the two figures converge into one at the center of the screen before Drach gets off the escalator—leaving Trintignant to move forward.

Les Violons du Bal proceeds into sustained color sequences set in 1939, in which Michel, his mother, grandmother, brother Jean (Christian Rist), and sister Nathalie (Nathalie Roussel) are uprooted and forced to leave Paris. Light-hearted and affluent, the family changes homes, names, and identities. Jean disappears to join his father in the underground; Nathalie—rejected by her wealthy Gentile fiancé's mother because of her religion—becomes a model in occupied Paris; as the situation grows increasingly dangerous for Jews, Michel is sent off to the country to spend a few months with a farmer's family. His mother and grandmother finally retrieve him, having arranged an escape into Switzerland. The supposedly good-hearted farmer, Monsieur Robert (Paul Le Person), leads them around in circles and takes their money, leaving the three refugees on their own to make a run for the border. Losing all their possessions along the way, they succeed in slipping through the fence just before German bullets can reach them.

This tale of suspense and sentiment is framed and punctuated by the realities of its cinematic fabrication. The effects of intercutting the present are twofold, suggesting a (perhaps forced) analogy between the Nazi era and the turbulent events of May '68, and acknowledging the indifference of producers to a Holocaust memoir that contains neither sex nor violence. Student demonstrations in black-and-white are juxtaposed with color shots of the Occupation, and when Trintignant takes his car from the garage, a bloodied protester lurks in the shadows. He is the same actor who played Jean earlier, and the crosscutting of this brother in the pastel past with the student in the grainy present implies either of two things: that this boy will play Jean in the film being made; or that the director helps the demonstrator because he reminds him of his brother. The parallel is developed when Monsieur Robert smuggles young Michel to the country while, in the present, Trintignant smuggles the demonstrator to Lyons. Although this equation ultimately cheapens the unique persecution inflicted by the Holocaust, it insists upon the degree to which the director's actions—and social conscience—are rooted in World War II.

More realistic is the reaction of the second producer—an Italian who proclaims proudly, "I promoted Mussolini"—when he sees the rushes midway through: he asks when they will film the sex part, and how many people die. "My characters don't die," says Trintignant with restrained fervor. "A dead Jew might sell," muses the producer, "but a live Jew—impossible." At the end of the film, this producer appraises the rushes with the comment, "It has the makings of a film." Trintignant's response, "But it *is* a film," means not only that *Les Violons du Bal* is completed, but that the film we are watching is not to be confused with reality. His cinematic exclamation point is to clap the clapboard before his face, acknowledging that the subject of the shot—and the film—is the director. This cinematic self-consciousness (or honesty) is appropriate to *Les Violons du Bal* for it locates the action firmly within Drach's personal recollections. It affirms his mediating presence as image-maker (worthy of the cousin of director Jean-Pierre Melville and former assistant to Jean Cocteau). Whereas a straightforward account of the past would have enclosed and sealed it, Drach's intrusive montage extends the Holocaust experience into the present.

CHAPTER 3

STYLES OF TENSION

Montage is not the only way for a filmmaker to create tension; the Holocaust experience can be expressed or approached through disorienting camera angles and movement, heightened lighting, distorting visual texture or color, stylized acting, contrapuntal soundtrack or music, and unconventional narrative structure. Films as seemingly disparate as *The Serpent's Egg, Cabaret, Kanal, Ambulance,* and *Passenger* proceed via dislocation and discomfort, refusing to simplify or prettify painful reality through filters. They suggest that the shocking dimensions of the Holocaust demand stylistic devices of disturbance rather than complacency.

The Serpent's Egg (1977) is not a pleasing film. Ingmar Bergman's English-language study of pre-Nazi Germany is morbid, depressing, and relentless in its tone of paranoia and inescapability. Through the relationship of an unemployed and alcoholic circus acrobat and a cabaret singer, the film presents three ominous aspects of 1923 Berlin: anti-Semitism; a ravaged economy; and scientific curiosity gone wild, severed from moral considerations. The serpent is an ancient animal; likewise, Nazism did not simply hatch: it was nurtured by historical antecedents, both economic and psychological. Beyond the story, however, Bergman weaves into *The Serpent's Egg* a troubled self-consciousness, questioning his own cinematic methods and purposes. By incorporating the films of a mad scientist within *The Serpent's Egg,* the director invites comparison between his images and those recorded by this chilling character.

Abel Rosenberg (David Carradine) is an American Jew—thus doubly an outsider in Berlin—who finds his brother Max dead in their hotel room. He informs Max's ex-wife Manuela (Liv Ullmann) that Max shot his brains out. The singer, distraught and naïvely generous, takes Abel into her apartment. Abel is questioned by an Inspector Bauer (Gert Frobe) who asks him if he is Jewish. The importance of his religion is developed in the next scene when Abel's former circus boss takes him to an elegant restaurant: he reads from a German newspaper the kind of anti-Semitic propaganda that began appear-

Joel Grey (the MC) in *Cabaret.*
MUSEUM OF MODERN ART/FILM STILLS ARCHIVE

ing regularly in publications like *Der Stürmer* in 1923. Abel doesn't believe "all the political crap," and claims that Jews get into trouble because they "act stupid"—unlike himself. It doesn't take long for the impoverished alcoholic to "act stupid" indeed, as when he rails at Bauer, "You're holding me because I'm a Jew" before attempting a futile escape. Manuela's cabaret is raided by armed thugs—probably members of the SA, the storm troopers of the early Nazi party, organized in 1921—who announce that "the sadistic filth" onstage is "part of the Jewish conspiracy." They beat the Jewish director's head to a bloody pulp before setting fire to the cabaret.

Manuela's sole remaining job is in a clinic where Hans (Heinz Bennent), a scientist they have known since childhood, performs suspicious experiments. She gets Abel a job in the archives and they move to an apartment in the clinic, trying to survive the rampant inflation and susceptibility to illness. When Abel finds Manuela dead and realizes that their life in the apartment had been constantly watched and recorded by unseen cameras as part of experiments, he breaks through the walls—behind the façade of the clinic—where Hans calmly awaits him. The elegant doctor projects (both in the present and into the future) for Abel his films of drug-induced human suffering: "In a few years, science will ask for these documents and continue on a gigantic scale," he proclaims. A pre-Mengele figure, Hans predicts the ripening of Nazism: "You can see the future like a serpent's egg. Through the thin membrane, you can clearly discern the already perfect reptile."

The bleak socio-economic conditions presented by Bergman convey the sense of a hopeless people. German marks are so devalued that their worth is a function of the paper's weight.[1] Meat is so scarce that a dead horse in the street is cut up and sold still dripping blood; Abel wakes up at 4:00 A.M. and observes silent bodies lining up for bread or boarding buses for work. His response, "I wake up from a nightmare and find the real world worse than the dream," is characteristic of the entire film, as each scene grows progressively darker. "Go to hell," he tells a young prostitute who invites his dollars in. "Where do you think we are?" she answers with a jeer. Religion, too, is impotent in this setting, as illustrated by Manuela's visit to a priest (James Whitmore) for solace. As in other Bergman films from *Through a Glass Darkly* to *Winter Light,* there is no balm for human suffering. The priest begs Manuela's forgiveness for his apathy and indifference, proposing, "We must give each other the forgiveness that a remote God denies us." By the end of the film, however, the combined physical and spiritual poverty has led people to sell themselves as human guinea pigs for Hans's experiments, abandoning all claims to dignity.

The Serpent's Egg's acknowledgment of anti-Semitism and economic devastation grounds Bergman's story in historical antecedents to Nazism, but its resonance comes from a self-conscious style that heightens the material. The film opens with a silent, black-and-white image of a crowd. In slow motion, the people move with desolate faces. A sudden cut to the opening credits is accompanied by upbeat music of the 1920s. When the crowd in slow motion returns a few moments later, there is once again silence. The persistent juxtaposition of the two modes introduces an uneasy relationship between the seen and the heard: the jazzy sound cannot coexist with the black-and-white image.

David Carradine (Abel)
and Liv Ullmann (Manuela)
in *The Serpent's Egg*.
CARLOS CLARENS

And the self-conscious alternation announces that the film is a mediator rather than recorder of history—not unlike the celebrated opening of Bergman's *Persona,* which calls attention to the celluloid and projector as characters in the ensuing drama.

This exploration of the film's materials and effects is developed in the last part of the film, after Abel finds Manuela dead. A camera takes a picture of his reaction, leading Abel to break all three mirrors—each of which was a one-way window concealing a movie camera. He enters the world the film came from, following the celluloid into the bowels of the clinic. There he finds the master "filmmaker" Hans, whose black-and-white cinematic documents prove far more bloodcurdling than anything in Bergman's stylized universe. The first film he proudly shows Abel traces the disintegration of a young mother locked in a cell with her infant who (through drugs) never stops crying. After twenty-four hours, maternal sympathy is replaced by anguish and guilt. Ultimately, she kills her child. Another film records a man who, after an injection of thanatoxide, feels as if his flesh is being torn apart—and kills himself. (Hans confesses that Max died in the same manner.) Finally, Hans shows Abel a man and woman under the effects of "Carter Blue"—alternately depressed, hostile, and tender—looking exactly like Abel himself and Manuela in an earlier scene.

Throughout this diabolical display, there are intercuts of the projector and flashing lights that suggest the degree to which it, and its contents, can be instruments of cruel voyeurism. (Indeed, Hans's identity as a voyeur is set up by the way Bergman introduces him: at the cabaret, he watches the show from

David Carradine (Abel) in *The Serpent's Egg.* CARLOS CLARENS

David Carradine (Abel)
and Liv Ullmann (Manuela)
in *The Serpent's Egg.*
CARLOS CLARENS

the side, unseen by the performers.) Hans's last film is the same as *The Serpent's Egg*'s opening—the sad crowd in slow motion. This coinciding of Bergman's image and Hans's record is deliberately ambiguous: Do both "directors" force human beings to portray agony in the service of something beyond themselves? Or is Bergman contrasting Hans's coldly captured images with his own sensitizing techniques?

This time, Hans provides a soundtrack for the silent group, as his voice-over predicts that, in ten years, there will be a revolution and they will use the hatred inherited from their parents. "Someone will make demands on them. Our world will go down in blood and fire." This is just after Hitler's failed Putsch; the irony is therefore that Hans's prediction will come true, but *not* with a new leader. The "demanding" figure will simply take further Hans's position: "We exterminate what is inferior and develop what is useful." The culmination of Hans's scientific voyeurism occurs when he swallows cyanide and grabs a mirror to watch his own death. His parting statement about seeing the future "like a serpent's egg" takes on another meaning, for the "membrane" can also refer to the celluloid: close-ups of the film stock do allow us to see outlines "of the future." Nevertheless, it is really the past; the result is a dizzying timelessness, which is appropriate to the notion of the serpent—of anti-Semitism—and of cinema.

Why all this cinematic self-consciousness? Perhaps, as in *Persona,* Bergman's aim is to guard against facile identification on the part of the viewer, and emotional manipulation on the part of the filmmaker. Intercuts of projectors and celluloid make us aware of the machines that determine our perception, distancing us from the action even while acknowledging their *modus operandi.* This seems particularly appropriate to the subject, for Bergman refuses to let the audience do what the Germans did: to get swept up in an emotional surge that ultimately suspends judgment and morality. Making his first film in the land of Bertolt Brecht, Bergman distances us from the horror at the same time that he forces us to look at its methods.

Surprisingly enough, one of the most successful American films in portraying the rise of Nazism is a musical, *Cabaret.* Directed by Bob Fosse in 1972, it is entertaining, engrossing, and ultimately chilling in its stylized tableaux of spreading swastikas. The credits unfold over a dark background which gradually comes into focus (like the film's concerns), a distorted mirror that reflects the cabaret clientele as a grotesque Grosz-like grouping. It is 1931 in Berlin, and into this eerie looking-glass pops the painted face of the Master of Ceremonies (Joel Grey)—our depraved guide, our disturbing narrator. His first song, "Willkommen," welcomes the viewer as well as the patrons of the Kit-Kat Club, making us part of the audience in and out of the cabaret. In narrative

Joel Grey (the MC) in *Cabaret.* **MUSEUM OF MODERN ART/FILM STILLS ARCHIVE**

terms, it welcomes the British student Brian (Michael York) to Berlin, where he takes a room across the hall from Sally Bowles (Liza Minnelli), an outrageous young American who sings at the cabaret. She bowls over the shy English tutor who finally falls in love with the vulnerable waif that exists under Sally's flamboyantly decadent surface. Concurrently, one of Brian's pupils, Fritz (Fritz Wepper), is entranced by another student, the wealthy Jewess Natalia Landauer (Marisa Berenson). The musical numbers within the Kit-Kat Club reflect, comment upon, and often parody the growing influence of the Nazis.

Sally meets Maximilian von Heune (Helmut Griem), an aristocratic German who showers gifts upon the delighted singer and her less-acquiescent boyfriend Brian. As Stanley Kauffmann said of *Jules and Jim,* the isosceles triangle becomes equilateral: "Screw Max!" yells Brian. "I do," responds Sally. "Well, so do I" is Brian's topper. Max thinks that the Nazis are "just hooligans" who are serving a purpose by ridding Germany of Communists, but a scene in a beer garden reveals their wide-ranging support as a crowd of ordinary-looking people joins in the singing of a Nazi song. While the situation for Jews worsens, Natalia refuses to marry Fritz—until he confesses that he is Jewish too. Brian asks the pregnant Sally to marry him but she realizes their life as a couple is doomed and decides to have an abortion instead. The Nazi-hating Englishman leaves Germany for home, and Sally remains at the cabaret. The last image is the misshapen mirror of the first shot, now reflecting a profusion of swastika armbands on Nazi patrons.

The distorted reflection corresponds to *Cabaret*'s musical numbers, which are consistently crosscut with the reality outside. By juxtaposing a production number in which the MC playfully slaps the chorines with the image of Nazis beating up the club's owner, Fosse insists on the cabaret as stylized microcosm rather than escape. Do the numbers neutralize the horror or heighten it? When the MC dabs a bit of mud under his nose like Hitler's mustache, is the character winking at the Führer's supporters or debasing Hitler? In any case, the crosscutting distances us from emotional identification with victimization and invites an intellectual appreciation of both the historical picture and its translation into spectacle. For example, the MC sings, "If You Could See Her Through My Eyes"—declaring his love for a woman in a gorilla costume—after Nazis have painted the word "Jew" on the Landauers' doorstep, and killed Natalia's dog. The number ends with the MC's conspiratorial whisper, "If you could see her through my eyes—she wouldn't look Jewish at all!"

The only musical sequence that does not take place within the cabaret, and is not developed by parallel montage, is the seminal number in the beer garden. Fosse begins with a close-up of an angelic-looking boy singing "Tomorrow Belongs to Me." A tilt downward reveals a uniform and a swastika armband. As the camera moves further back, it includes other young people standing to join in the song, and then older German citizens, until a long shot presents a throbbing crowd of incipient Nazis. Brian turns to Maximilian and asks, "Do you still think you can stop them?" The most disturbing element in the scene is Fosse's eschewing of distancing devices: he leaves the audience vulnerable to the emotion of the song, and it is only at the end that we pull back, horrified at the ease with which unified voices can become viscerally seductive. This scene affords an insight into the rise of Nazism, for it is the only number that gives the audience a chance to get into the act. These Germans feel important, part of a movement that offers a hopeful tomorrow. Their insidiously wholesome faces serve as a contrast to the comparatively more harmless decadence in the Kit-Kat Club, for the latter at least allows for liberating irony about the Nazis.

A case in point is the eighth musical number, which plays with various displacements. After presenting a row of chorus girls in pink corsets, the camera pauses on the back of a dancer who turns out to be the MC. The host in drag subsequently turns his hat around so that it becomes a helmet, and the chorines shoulder their canes like rifles. They goose-step about the stage, suggesting a perversity that underlies Nazism; indeed, the overt sexual decadence in the Kit-Kat Club consistently de-eroticizes and de-personalizes (mutually dependent processes). The lewd jokes and abstract female flesh suggest that Nazism is predicated upon a denial of love and sex, a display of flesh to be automatized into parade formation. (Fosse's choreography and constant cuts intensify these impressions by fragmenting the dancers' bodies into often faceless patterns.) If, as Sally's last song puts it, "Life is a cabaret, old chum," the corollary is also true: the cabaret *is* life, but life translated into a spectacular reflection. Like the club's patrons, we enter this musical world to forget about reality, only to find that it cannot be kept outside.

The Polish cinema has proven more brutally direct in its representations of World War II destruction. In particular, Andrzej Wajda's *Kanal* (1957) is a relentlessly harrowing reconstruction of the last part of the Warsaw Uprising. Along with *A Generation* (1955) and *Ashes and Diamonds* (1958), it is the centerpiece of what has come to be known as his war trilogy, a three-part exploration of the possibilities for Polish heroism during and immediately after Nazi oppression. *Kanal* is the darkest of the three, a haunting acknowledgement of the doomed Polish Resistance.

A modern analogue of Dante's *Inferno, Kanal* presents a literal and figurative descent: the film begins with aerial documentary footage of Warsaw in rubbles, moves to ground level after the credits, and finally curves underground to the sewers, where the last part of the Uprising actually took place. Shot in the sewers of Warsaw, *Kanal*'s realism of detail is often stomach-churning, as we see the characters wading in excrement. Wajda intensifies the claustrophobia through lighting and camera work: the only illumination in the underworld comes from flashlights or matches—bright dots surrounded by blackness. Moreover, the camera (usually positioned at low-angle) not only renders the figures heroic, but makes us feel their entrapment, with the ceilings bearing down on them.

As Chapter 9 will develop, Wajda uses close-ups sparingly, preferring group shots that stress relationships and place the characters within a palpable historical space. Thus, when he finally does make an entire landscape of a face, the effect is gripping. It is appropriate that the most memorable close-up is given to the proud musician (Wladyslaw Szeybal) who joins the Resistance at the last moment and is not an experienced soldier like the others. He begins

Tadeusz Janczar (Korab) and Teresa Izewska (Daisy) in *Kanal*.
KINO INTERNATIONAL CORPORATION

to go mad in the swirling dark—playing an ocarina as he wanders in the dank mist—and a stark close-up serves to isolate him, expressing his self-enclosure.

Kanal commemorates a hopeless situation, a last stand of martyrs who perished in noxious circumstances. There is no way out but death, as two scenes demonstrate: after Commander Zadra (Wienczyslaw Glinski) emerges into daylight and learns that his company has not followed, he returns to the fatal bowels of the sewers. And when the injured hero Korab (Tadeusz Janczar) and his spunky girlfriend Daisy (Teresa Izewska) glimpse an exit into the sea, a subjective camera from their point of view leads us to the light with them—only to find the exit barred. This caged portal, in the shape of a headstone, is like an epitaph for the Polish men and women who perished there in 1944.

One of Wajda's assistants on *Kanal* was Janusz Morgenstern, who went on to make his own poignant commemoration of Polish martyrs: *Ambulance* (1962) illustrates how a story can be told cinematically using a minimum of means. Without a word of dialogue, the 15-minute film dramatizes an incident with symbolic resonance. A tracking shot on a receding road introduces both a backward glance and a subtle feeling of dislocation because one can't see what lies ahead. The sound of Hitler's ranting yields to a military march, immediately establishing the film's context. As an ambulance stops beyond a fence, we hear the exhaust whose mechanical exhalation seems to blend with the preceding sounds. A group of children is playing next to the ambulance, watched by a grave-looking man. The first child we see is blindfolded in his game, an appropriate image for their ignorance (and ours) as to the purpose of the ambulance. An SS officer calmly and methodically goes about his work —checking the exhaust valve and accelerator, pouring gasoline, and sealing the carbon monoxide fumes within the van. The children play more and more apprehensively, especially when one little girl is pushed aside by the officer and drops her shoe. The snarling dog held by another officer keeps her—and the serious-looking man—from retrieving it. This image of dispossession is juxtaposed with a shot inside the back of the ambulance as it fills up with dark smoke. By placing the audience in the position that the prisoners will occupy, with the doors banging shut in our faces, the film creates a visceral foreboding.

A boy plays with a flying toy whose ejection into the sky causes the dog to suddenly break from its master. The dog runs after the object as the children are herded into the van. The grave-looking man reassures them as he quietly enters alongside. His last look at life—a long take from his point of view of birds flying—provides a poignant opposition between freedom and the earthly hell of fumes awaiting him and his charges. The dog suddenly reappears, offering the child's shoe to its owner; the doors bang shut upon us and we hear the dog's whimper, presumably after being hit. The ambulance goes on its way with its Red Cross—an insignia of salvation—concealing a mobile gas chamber.

Each carefully composed shot of *Ambulance* suggests rather than states a horrific aspect or moral question of the Holocaust. A knowing leap of the imagination turns the exhaust pipes into crematoria chimneys, and the fenced-in yard into a concentration camp. The dog's reversal leads us to question whether a natural creature is inherently evil, good, or simply dependent on the hand that feeds/strikes him. Along with the murder of innocent children and the helplessness before the implacable machinery of death, the film presents the dilemma of resistance: the teacher figure does not revolt physically, but he does defy the Nazi attempt at dehumanization. By comforting the children, he enacts a resistance of the spirit that renders his death a humane choice. It is probable that this character is based on Janusz Korczak, the Polish teacher, social worker, and author whose heroism during World War II created an enduring legend. His progressive orphanage was relocated within the Warsaw Ghetto, where he fed the children both physically and spiritually. In *The Witnesses* ("Le Temps du Ghetto"), Frédéric Rossif's fine documentary of 1962, a survivor chronicles Korczak's refusal of Nazi mentality: an SS officer offered the teacher his freedom if he would round up the children quietly. Knowing they were bound for the death camp of Treblinka, he replied, "No, I will stay with my children." *Ambulance* leads us to provide our own dialogue —necessarily riddled with questions about what we could or should have done in this man's place. If, as George Steiner claims, "the world of Auschwitz lies outside speech as it lies outside reason,"[2] perhaps it can be touched by images.

The complexity of *Ambulance* is shared by another Polish film of the same year, *Passenger* ("Pasażerka"). It is a challenging film of unresolved tensions partly because its director, Andrzej Munk, died in a car accident in 1961 before completing the film. When his colleagues—especially Witold Lesiewicz—

pieced the work together, they built this fact into *Passenger*'s opening, thus asking from the outset, how does one make a film about fragments of the Holocaust? The response is a series of images in at least three tenses—the present, the past, and the conditional (what might have happened)—that pit a German woman's self-justifying recollection of Auschwitz against a more likely account. *Passenger* begins with photographs of Munk while a dispassionate male voice-over explains what happened to the filmmaker. These "real" documents are succeeded by stills from the film he was shooting—frozen images animated by camera movement and the verbal narration. Not wanting to speculate on Munk's answers, "we can succeed only in presenting the questions he wanted to pose," acknowledges the voice.

The story begins "today" on a luxury liner, "a floating island in time" that permits its passengers freedom from biography and society. The woman in the stills is Liza (Aleksandra Slaska), returning to her native Germany with a new husband. Her face grows clenched as she spots Marta (Anna Ciepielewska) boarding at Southhampton. Liza's shared and troubling past with this young woman is suggested by the sudden whiteout to an eerie nighttime scene depicting naked women trapped inside a circle of dressed women, with dogs barking nearby. Quick shots of a number being tattooed on an arm and heads being shorn establish the concentration camp origin of Liza's memories. The tattoo, followed by a shot of her husband's hand on her arm, prepares us for Liza's version of herself as a victim of sorts. It is noteworthy that the screen suddenly stretches to accommodate her frightening recollections: scenes of the past are in Dyaliscope (wide screen) while shots of the present conform to a more narrow ratio. The alternation between the two formats implies that the present offers a limited frame: only with the informing past can a fuller image be presented.

"I was an overseer. I didn't hurt anyone. If she's alive, it's thanks to me," Liza explains to her husband in a voice-over. This leads into the first version of her time in Auschwitz, where she took charge of the storehouses. "I never dealt with the prisoners, only their things," she claims. "I just did my duty. I always tried to help these women." The images support the self-righteous narration as she selects Marta to be her assistant—even enabling the young political prisoner to see her fiancé Tadeusz (Marek Walczewski). This first "noble version," in the male narrator's words, ends with Marta being summoned to the death block.

A return to the present shows Liza watching the woman who might be Marta in fragments—stills of shipboard parties—as the male narrator tells what Munk intended to include between the two versions. The second account begins with Liza's confession, "I was stupid enough to feel sorry for her," and proceeds to flesh out the sketchy moments of the preceding one. It becomes increasingly apparent that the storeroom is a privileged space where political prisoners are decently dressed and fed—a contrast to the scene Liza observes beyond the fence: in the camp itself, a group of children wearing Jewish armbands are led into a building. That they are about to be gassed is indicated by shots of a soldier putting on a mask and pouring the Zyklon into the appropriate holes. Furthermore, black smoke is visible from the chimney, casting a dark shadow over the camp.

The extermination of the Jewish children in Auschwitz is subtly confirmed by the next shot of empty baby carriages being rolled into the storehouse. Here, Marta shows her first act of defiance when a baby is heard: she runs to check the sound, brings back a doll that makes crying sounds to appease the Commandant's vicious curiosity, and proceeds to hide a sobbing Jewish child with the help of the other prisoners. She and Tadeusz are not merely lovers, but active resisters engaged in a cat-and-mouse game with Liza. The overseer is jealous of their love but needs Marta; as her superior tells her, they must win the trust of the best prisoners to establish order in the camp. Specifically, she needs the young dissident to give the "right" answers to an international commission visiting the camp. Marta does not answer their questions, but to save her fiancé's skin, she is forced to admit that he visited her in the hospital.

Liza exults in learning that she will be promoted and transferred to Berlin, but Marta sours her last moments in the camp by confessing to subversive activities. The film returns to the present in which the male narrator says of Liza, "If she always sought to justify herself, it's only human." The hypothetical ending is that the young woman disembarks at the next port and that Liza remains unchanged by the encounter: "It is doubtful that Liza will be challenged with truths that remain buried in the mud of Auschwitz. Nothing can trouble her" for she is among those "who prefer not to remember yesterday's crimes, among people who even today . . ." The narrator breaks off here, forcing the viewer to finish the sentence, and the film. For *Passenger* ends like a stimulant rather than a tonic, insisting that the chapter is not closed. Perhaps the end of the sentence can be found in the last shot—a still of the luxury liner —implying that we remain isolated, unconnected to events, unable to see and touch what is happening around us.

The fact that this film forces us on a formal level to participate in piecing the fragments and versions together ties in with its moral invitation to action. For if Liza's first version presents Marta simply as a lovesick child, the second insists on her being a political resister and a heroic figure. For example, Marta is the only prisoner who yells to a naked and humiliated woman on display to stand tall. When Liza finds a note in the barracks and asks Marta to translate it aloud, she invents a love letter rather than read the names and numbers of SS officers listed. (A subsequent scene clarifies that such notes were smuggled out of the camp to be used by Radio-London on its broadcasts indicting war criminals.) And when Liza threatens that the whole group will be punished if the author of the note does not admit to it, Marta steps forward in an act of solidarity with the covert resistance network operating in the camp. (In the documentary *Genocide* (1975)—part of Great Britain's "World at War" series—we see photographs of the camps that were indeed smuggled out by organized political prisoners during the war.)

A major question raised by *Passenger* is whether postwar justifications by Germans are trustworthy or merely self-serving. The interplay between Liza's self-justifying memory and the political realities of dissenters in Auschwitz uses similar visual material with divergent interpretations. That the first version is Liza's subjective story is evident from the camera work: we do not ever really see Liza, except as a reflection in a mirror or glass window. Rather, we see *through* her eyes in point-of-view shots, such as the long tracking shot of the female prisoners from whom Liza will choose an assistant. Another telling shot is revealed to have been subjective only in the second half: a lengthy pan of the hospital that ends on Marta is repeated later, but this time begins further back—with *Liza*—before following her glance. The camera movement is also slower the second time, permitting us to see more details.

The only dialogue in the first account is Liza's narration. The second version finally presents direct dialogue, and because this convergence of sound and image is in keeping with cinematic convention, the section seems more subtly "real." It also develops the deadly circle game that flashed into Liza's mind at the opening of the film; with persistent unraveling, it establishes that Liza was responsible for choosing the prisoners who would be caught in the circle. She does indeed save Marta in this scene, but the defiance visible in the prisoner's face suggests that Liza's compassion is a lesser motive than the need for a partner in her own game. Her aim is to break down Marta's integrity by making her a privileged prisoner. Marta's role is akin to that of Antigone in Jean Anouilh's play, who states to the king, "I am here to say no."

Rather than merely substituting this psychological tug of war for a depiction of concentration camp realities, Munk uses the background to show the harshness of existence. Bodies are beaten behind Liza, and *Passenger*'s ultimate condemnation of the overseer is the narrator's assessment, "In the vague, unreal background, there are always people dying anonymously, quietly, over whom she walked unseeing." For those who might feel that the presentation of Auschwitz is too bland, the fact remains that the locale is always mediated by Liza's memory. As the director explained two days before his death,

In the film, Auschwitz is shown from a distance of twenty years and it is seen through the eyes of an S.S. woman. She relates facts coldly while retaining a clear conscience.[3]

For Munk, a Jew from Cracow, the point is not an objective reconstruction of camp life but the gradual revelation of a relationship between overseer and privileged prisoner; nevertheless, the psychological and political resonance of *Passenger* extends beyond this relationship—not unlike its frame which widens into Dyaliscope. The viewer is led to ponder this extension by the film's unfinished ending: isn't the situation of a film spectator analogous to that of a ship's passenger? Do we not also enter the theater to be taken on a trip that frees us from history, memory, biography? And don't we have to reconnect with reality when the voyage ends?

CHAPTER 4
BLACK HUMOR

omic films about the Holocaust raise two major questions: to what extent is humor appropriate when dealing with such devastation? And what illumination can a perspective of humor provide that is not possible in a serious approach? Mel Brooks's *The Producers* is certainly not about the Holocaust, but its protagonists are right on target when they select Nazism as the most outrageous and tasteless subject for comic or musical treatment. The aim of these producers (Zero Mostel and Gene Wilder) is to make a quick buck, but this hardly describes the situation of filmmakers who use comedy as a weapon. The type of humor exemplified by *The Great Dictator, To Be or Not to Be,* and *Seven Beauties* is of course "black"—the kind that leaves a bitter taste after the laugh.

To give Hitler, Mussolini, and other mad megalomaniacs a comic kick, Charles Chaplin wrote and directed *The Great Dictator* (1940). In this satire, he played both the ranting Adenoid Hynkel and the victimized little Jewish barber. There was something curiously appropriate about the little tramp impersonating the dictator, for by 1939, Hitler and Chaplin were perhaps the two most famous men in the world. The tyrant and the tramp reverse roles in *The Great Dictator,* permitting the eternal outsider to address the masses, and the dreaded icon to seem a buffoon. The film opens with a title that sets the rather serious tone of Chaplin's brand of comedy:

This is a story of a period between two World Wars—an interim in which Insanity cut loose, Liberty took a nose dive, and Humanity was kicked around somewhat.

This establishment of an absurd universe is developed in the World War I sequence that begins the film's action: the tramp as a soldier (looking very much like his earlier persona in *Shoulder Arms* of 1918) pulls a string to release a bomb. However, the unexploded shell follows the tramp with a mind of its own—an agent of destruction out of control. A Big Bertha cannon that circles

"Springtime for Hitler" in *The Producers.*
IMAGES FILM ARCHIVE

till it faces the tramp continues this idea of man-made instruments turning against their creators, as does a plane that whips around and flies upside down with the tramp and Major Schultz (Reginald Gardner). This is an appropriate image for war: a topsy-turvy situation devoid of human guidance. The tramp saves Schultz's life, learns that the war is over, and is taken to a hospital where amnesia detains him until Hynkel takes power years later.

In the film's present tense, we find that the little soldier is a Jewish barber —and a dead ringer for the dictator of "Tomania." Hynkel's first speech combines barking, broken German, and English in a verbal assault on the Jews. (This scene should be appreciated in the context of Chaplin's own ambivalence toward sound. If Hitler aped Chaplin's image, the silent comedian gets even by draining the dictator's speech of meaning.) So heated is his discourse that microphones droop, bend, and twirl away from his face. When he leaves the cheering and saluting crowds, even the statues have raised arms: the traditionally armless Venus de Milo is in "heil" position, as is Rodin's Thinker. While these are basic sight gags, they contain darker implications: art and culture have been recast in a Nazi image and perverted into propaganda. The sequence ends with Hynkel's adviser Garbitsch (Henry Daniell) suggesting that violence against the Jews will make people forget their empty stomachs.

The action shifts to the ghetto, where storm troopers harry the Jewish inhabitants. The amnesiac barber has just returned from the hospital, unaware that Jews must now accept humiliation and defacement of property. Along with Hannah (Paulette Goddard), a young Jewess who hits the troopers over the head with a frying pan, the tramp resists the hooligans. Major Schultz (now a Nazi) suddenly arrives on the scene and, remembering that our little hero once saved his life, has him released.

Garbitsch and Herring (Billy Gilbert) continue to feed Hynkel's delusions of limitless power; as the ghetto burns, the Jews escape to idyllic "Osterlich," and the dictator decides to invade this neighboring country. His obstacle is Benzini Napaloni's army (from "Bacteria")—already massed at the border. Hynkel invites his flamboyant fellow dictator (Jack Oakie) to a lavish dinner where they try to upstage one another. Both are undone by mouthfuls of hot English mustard, as it becomes clear that they have bitten off more than they can chew. The barber escapes from prison in a Nazi uniform with Schultz, while troopers mistakenly arrest Hynkel as he is out duck-shooting. This ultimate reversal leads the barber onto the rally platform, before which a huge assemblage awaits Hynkel's major address. The comic parody of Riefenstahl's insidious *Triumph of the Will* (1935), even to the use of looming shadows and over-brilliant lighting, suddenly shifts gears: the audience is faced with Chaplin the polemicist's straightforward plea for peace, brotherhood, and an end to oppression everywhere.

The undisguised parallels, such as Herring/Göring and the realism in the ghetto sequences, were quite courageous for an American film of 1940. At a time when the swastika was a feared symbol, Chaplin transformed it into a double-cross (an all-too-perfect mark for what Hitler was doing to Germany). *The Great Dictator* acknowledges the existence of concentration camps, as when a customer tells the barber that all the men have "gone there." Indeed, the images and conversations of the ghetto display both an ethnic realism

Adenoid Hynkel in *The Great Dictator.* CARLOS CLARENS

("Jewish" faces and Yiddish speech rhythms) and a historical one (destruction of property and brutal SS pranks). The one element that might strike some viewers as less than realistic is open resistance, which Chaplin presents as a constant possibility and responsibility. Almost every scene in the ghetto contains an illustration of Hannah's line, "We can't fight alone, but we can lick 'em together."

This spunky young woman talks back to the SS, smacks them with a skillet, and becomes a symbol of hope by the end of the film. Mr. Jaeckel (Maurice Moscovich), the ironic resident sage of the ghetto, tells the men they have to make a stand. And when Schultz escapes from the camp to this group, he immediately arranges a meeting to organize resisters. These scenes serve to encourage Jewish resistance while parallel scenes undercut Hitler: the underdog seems stronger while the omnipotent ruler looks merely inflated. This image is most cleverly presented in *The Great Dictator*'s famous globe scene: Garbitsch strokes Hynkel's ego by predicting he will rule the world after "wiping out the Jews. Then the brunettes." Hynkel cackles and then picks up a giant globe that turns out to be a balloon. In an exquisitely choreographed dialogueless sequence, accompanied by music from Wagner's *Lohengrin,* he twirls, caresses, and kicks the world around (including a memorable backside kick). But the balloon bursts: Hynkel cannot hold onto his image of the world.

The next scene portrays the barber succeeding where the dictator could not: in a more restrained but equally choreographed number, he shaves a customer to the brisk rhythms of a Brahms gypsy melody (perhaps an allusion to the

Storm troopers come to the Jewish ghetto in *The Great Dictator*. CARLOS CLARENS

vitality of the "brunettes" that are second on the Nazis' wipe-out list). Unlike his look-alike, the little barber knows just how far to press, and his sharp instrument does not prick what he holds. Moreover, an instrument of potential terror used appropriately acquires aesthetic "rightness." The juxtaposition of these two scenes suggests that the barber's razor will be the agent of Hynkel's deflation—as, indeed, Chaplin's keen humor is to Hitler's image in this film. A similar example of creative editing occurs when the ghetto burns: there is an intercut of Hynkel playing the piano before a shot of smoke designating the destruction of the Jewish neighborhood. A twentieth-century Nero, Hynkel is not even a very good musician.

The dictator is most resoundingly mocked when he speaks, for his emphatically guttural rantings result in nonsense speech. The overemotional speaker gets so carried away with his histrionics that he splashes water into his pants. Hynkel jumbles German and English until the only recognizable word is *Jüden,* emitted with much facial contortion. The final speech is consequently a complete reversal of *The Great Dictator*'s comic tone, methods, and impact. Although it is not the film's first serious declamation—Hannah had earlier addressed the camera with the hope that her people might be left alone and not forced to go away—the ending disrupts the dark humor that precedes it.

Mistaken for the Führer, the barber entreats the crowd to refuse the yoke of oppressors. "Greed has poisoned men's souls," he laments, but "the power they took from the people will return to the people." With increasing passion, he quotes St. Luke about the kingdom of God being manifest in men, and closes with a social democratic vision of the future. "Look up, Hannah," he intones, as sentimental string music accompanies a close-up of her tearful, hopeful face. While many have attacked the ending's clichéd sentiments, forced optimism, and disruption of tone, it can be seen as Chaplin's acknowledgement that the preceding comedy is inadequate to the gravity of the events depicted. Although *The Great Dictator*'s procedure is comic, its aims are serious—as announced in the opening titles. André Bazin was perceptive when he claimed that Hitler had stolen Chaplin's mustache and *The Great Dictator* was his way of getting even;[1] this film was also an attempt at *liberating* laughter, whereby Chaplin could toy as deftly and maliciously with Hitler's image as Hynkel with his ephemeral globe. The year was only 1940, and war was declared during the film's production. In Chicago, with its large German population, the film was banned.

Under the sign
of the double-cross
in *The Great Dictator*.
CARLOS CLARENS

Above, Charles Chaplin as the little barber and below, the barber's resistance in *The Great Dictator.* CARLOS CLARENS

Public response was less than kind two years later, when Ernst Lubitsch made *To Be or Not to Be.* Black comedy was hardly a familiar experience for film audiences in 1942, which may explain why this film was so misunderstood and savagely criticized. The director of such treasured comedies as *Trouble in Paradise, Ninotchka,* and *The Shop Around the Corner* was clearly taking some gargantuan risks: a comedy about the Nazi occupation of Poland? Jack Benny as a Polish actor playing Hamlet? A character who looks exactly like Hitler responding to a chorus of "Heil Hitler!" with "Heil myself"? And, if the film didn't have enough problems, the sudden death of its female star, Carole Lombard, in a plane crash shortly before the film's premiere, made it that much harder for audiences to roar with laughter.

Now that films like *Dr. Strangelove* have accustomed viewers to savage satire, *To Be or Not to Be* can be better appreciated in its juxtaposition of farce and melodrama. Now that *Hogan's Heroes* has made bumbling Nazis a staple of television culture, Lubitsch's prototypes—especially the saucer-eyed Sig Ruman as "Concentration Camp Ehrhardt"—no longer seem to be in bad taste. Forty years later, we can see how Lubitsch translated painful events into a timeless meditation on ego, vulnerability, role-playing, and the need for humor. From a story by Lubitsch and Melchior Lengyel, Edwin Justus Mayer fashioned a pungent screenplay full of provocative Lubitsch touches—innuendo, wry wit, affectionate deflation of characters—and an almost unrecountable plot. The Nazi blitzkrieg of Warsaw provides the backdrop for the exploits of a band of Polish actors that never stops "performing"—whether to the thunder of applause or bombs. Occupying center stage are Jack Benny as the vain, hammy, and jealous Josef Tura, and Carole Lombard as his clever, luminous, and less-than-faithful wife, Maria.

Josef and Maria Tura adopt a series of poses in order to sabotage the Nazi invaders. Maria improvises alluringly with the suave Professor Siletsky (Stanley Ridges), who is a Nazi spy, and then with the buffoonish Colonel Ehrhardt. Josef impersonates Ehrhardt with the real Siletsky, and then Siletsky with the real Ehrhardt. Each encounter builds upon, reflects, or reverses a preceding one. Ehrhardt is informed of Siletsky's death while Tura is in his office posing as Siletsky. The masquerade leads to a macabre scene in which the impostor is placed in the same room with Siletsky's corpse. The two look identical, but Tura quickly masters the situation with a handy razor. He removes the corpse's beard and then pastes it back on to make it appear that the real Siletsky was a fake. This scene partly accounts for the difficulty audiences of 1942 had in accepting the film. It is predicated on the kind of dark humor that would seem palatable only thirty or more years later, with Hitchcock making macabre fun of rigor mortis in *Frenzy* (1972) or Blake Edwards playing with corpses in *S.O.B.* (1981).

The mixture of genres and tones was equally disconcerting, for *To Be or Not to Be* moves swiftly and unpredictably from comic inventiveness to frighteningly authentic-looking war footage, and back again. Suddenly there are scurrying bodies illuminated only by bursts of fire against a black sky; the storefronts that introduced us to the film's comic world with a series of Polish names are now shattered. In a letter defending his work, Lubitsch felt it necessary to underscore the gravity of these scenes, despite the satirical tone pervading the film:

An impassioned Hynkel in *The Great Dictator*. CARLOS CLARENS

When in *To Be or Not to Be* I have referred to the destruction of Warsaw, I have shown it in all seriousness; the commentation under the shots of the devastated Warsaw speaks for itself and cannot leave any doubt in the spectator's mind what my point of view and attitude are toward those acts of horror. What I have satirized in this picture are the Nazis and their ridiculous ideology. I have also satirized the attitude of actors who always remain actors regardless of how dangerous the situation might be, which I believe is a true observation.[2]

Other disturbing touches include the ultimately uncomfortable humor when a Polish actor impersonating Hitler orders two German pilots to jump from a plane. With no more than a "Heil Hitler!"—and without parachutes—they obediently jump. Funny, but . . . As Theodore Huff wrote in his *Index to the Films of Ernst Lubitsch,*

. . . the Lubitsch burlesque, laid in Nazi-invaded Warsaw, was called callous, a picture of confusing moods, lacking in taste, its subject not suitable for fun making. While others felt that such merciless satire and subtle humor were good anti-Nazi propaganda, the picture was, perhaps, ill-timed.[3]

The Philadelphia *Inquirer* called it "a callous, tasteless effort to find fun in the bombing of Warsaw," and the National Board of Review, while favorably disposed to the film, cautioned, "Sensitive people won't like it."[4] The line for which Lubitsch was most vociferously attacked was Ehrhardt's answer to

Tura's repeated question, "You've heard of that great, *great* Polish actor, Josef Tura?" The colonel recalls with amusement, "What he did to Shakespeare, we are doing now to Poland." Lubitsch refused to delete the line because he did not believe that he was making a joke at the expense of the victims.

Lubitsch was so distressed by the response to *To Be or Not to Be* that he wrote an open letter to the Philadelphia *Inquirer:*

Never have I said in a picture anything derogative about Poland or the Poles. On the contrary, I have portrayed them as a gallant people who do not cry on other people's shoulders in their misery, but even in the darkest day never lost courage and ingenuity or their sense of humor. It can be argued if the tragedy of Poland realistically portrayed as in *To Be or Not to Be* can be merged with satire. I believe it can be.[5]

But the mixture of tones created a pervasive ambiguity. The Nazis are, finally, not easy "villains" at all: that Ehrhardt and Tura display the same childish narcissism ("So they call me Concentration Camp Ehrhardt!"/"You've heard of that great, *great* Polish actor, Josef Tura?") underlines the shared human emotions beneath their national identities. Tura, in his role-playing, suggests the universal fallibility and the occasional charm that can be attributed to every character in the film.

Should Lubitsch be praised or blamed for never really damning his characters, whether Nazi pigs or Polish hams? In 1942 it might have seemed a cop-out to show that the Nazis' most powerful motivation was fear of their own superiors. Nevertheless, *To Be or Not to Be* did deflate the image of a national enemy: Hitler is ultimately "just a little man with a mustache," not unlike the buffoon incarnated by Chaplin in *The Great Dictator.* Moreover, the fact that the Gestapo constitutes a source of humor rather than horror becomes fairly horrifying itself, for Lubitsch invites an awareness of our own responses through the juxtaposition of moods. Forty years validate to some extent how Lubitsch's famed art of indirection was appropriate not only for sex but also for politics; he believed not in direct attack but in subtle subversion. *To Be or Not to Be* proposes that the way to undercut tyranny is to play your roles cleverly till you amass the power to direct. As the title implies, the source of these characters' strength is theatrical—whether they perform as thespians or as spies.

The film opens with a voice-over narration establishing a real time and place, 1939 Warsaw, and a real figure, for we witness Adolf Hitler staring at Maslovsky's Delicatessen. How did he come to be there? wonders the narrator. A scene at Gestapo headquarters provides the answer, as Hitler is greeted by the officers and answers (deadpan), "Heil myself." But these seemingly real scenes turn out to be a play in rehearsal, and Hitler is an actor named Bronski (Tom Dugan), who ad-libs because "I thought it would get a laugh." Bronski's arguments with the director—who doesn't think he looks enough like Hitler —lead him to test his costume in the street.

The interplay between theatrical artifice and reality continues as the actors break and listen onstage to a radio broadcast of the real Hitler. This intrusion of reality is extended when government representatives enter to cancel the show because they fear it will offend the Führer. A safe classic is substituted, with Tura playing Hamlet. During the famous soliloquy, a handsome young flier, Lt. Sobinski (Robert Stack), gets up from the audience and visits Maria in her dressing room ("To be or not to be" being the prearranged signal for him to come backstage), where she puts on another act that is more compatible with her sweet, fan-magazine image. But all these roles explode in the face of the sudden invasion: the actors now know that "the Nazis are putting on a bigger show than ours," and that "there are no censors to stop them." From this point on, the art of acting will be utilized for the sake of survival.

Theater and life intermingle when Maria puts on for Siletsky's dinner the dress she intended to wear in the play's concentration camp sequence. (The costume is more appropriate for the dinner since it is as sexy, glittering, and playful as its owner.) Her act with Siletsky is a Lubitsch mélange of sex and politics, with unmistakable gestures and inimitable metaphors, as Siletsky tempts her to become a spy for the Nazis—and also to succumb to his charms. "Shall we drink to a blitzkrieg?" asks the professor seductively. "I prefer a slow encirclement," she sighs. As he plies her with champagne during this "affair of state," he insists that "by the end of the evening, I'll have you saying 'Heil Hitler.' " Between kisses, she murmurs the phrase, now comically defused.

The most effective and poignant example of the space shared by stylization and authenticity in the fluid Lubitsch universe is Shylock's speech from *The Merchant of Venice,* which another of the actors, Greenberg (Felix Bressart), delivers three times: the first is backstage, where he is merely an extra in

Bronski (played by Tom Dugan) playing Hitler in *To Be or Not to Be.*

Jack Benny (Josef), Carole Lombard (Maria), and the theatrical troupe in *To Be or Not to Be.* IMAGES FILM ARCHIVE

Hamlet, indulging in every bit player's wishful dream of stardom; the second is in a rubble-strewn street, where Shakespeare's plea for tolerance in the mouth of a Jewish actor acquires a concrete significance—beyond humor; and the third is at the film's climax, when the lives of all the actors in the troupe are at stake. Greenberg performs Shylock for an unwitting audience of Nazi soldiers and their supposed Führer (who is, in fact, the actor Bronski). Greenberg plays his part on a level where poetic text, staging, and memorizing lines constitute rehearsals for resistance, solidarity, and survival.

It is finally survival that *To Be or Not to Be* is about; it explores with sympathy and irony characters who must act in order to live, or adapt and improvise in order to subvert and overthrow. Lubitsch—a German Jew directing in America in 1942—may have been taking action in the only way available to him: the film asserts that art can heighten and transform experience to the point of effecting social change. *To Be or Not to Be* can be interpreted as an affirmation of its own capacity to delight *and* disturb, or to face horror with the ammunition of sharp humor. It suggests that art (including films) can prepare for life—a stage where the two meanings of "to act" are inextricably linked.

These black comedies made during World War II are necessarily more naïve and optimistic than a postwar film that acknowledges the extent of the devastation wrought by Nazism. Lina Wertmüller's *Seven Beauties* ("Pasqualino

Giancarlo Giannini (Pasqualino) in *Seven Beauties*. CINEMA 5

Settebelezze") (1975) goes further than these American treatments with a controversial study of survival that tests audience thresholds of laughter and horror. The story begins during World War II with the escape of Pasqualino "Seven Beauties" (Giancarlo Giannini) from a train carrying soldiers to the front. He meets a friend and as they roam the dangerous terrain, he begins to recount his past adventures. Through flashbacks to a colorful, music-filled, prewar Naples that is a far cry from the bleakness of Pasqualino's present, we meet a character seemingly different from the prisoner. Pasqualino enters a Felliniesque music hall where one of his sisters is performing a hilariously lascivious song and dance: from Pasqualino's gangster suit, mustache, cigarette holder, cocky hat angle (not to mention the red light in which he is bathed), we know immediately that this is a comic-strip "Godfather." He threatens to kill the pimp who has "ruined" his sister now dancing onstage. Pasqualino must maintain the "honor of the family"—seven-less-than-beautiful sisters (whence his ironic nickname) and his mother—who work long hours at stuffing mattresses while he struts around. Pasqualino says repeatedly that the most important thing is respect, and finally kills the pimp.

The story of survival unfolds as Pasqualino and his road buddy Francesco (Piero di Iorio) are thrown into a German concentration camp. This prison is depicted with a poetic but brutal realism that might be grueling to sit through if Wertmüller did not continually flash back to more vibrant past sequences. For example, the introductory shot of dead naked bodies incessantly filling the screen, accompanied by Wagner's "Ride of the Valkyries," is a visual echo of the rows of beef in the slaughterhouse of Wertmüller's earlier

All Screwed Up (1973). The camp is run by a ruthless Commandant (Shirley Stoller), whom Pasqualino decides he must seduce if he is to survive. His earlier histrionics over his sister's "whoring" give way to his own attempts to "sell" his body, with erection a prerequisite for respect. The final scenes, during which he becomes a Kapo to stay alive, are not quite as amusing as those in Naples: the notions of honor and respect, which contain comic resonance in the flashback sequences, become both derisive and poignant toward the end. To maintain his "family"—the men under his command in Stalag 23 —Pasqualino must sacrifice six men; along with the seventh who commits an especially grisly suicide, they form bitter counterparts to his seven women. Finally, when he is ordered to shoot Francesco, we are plunged into a moral limbo as gray and nebulous as the air of the camp itself.

The last part of the film is discomfiting in its depiction of not only massacred bodies, but the psychic destruction of a victim-turned-oppressor. Pasqualino knows that if he refuses to shoot his friend, someone else will do it. As he holds the gun above Francesco who pleads with him to pull the trigger, *Seven Beauties* raises—and forces the viewer to grapple with—questions about acting humanely and the price of survival. By prolonging the moment, Wertmüller seems to ask, "What would *you* have done in Pasqualino's situation?" After he fires, the camera pans around the entire room in a chilling movement that stops at Pasqualino's face before rising into the eerie smoke. This shot gives us time to ponder Pasqualino's choice and its potential effects. A cut to the bright city of Naples (where his mother, sisters, and fiancée are now all

**Shirley Stoller
(the Commandant)
in *Seven Beauties.*
CINEMA 5**

Pasqualino escaping in *Seven Beauties*. CINEMA 5

prostitutes) brings us back to the "world of the living" with a lurch. Our "hero" returns, but in a manner that suggests the absence of a fully human being: rather than seeing Pasqualino entering the family apartment, we view its contents through his eyes. The insistently subjective camera does not let us see Pasqualino—only to see through him. His face becomes visible *in the mirror,* a reflection that says, "Yes, I'm alive," while his tired eyes seem to ask, "At what price?" The director neither supports nor condemns her protagonist: she simply presents him to us in both his weakness and his endurance.

As in *Swept Away* (1974), Wertmüller alternates between eliciting sympathy and scorn for the protagonist. She balances close-ups and a subjective camera viewpoint, which evoke empathy, with objective long shots that invite detachment. Critics who assumed that the director was endorsing her protagonist simply by having him survive tended to ignore the cinematic means through which Wertmüller was examining her hero. *Seven Beauties* refuses the complacency of a fixed moral structure. It doesn't tell us what to think; it doesn't offer answers. It makes us laugh, and consequently leads us to ask how the hilarious and the horrifying can be so close. There is no question that Wertmüller works in broad strokes. She was, after all, an assistant to the master of the human grotesque, Fellini, and began her career as a puppeteer. There is therefore a tendency in her films to substitute caricature for character, and spectacle for insight. Nevertheless, the style of *Seven Beauties* contrasts Naples' cartoon world of exaggerated acting, make-up, swagger, color and so on, with a world drained of color. And for those who would argue that Wagner's "Ride of the

Valkyries" accompanying Pasqualino's arrival at the concentration camp is not exactly subtle, its use is consistent with Wertmüller's dislocating technique.

From *Seven Beauties'* first sequence—newsreel footage of Nazi destruction to the beat of rock music—the film juxtaposes historical fact with a contemporary sensibility. We see Mussolini, Hitler, and bombs flying, while a voice-over intones, "Oh, yeah." A similar counterpoint between image and sound can be found at the end when Pasqualino's face hardens into a still while a kind of derisive music persists. Whereas Pauline Kael's negative review, "Seven Fatties," maintained that "Wertmüller turns suffering into vaudeville not as part of a Brechtian technique, but, rather, as an expression of a roller-coaster temperament. The suffering is reduced to fun-house games,"[6] her soundtrack does serve to distance us from a facile identification with Pasqualino. The film was vociferously attacked by eminent writers like Jerzy Kosinski and Bruno Bettelheim too, but a far more incisive as well as sympathetic analysis was offered by Terrence Des Pres in *Harper's.* For the author of *The Survivor,* the Wertmüller method is

to give us rough slabs of reality stewing in their own exaggeration. Our first response will be . . . a laughter which trails off finally into profound awareness of the deformity of life as it is . . .[7]

Wertmüller's strokes are sometimes excessive, but perhaps this is one of the ways a contemporary filmmaker can combat the lulling effects of cinema and television. Kael is right in stating that "Wertmüller keeps her films moving by hurling salamis at the audience," but maybe salamis are necessary to stimulate an audience spoon-fed by formulas. Wertmüller's use of laughter is tantamount to assault. The target? Our own complacency, whether in a movie theater or a wartime situation. Wreaking havoc with genre, expectation, and propriety, *Seven Beauties* illustrates how a grotesque era of history might by illuminated by a "roller-coaster" style. By having the anarchist (Fernando Rey) commit suicide by jumping into a pool of excrement, Wertmüller gives the laughter an exceedingly bad taste to render a potentially comic moment quite horrifying. One is therefore not likely to forget this scene, nor his words before the fatal leap: "Man in disorder is our only hope." Given the degree to which Nazi behavior was characterized by order and efficiency, from robot-like salutes to well-run crematoria, the disorder inherent in black comedy can be a powerful antidote to systematic insanity. In the words of Eugène Ionesco,

Humor makes us conscious with a free lucidity of the tragic or desultory condition of man. . . . Laughter alone does not respect any taboo; the comic alone is capable of giving us the strength to bear the tragedy of existence.[8]

PART II
NARRATIVE STRATEGIES

CHAPTER 5

THE JEW AS CHILD

Many films dealing with the Holocaust focus on children or adolescents: among these, *Black Thursday, The Two of Us,* and *Les Violons du Bal* explore the German Occupation of France through its effects on Jewish children, while *The Evacuees* and *David* depict hunted boys in wartime England and Germany. The most salient feature of this narrative strategy is that it highlights the intimacy of family, insisting upon the primacy of blood ties even as it demonstrates that individual survival was predicated on separation. There are also films that do not center on a young Jew—such as *The Damned* and *The Tin Drum*—but yoke childhood and Judaism together to express weakness and victimization. In a perceptive article entitled "The Jew as a Female Figure in Holocaust Film," Judith Doneson has noted that many Holocaust films focus on the Jew "as a weak character, somewhat feminine, being protected by a strong Christian-gentile, the male, in what comes to symbolize a male-female relationship."[1] While this is clearly the case for films like *Black Thursday,* some of the darker visions of the Holocaust depict the Jew as child—whether male or female—both literally and figuratively. In the case of Visconti's *The Damned* (1969), which will be analyzed in Chapter 8, the only Jewish character is indeed a little girl, Lisa. The perverse Martin (Helmut Berger) is attracted to this wide-eyed girl who lives next door to his mistress, and he gently seduces her. When he returns to the room she occupies, Lisa (Irina Wanka) quietly gets out of bed, walks out of the room, and (we learn later) hangs herself. The response of the police is that because she is Jewish, it was not even a crime for Martin to have led her to her death.

The helplessness of the Jewish victim before the Nazi onslaught is also touched upon in *The Tin Drum* (1979), directed by Volker Schlöndorff from Günter Grass's novel. Given its focus on Oskar (David Bennent), a German child who decides at the age of three to stop growing, this portrait of the rise of Nazism creates intriguing rhymes among the child, the Jew, and the midget. It is the wise old midget Bebra (Fritz Hakl) who says *"Mazel tov"* to Oskar, and warns him, "The *others* are coming. They will preach our destruction," before a cut to children yelling, "Heil Hitler!" Bebra also tells Oskar that they must be onstage in order to avoid being controlled. It seems more than coincidental that the only Jewish character, Sigismund Markus (Charles Aznavour), is diminutive; he has a toy store and deals in objects for small people (it is Markus who gives Oskar his tin drum); and, like Bebra, he adopts a role—by becoming baptized. That the midget might be a double for the Jew is implied by the fact that both Bebra and Markus give Oskar a surface to play on—the drum and the stage—or a means to resist control. In this sense, the notion of the Jew as child is pushed into the stylized and even grotesque image of a little outsider who is unable to assume full human proportions while the Nazis run the show.

The country that has produced the most significant number of films dealing with the Jew as child is France—whose wartime behavior was particularly abhorrent: as we learn in *The Sorrow and the Pity,* thousands of Jewish children were arrested by the French police. They were among the 75,000 Jews that France rounded up and deported with a compliance bordering on eagerness. Robert Paxton and Michael Marrus have chronicled in *Vichy France and the Jews* how France and Bulgaria were the only countries in Europe that (while retaining sovereignty over part of their territory) *proposed* to the Germans the roundup and delivery of Jews.[2] Under the Pétainist regime, 1941 saw a well-attended anti-Semitic exhibition in Paris: "*Le Juif et la France* au Palais Berlitz sous l'égide des questions juives" included a pamphlet with directives such as,

The exhibition shows you the racial characteristics of Jews: you will be enlightened by the text and image on their penetration into our country and the harm they have done here; you will therefore understand why so many Frenchmen are dead.[3]

The recent French films on the Holocaust acknowledge and reject the anti-Semitism that claimed so many children as victims during World War II.

Black Thursday ("Les Guichets du Louvre") follows two adolescents through occupied Paris on July 16, 1942—the "black" day that the French police rounded up 14,000 Jews into a winter sports arena for deportation. Against this backdrop of the "La Grande Rafle du Vel' d'Hiv," Paul (Christian Rist), a Christian student, tries to save Jews in general and Jeanne (Christine Pascal) in particular. Directed by Michel Mitrani, this 1974 film quietly indicts not only French anti-Semitism but Jewish passivity. *Black Thursday* begins with French policemen sharing food in a bus: these ordinary men are about to commit extraordinarily monstrous acts, rounding up France's "undesirable" citizens. Paul's motto is "Help the hunted, not the hunter," and he tries to persuade various persons—whose Jewish badges are tantamount to death warrants—to follow him to safety. No one listens. An elegant woman (Judith Magre) responds, "I have nothing to fear: I'm French. And my husband is a POW." A few scenes later, she will be glimpsed in the window of a bus headed for the transports. Paul finally convinces Jeanne that Parisian Jews are doomed when she learns that both her mother and sister have been taken. He leads the hesitant young woman to the safety of the Left Bank, but just before they cross

**Above, David Bennent (Oskar) and Fritz Hakl (Bebra)
and below, Charles Aznavour (Markus) and Angela Winkler (Agnes)
in *The Tin Drum*. CARLOS CLARENS**

Christine Pascal (Jeanne) and Christian Rist (Paul)
in *Black Thursday*. KEN WLASCHIN

Fleeing the French police in *Black Thursday.*
LEVITT-PICKMAN FILM CORPORATION

the bridge, she decides to return to her people. A closing title taken from the New York *Times* states, "Only thirty adults survived that 'Great Roundup.' Not a single child returned."

Black Thursday does not flinch from presenting the complacent French, whether they be policemen who hardly balk at "cleaning up" the Jewish neighborhoods, or Gentiles who loot apartments only moments after the Jewish tenants have left. One policeman speaks in disbelief of a Jewish woman who threw her children and then herself from a window rather than be taken: "After all, we're not the Germans," he rationalizes with smug comfort. Nevertheless, the Jews in this film are equally blind to the situation; in a symbolic touch worthy of Marcel Carné, Mitrani even includes a blind man with a cane whom Paul tries vainly to assist: he turns out to be Jewish as well. These characters can all be seen as children who are in need of protection (by a Christian) or who obey authorities. When Paul implores Jeanne to remove the Jewish star sewn onto her coat, she refuses. After learning of her mother's disappearance, she is offered scissors by a kindly woman. Instead of removing the star, Jeanne points the scissors at herself with the implication of suicide —and the woman tears off the badge for her. When Jeanne warns her religious relatives about the roundup, they are horrified that she has removed her star, and the eldest says in Yiddish, "We have to live according to God's will."

The focus of the film is consequently the Christian youth and his futile generosity. Paul, who began his mission because of an abstract desire to do good deeds, gradually falls in love with Jeanne. When he urges her to go away with him to the country, he declares, "I need your eyes to see," suggesting that the Christian needs to assume the Jewish victim's burden for his own redemption. In her article, Judith Doneson claims that *Black Thursday,* along with other films, presents a symbiotic relationship between the Jew and the Gentile:

For the Jew this means a reliance upon the Christian for his survival, while the Christian depends upon the Jew as both a witness to his own theology and as a humanizing factor which helps bring out the "goodness" incumbent upon noble Christian souls. This mutual need is represented as a couple, the Jew being the female, the Christian . . . the male.[4]

Jeanne refuses to tell Paul her name until the last scene, and only after she decides to rejoin her people. She thus acquires an identity only by embracing her fate as a victim. Doneson argues that "[Jeanne] takes on the role of a martyr by figuratively choosing to return to the fire and die as a Jew with her people. Thus does she come to resemble an early French martyr and nationalist [Jeanne d'Arc], a hero to her people. . . ." This theological interpretation does not, however, take account of a simple emotional fact: Jeanne has been separated from her mother and, like Edith in *Kapo,* she chooses the transports in order to be with her. It is this identity—the child torn from parents, rather than prospective martyr—that impelled Jews like Jeanne to reject personal safety.

Claude Berri's 1966 film *The Two of Us* ("Le Vieil Homme et l'Enfant") acknowledges and mocks French anti-Semitism through the touching story of a nine-year-old Jewish boy (Alain Cohen) who is sent to the French countryside when Paris becomes too dangerous. A prefatory title states that this is a true story, and the protagonist's voice-over narration adds to the illusion of history. The boy's overwrought father (Charles Denner) realizes the child will survive more easily under an assumed name—Claude Longuet—and in the care of a Christian couple. He and his wife entrust him to the parents of a friend. Claude's new "Pépé" (Gramps, played by the celebrated French actor Michel Simon) is a determined but lovable anti-Semite. "In 1939," he expounds, "three percent of the French population was Jewish, but eighty-one percent of the government was Jewish." In the course of the film, he trots out other clichés including "You can always recognize them by the smell" and "They have flat feet to keep them out of the army, but are the fastest to run to the bank." Never suspecting that the child he is growing to love is "one of them," the old grouch spouts Vichy rhetoric, and complains that his daughter "loves Jews and Reds." The Liberation finally comes, and Claude's parents take him home.

The old xenophobe never learns that his "adopted grandson" *is* Jewish, and François Truffaut proposed that "Berri had the tact, the intelligence, the sensitivity and the intuition not to clear up the misunderstanding."[5] However, Gramps' lack of illumination further encloses the film within the domain of tranquil recollection. The voice-over establishes that like *Les Violons du Bal,* the boy's backward glance retains familial warmth rather than the complexities nurtured by the Occupation. The child never really confronts the father figure, and *The Two of Us* is very much a film that accepts patriarchy—in both visual and narrative terms. When Claude's father recounts a story while feeding him dinner, a long-take three-shot maintains the child and mother spatially below him. Likewise, Gramps is the one who runs the home, and Granny's obedience extends into the political realm when she speaks of Maréchal Pétain as a hero.

Nevertheless, the film is charming and effective through Alain Cohen's dark expressive eyes and Simon's characterization of the lovable bigot. Moreover, Charles Denner's grave and pinched features give the early sequences a feeling of authenticity: in his twitching face, we see the vulnerable Jew who must send his beloved son away until the craziness of war subsides. The farewell scene is especially well designed because the camera is located within the train, behind the child, as the parents try to keep up with its receding movement. At such moments, *The Two of Us* seems worthy of Truffaut's appraisal:

For twenty years I have been waiting for the *real* film about the *real* France during the *real* Occupation, the film about the majority of Frenchmen, those who were involved neither in the collaboration nor the Resistance, those who did nothing, either good or bad, those who survived like characters in a Beckett play. . . . Now Claude Berri's first film, *The Two of Us,* makes the long wait worth it.

The Evacuees (Great Britain, 1975) is directed by Alan Parker in a far gentler key than his subsequent films, *Midnight Express, Fame,* and *Shoot the Moon.* Made for the BBC, it traces the provisional exile of two Jewish youths from Manchester to Blackpool, by the sea. *The Evacuees,* written by Jack Rosenthal, begins on September 1, 1939, with a teacher named Goldstone reading off the Jewish boys' names in class. It turns out that they will be matched up with temporary foster parents. After bidding their own families good-by, they follow Goldstone as he asks people to take in these evacuees. Many feign excuses; one housewife asks, "Are they clean?" and then says, "I'll try one"! The Miller brothers are taken in by Mrs. Graham, where their first humorous problem is the pork sausage being served: they try to say a Jewish prayer over the pork, each holding a hand over his head. The effect of their absence upon their own family is beautifully expressed by a shot of the Millers' dinner table: the camera begins and remains on the empty chairs for a long moment before panning to the parents and grandmother eating silently.

By January of 1940, Mrs. Graham is running the show, pocketing the letters and food that the mother sends the boys. She is sweet on the surface, but steely inside: when Mrs. Miller comes to see them, Mrs. Graham interrupts her embrace. Finally, the brothers write a veiled letter home that reveals what has been happening to their mail and food. Their mother takes them back to Manchester, leaving Mrs. Graham who claims tearfully to her husband, "I taught them respect for their betters and elders; I call that love." Her self-justifying attitude is contrasted with the love that emanates from the Millers'

Chanukah celebration at home. By March 1941, the children in Manchester are cruel to a new evacuee from London—suggesting that it is not simply in Nazi Germany that people must guard against intolerance. *The Evacuees* is a lovely little film, with humor and pain delicately balanced. Nevertheless, the portrayal of these Jewish boys in the early stages of World War II is relatively mild, containing more humorous recollection—like Mrs. Miller and her mother wearing pots on their heads for air raids—than serious reflection.[6]

Like *The Evacuees,* Peter Lilienthal's *David* (1979) is about adolescence—not only in terms of the protagonist's age, but Nazism itself; like *Les Violons du Bal, The Garden of the Finzi-Continis,* and *Lacombe, Lucien,* its context is the rise of human monstrosity. *David*'s early image of a chained strong man performing in 1933 might represent the brute strength of Nazism that was about to explode in the mid-thirties. Nevertheless, the focus of this German film, which won the Golden Bear Prize at the Berlin Film Festival, is quietly intimate: it succeeds best in its communication of the warmth and solidarity in a rabbi's family. *David* begins in 1933 Liegnitz where little David Singer (Torsten Henties) is beaten up by three Hitler Youth children who scream,

Walter Taub (Rabbi Singer) and Mario Fischel (the grown David) in *David.*
KINO INTERNATIONAL CORPORATION

"Jewish pig!" His father (Walter Taub) is the rabbi who, while conducting a synagogue celebration of the holiday of Purim, offers a historical precedent for the oppression and exile of Jews: "Get thee to the mountain that thou shalt not perish." During dinner one evening, a parade passes by outside that is punctuated by the cry, *"Juden raus! Juden raus!"* The rabbi thinks they're saying, "Youth, come out" *(Jugend raus),* but we learn that the words are actually "Jews, get out!"

A cut to 1938 finds David (Mario Fischel), now a teen-ager, in a train to Berlin. Having been kicked out of *Gymnasium* for being a Jew, he and his brother Leo (Dominique Horwitz) go to a trade school, along with other Jews. The title, "November 1938—Nationwide Pogrom," establishes that the scenes of desecration, looting, and synagogue-burning represent the infamous *Kristallnacht.* The rabbi and congregation are humiliated and forced to watch their house of worship go up in flames. David is then sent to an agricultural training camp to prepare for his eventual emigration to Palestine. A sudden call from his father demanding David's immediate return causes David to be absent during the roundup of the young members of the training camp—who are led into a building from which none ever emerge. When David's parents are later taken as well, he hides out in their ransacked apartment, teaching himself Hebrew. His next hiding place is with a shoemaker whose relationship to David and his sister (Eva Mattes) smacks of greed more than altruism. They know it is time to move on when the shoemaker's grandson comes back from army service crying, "They gassed them during the day and burned them at night." After a kind factory owner (played by Rudolf Sellner, former director of the Berlin Opera) gives him false papers, David escapes to Vienna and onto a boat, the soundtrack suddenly alive with joyous music. Although the film does not state his destination, Lilienthal explained that David goes to "the only place in the world where, in 1943, a Jew could be greeted by people singing and dancing: Palestine."[7]

The understatement of the ending is in keeping with the tone of the entire film. The Nazis' systematic destruction of Jewish life—dispossession and deportation to concentration camps—is presented with a respectful distancing from the subject. Without actually showing the horror of the concentration camps via reconstruction, Lilienthal suggests the cruel indifference that permitted genocide to take place. As Carlos Clarens wrote:

In *David* there is none of the *retro* soft-focus of *The Garden of the Finzi-Continis* . . . there are no predictable melodramatics as in the TV miniseries *Holocaust:* Lilienthal proceeds through accumulation of detail. Nor is *David* a UFA-style fantasy like *Lili Marleen.* . . . What's left, then, once you take away any sentimentality, melodrama, and comfortable outrage? Just a tale of madness so epidemic that it eventually spread, in the form of hope and self-delusion, to the Jews themselves.[8]

For example, after Rabbi Singer is arrested, he comes home and reveals a swastika branded on his scalp—but the branding took place off-screen. In fact, the director admitted in an interview that he cut one sequence that would have been more violent—and thus potentially exploitative:

There is one scene . . . of the Nazis coming to the Jewish pension in the evening. They take people out in their pajamas and kick them under the tables. I never gave any direction of insult, but suddenly they found the old vocabulary. It would have been the only violent scene in the film, adding nothing new. It was against the spirit of the film, so I took it out. For me, blood is blood even if it's ketchup. That's where direction ends, for me.[9]

A literal depiction might have been less moving for, as one of the characters remarks, "there's nothing people get used to faster than seeing others suffer." Rather, the film moves slowly and tenderly (though never sentimentally) through the events that uproot and disband a family.

David is one of the rare Holocaust films that conveys the joy and pride of being Jewish. Unlike the blue-eyed blondes of *The Garden of the Finzi-Continis* and *Lacombe, Lucien,* the characters in *David*—many of them played by nonprofessional actors—have a palpable authenticity. Lilienthal found some of his performers in the Warsaw Yiddish Theater, and chose a cinematographer who is particularly sensitive to idiosyncratic faces—Al Ruban, known for his work with John Cassavetes. When questioned about the source of the celebratory Jewish tone of the film, Lilienthal confessed, "At first it was a counter-reaction, because many immigrants were not proud of being Jewish.

Mario Fischel (the grown David) in *David.*
KINO INTERNATIONAL
CORPORATION

Therefore, I had to be. And when I learned about persecutions, that was another reason to be proud."[10] Indeed, Lilienthal's own biography has profound connections to *David* and accounts for much of the film's integrity. This German Jew left Berlin for Uruguay with his mother in 1939—at the age of ten—and returned to his homeland in 1956. His formative years in South America gave him a keen perspective on social unrest and solidarity. After making a number of explicitly political films, he adapted Joel König's autobiographical book in two stages: "I wrote the first version with Jurek Becker. The final draft I did alone, to combine David's character with my own, and his experiences with mine." For example, David washes dishes in a Chinese restaurant toward the end of the film, an episode from Lilienthal's past:

The only restaurants that weren't hostile to Jews in 1939 were Chinese. Other places had signs saying Jews and dogs not allowed. We couldn't buy ice cream, and we sat on special yellow benches. We weren't allowed into swimming pools. But I thought that this made us very special. I considered it a privilege, not a punishment.[11]

König served as an adviser on the film; the result is a poignant backward glance that, like *The Boat Is Full,* resists melodramatic clichés, manipulative music, and simplified behavior by "villains" or "heroes." As with many victims of the Holocaust, David is hidden by a variety of individuals: he is exploited by some, saved by others. He is intelligent but unremarkable, resourceful but not especially "heroic," hopeful but not visibly passionate. As Robert Liebman pointed out,

His father taught him that when the authorities forbid you to pray, you can outsmart them by praying to yourself. His father also declared that a swastika on one's head is insignificant if one is alive to talk about it: "I'm here, I'm here; that's all that counts." Lilienthal sums up David's familial heritage by simply noting that "he had a strong reason to live—the Jewish religion."[12]

Although the boy progressively loses members of his family, *David* celebrates the spirit that binds him to his rabbi-father, and thus to a rich—if vulnerable —heritage.

CHAPTER 6
IN THE HIDING/ON STAGE

I n the art of motion pictures, the depiction of claustrophobia is a challenge: what can a filmmaker do with the inherently "theatrical" concept of enclosure in which spatial restrictions and protagonists' paranoia—as in films dealing with the Holocaust—conspire to prevent free movement? What "landscape" is possible when characters are essentially defined by fear, impatience, or passivity? The answers afforded by films like *Samson* and *The Boat Is Full* suggest that the magnification of a face can be as cinematic as the mobility of a camera—especially when the character being hidden is himself hiding an emotion. The limitation of action to a single room might feel like theater, but the close-up (when used judicially and subtly) makes such scenes radically filmic. Moreover, films like *The Condemned of Altona* and *The Last Metro* concern themselves explictly with theater as an integral component of hiding. By exploring dependence, choice, and occupation within personal relationships, they illuminate these themes on wider political and moral levels as well.

Theater is both the source and narrative center of *The Condemned of Altona* ("I Sequestrati di Altona"). Adapted by Abby Mann and Cesare Zavattini from Jean-Paul Sartre's play, this 1962 Italian-American co-production directed by Vittorio De Sica masterfully incorporates Brecht's play *The Resistible Rise of Arturo Ui*. Like *Hamlet*'s strategy—"The play's the thing/Wherein I'll catch the conscience of the king"—the interplay of theater and actuality provides much of the drama. The German magnate Gerlach (Fredric March) claims that his son Franz (Maximilian Schell)—a former Nazi officer whose entire company was killed in Smolensk in 1941—died after being tried in Nuremberg. Actually, he is locked in a hidden part of his father's mansion, seen only by his sister Leni (Francoise Prévost). She reads him newspapers from 1945 as current events to maintain his illusion that Germany is still at war. When Gerlach learns that he is dying of cancer, his other son

Werner (Robert Wagner) returns to the house with his wife Johanna (Sophia Loren). She discovers Franz's existence and persistently tries to free him from his spatial and psychological prison.

Faithful to the artistic source of the film, De Sica sets his scenes with theatrical devices from the outset: when the doctor tells Gerlach that he has only six months to live, he pulls down a window shade whose shadow descends on the patient like a curtain. Gerlach then speaks through an X-ray machine, which creates the frightening image of a disembodied voice. This image subsequently links Gerlach with Hitler, whose voice is heard on the radio, and with Franz who continually tapes and plays back his own harangues. Indeed, all the major characters in *The Condemned of Altona* are agents of voice or exist primarily through their speech, in true theater style: Johanna is a stage actress, Werner is a trial lawyer, Leni reads aloud deceptive newspapers, Gerlach has cancer of the throat, and Franz's self-mystification ("One voice shall remain to cry no, not guilty," he screams) and subsequent disruption of the Brecht play are enacted through declamations.

Franz is introduced via voice: we hear a few words and then a tape rewinding. Only afterward do we see fragments of a face—close-up of mouth and then eyes—with a tape recorder and microphone. Franz's first action is to make Leni "testify that all is rubble." He directs his living scenario before walls painted with horrific faces reminiscent of Munch's "The Scream." These skeletal visages of mute agony (corresponding to the pre-credit sequence in Smolensk that ends with a freeze frame of a soldier's silent scream) externalize Franz's character. And his aggressive action vis-à-vis Johanna is to shine a bright light on her. Johanna and her brother-in-law are linked by two scenes that take place in a theater: after we see Werner accusing four punks in a courtroom of anti-Semitic activity, there is an abrupt cut to a man and a woman listening to Hitler on the radio. It is only later that we learn they are onstage, rehearsing Brecht's play; Johanna reads a letter aloud, her voice vying with that of the Führer's. When Franz is finally persuaded to leave the house, he goes to Johanna's theater and wanders zombielike into the performance. Assuming that the actor *is* the Führer, he berates the audience to respect Hitler, yelling "Pigs!": his voice competes with Hitler's on stage, as Johanna's did earlier.

In a larger sense, *The Condemned of Altona* is about overcoming the voice of the father. Gerlach loses his power of speech, and is later definitively silenced by his son in Franz's closing suicide/patricide; Hitler is drowned out by Johanna and then Franz. Both characters enact a denial of the patriarch/dictator through theater—Johanna in a literal sense, and Franz by turning his room into an expressionist stage, replete with grotesque décor, high-contrast lighting, elaborate *mise en scène,* and his own Nazi "costume."

Expressive camera work heightens Franz's theatricality. He is seen from a high angle when he puts on a blanket and talks like a machine gun, returning to Smolensk in 1941. As he assumes different voices, the camera alternates between this high angle and a low one, giving visual form to his different identities. His performance is a rehearsal rather than a revival, for Franz's stage is a projection into the future—a trial in the year 3059. He is concerned with how the "decapods" (crablike inhabitants of the thirty-first century) will

Maximilian Schell (Franz) in *The Condemned of Altona.*
MUSEUM OF MODERN ART/FILM STILLS ARCHIVE

judge twentieth-century man, and tries to remain the voice that cries "not guilty." When he finally does emerge into the night air, his face is reflected in a pool of water. He wipes away the reflection, unable to look at the self-image he created. At this point, Franz goes to the theater whose façade contains pictures of Johanna and of another consummate performer—Adolf Hitler. But Franz cannot accept the fact that the theater is greater than Hitler's image, nor that *Arturo Ui* is performance rather than life. As a theatrical spectator whose disbelief needs no suspending, he hyperbolically supports Johanna's earlier comment, "The theater is the world compressed and with meaning."

Theater liberates Johanna and Franz in different ways, as both insist on discovering the truth. In the Brecht scene, it shatters his illusions, allowing him to stop living in "bad faith" and to start facing a new world. And yet, the film seems to ask, is this world (of 1959) really a new one? A Hamburg where people on the street hardly blink at this man in a Nazi uniform? Where "schoolbooks say Hitler was like Napoleon," according to Johanna? A courtroom in which teenagers are charged with defacing a Jewish cemetery? A brother who is clearly capable of becoming another unscrupulous Gerlach? Johanna's response, the imaginative transformation of theater, is thus a perpetual antidote to what she perceives as a chronic disease: "You are afflicted with a national infirmity—a lack of imagination for the suffering of others."

Franz's situation is quite different from that of the other hidden characters throughout Holocaust films. "If I wanted to escape," he boasts, "I'd have gone to the Argentine long ago." He does not even realize that his hiding is imprisonment, because Leni fuels his delusion that war continues to rage beyond his room. However, his situation is somewhat analogous to that of the character Samson in Andrzej Wajda's 1961 film of the same title, a man who is similarly caught between two women—one who continues his imprisonment (Kazia) and one who represents liberation (the actress Lucyna). Franz and Samson are prisoners without a sense of time; dependent on Leni and Kazia for news of the outside world, they are persuaded that to go outside is dangerous; the women want them to remain within.

Samson opens in a Polish university where the young hero Jakub Gold/ Samson (Serge Merlin) is the victim of growing anti-Semitism. When he accidentally throws a brick at the one student who tried to help him, he is sent to jail. This first enclosure is rendered visually compelling through Wajda's typically expressive composition, lighting, and camera work. He meets the heroic professor Pankrat (Tadeusz Bartosik), and one shot balances Pankrat's cell on the left with Samson's on the right: there is light only on each face, a glimmering bond in the pervasive dark. The faces are further linked by a panning camera movement. An explosion gets Samson out of jail, but his next prison is the Warsaw Ghetto. A magnificently layered shot expresses the situation through economical deep focus: the soldiers in the foreground hammer in bars, closing off our view of the midground where the crowd faces us, and in the background more soldiers are visible. Samson survives in the Ghetto by burying the dead inhabitants. When he must carry his own mother (Irena Netto) to burial, he accepts a friend's offer to escape, and heads for the Aryan sector. Here, he takes refuge with Lucyna (Alina Janowska), an actress who tries to keep him from returning to the Ghetto. When she finally confesses that she too is a Jew—"I escape from the Ghetto every day"—we become aware of the fundamental role-playing necessary for survival under the Occupation. Lucyna is an actress on stage and off, and she extends her ability to assume a persona into her efforts to protect Samson: she dyes her hair blonde, and then cuts it to change her appearance.

Samson leaves her apartment and her love—a departure foreshadowed by a shot of the couple in bed through the bars of a chair, suggesting imprisonment—and meets a group of street performers who put a mask on him. Wajda shows the solidarity of theater people and their ease in adapting to maleficent conditions when they help him regain the path to the Ghetto. Samson finds the apartment of Malina (Jan Ciecierski), his former cell-mate, who lives with his daughter Kazia (Elzbieta Kepinska). That she will destroy his identity is hinted when she washes Samson's sweater—inadvertently removing the Jewish star—and reinforced when she cuts the hero's hair. This "Delilah" falls in love with the hidden boarder, and when the actress comes looking for him, Kazia tells her the only place to find her former lodger is Gestapo headquarters. Lucyna gives herself up to the Nazis while Kazia tries to win Samson's love by assuming the role of protector, not unlike the actress in Wojciech Has's 1963 film *How to be Loved* ("Jak być Kochana") who hides the reluctant hero played by Zbigniew Cybulski—and both scripts are by Kazimierz Brandys.

Theatrical lighting once again connects the film's prisons as Samson's rocking chair casts intermittent bars on Kazia's face; when Samson lowers his head, he places them both behind reflected bars. He rocks himself into a lamentable passivity, claiming that he will never leave the cellar, until he is roused by the memory of his mother's admonition: "Our ordeal has gone on for more than five thousand years. You have to be as strong as Samson." After Malina is struck by a German van and carried away, Kazia brings her charge upstairs: the screen goes white as Samson leaves the cellar, a subjective burst of illumination signifying escape from the dark. (This is the case for the audience as well, for we have been seeing only as much of the outside world as the prisoner.)

Samson abandons the clutching Kazia and finds what will become his last hiding place, inside the printing plant of a clandestine newspaper. Now allied with Pankrat and the Communists, he enacts a heroic finale by throwing a grenade at snooping German soldiers. A beam falls on him, killing him, and *Samson* ends with a whiteout; this rhymes visually with the earlier explosion of light, suggesting a final escape—and illumination through heroic action. *Samson*'s voice-over narration changes from an objective (if poetic) third-person to the first-person—the hero's inner voice inciting him to act. Thematically, this shift represents a movement from manipulated object to ruler of his own destiny, no longer at the mercy of women. The dark woman in *Samson* cuts his hair, implying the emasculation of the male; the fair woman cuts her own hair, prefiguring her self-destruction. These symbolic actions point to the mutual dependency or psychological occupation experienced by characters under political occupation.

In both *Samson* and *The Condemned of Altona* (shot the same year), the women are curiously polarized into the savior-actress (Lucyna and Johanna) and the possessive protector (Kazia and Leni), but all of them ultimately shield or prod the vulnerable male because of their own frustrated needs. They are, in a sense, director figures, *metteuses-en-scène* who manipulate the lead actor. This reflects how the "hiding" hero of films about the Holocaust must be— or become—a performer, able to assume and play roles, create a set/home, constantly improvise, and be prepared to "take the show on the road." Perhaps the most masterful elaboration of this theme is François Truffaut's 1980 film *The Last Metro* ("Le Dernier Métro") in which a Jewish theater director and his actress-wife play out an offstage drama in order to elude the Gestapo and the French police.

The Last Metro takes place during the German Occupation of Paris, just as the Free Zone is about to be invaded. Lucas Steiner (Heinz Bennent), a German-Jewish stage director, is forced to go underground amid mounting anti-Semitism in 1942. He entrusts the management of the prestigious Théâtre Montmartre to his wife Marion (Catherine Deneuve). She must surmount the subtle threats of the pro-Nazi drama critic Daxiat (Jean-Louis Richard),* the romantic appeal of her new leading man Bernard (Gérard Depardieu), and the curfew that requires their curtain to come down in time for the night's last subway service. Thus, the limitations imposed by war define the possibilities of theater. Marion's central preoccupation, however, is her husband: he is not in South America, as everyone believes, but hidden in the cellar of the theater. The play the company puts on is *La Disparue* ("The Woman Who Disappeared") but it is really Marion who disappears every night—under the stage.

Like Kazia, Marion cuts Lucas' hair, and like Leni, she prevents the man

---

*Daxiat is modeled on Alain Laubreaux, a Jew-baiting French drama critic of *Je Suis Partout,* the most virulently collaborationist newspaper during the Occupation.

Above,
François Truffaut
directing Heinz Bennent
and Catherine Deneuve.

Below,
Catherine Deneuve
(Marion) and Heinz
Bennent (Lucas) in
The Last Metro.
LES FILMS DU CARROSSE

from going outside—even going so far as to club Lucas over the head when he tries to leave the hiding place. Nevertheless, Marion's actions are unselfish and she is closer to Johanna in *The Condemned of Altona*—strong in her identity as actress. Role-playing, improvisation, and a vivid imagination enable both Lucas and Marion to survive as well as mount good plays. The 813 days he spends literally underground are bearable only because Lucas devises a way to participate in the performances above: through a utilities duct in the wall, he can hear the rehearsals, and he prepares notes that become Marion's suggestions to her director Jean-Loup (Jean Poiret). While the set is being constructed onstage, Lucas builds his "apartment" below with props. And when the French police arrive to search the cellar, he quickly "strikes the set" so that the Gestapo find no trace of a hidden Jew.

Theater is a cover in *The Last Metro*—literally for Lucas who is really underground and wants to be onstage, and figuratively for Bernard who is onstage but really wants to be in the Resistance. Bernard is the only one in the theater company who refuses to assume a compliant persona vis-à-vis the authorities: after Daxiat pans the show, Bernard beats him up in a restaurant. This is the sort of flamboyant gesture an actor might indulge in (as, indeed, did Jean Marais at the time), but *not* a member of the Resistance. Similarly, *The Last Metro* often translates a political question into a theatrical concern. One way to read the film is in terms of displacement: we constantly see characters being moved around, not only onstage but up and down the stairs: Bernard refuses to take the place of Rosen, the Jewish actor with Aryan papers; and we don't really see anti-Semitism as much as French individuals who want for themselves the desirable situations occupied by Jews—their theaters, their women, their artistic authority. (Lucas reads to Marion that French fascists claim of Jews, "they steal our most beautiful women," and Daxiat tells Jean-Loup that the only way to keep the Théâtre Montmartre is to allow him to be co-director.) The Nazi impulse in Paris is depicted in terms of expulsion—"France is off-limit to Jews," declares Daxiat on the radio—or loss of place. More specifically, it is symbolized by Lucas being forced off his stage into placelessness—a room as self-enclosed as a stage.

We do not see any truly painful images of Nazi behavior in *The Last Metro*, for Truffaut's concern is clearly more with his characters than with the German Occupation. For example, there are very few Germans in the film—a soldier who pats a boy's head, another who paints the Sacré-Coeur in a Paris street, the genteel husband of a French woman who attends the opening night party, and (the most dangerous) a lieutenant at Gestapo headquarters whose admiration of Marion is expressed by his holding her hand too long. Truffaut's premise seems to be that there was as much to fear from the pro-Nazi French as from the Germans. Marion tells Lucas that the number of letters denouncing Jews is up to 1,500 a day—an acknowledgment of a French rather than German phenomenon. "That's why there are almost no Germans in the film," Truffaut admitted in an interview.[1] "One of the most monstrous things during the war was the 'Rafle du Vel' d'Hiv,' and it was the French who did it," he elaborated, referring to the roundup of 14,000 Jews by the Paris police on July 16, 1942. (This event, which facilitated deportation to concentration camps from Paris' sports arena, the Vélodrome d'Hiver, is also treated in *Black Thursday* and Joseph Losey's *Mr. Klein.*)

Despite *The Last Metro*'s sensitivity to the plight of Jews in wartime France, anti-Semitism is hardly its main theme. While the film calls attention to the fact that actors had to have an Aryan certificate in order to appear on stage or screen, it does not dwell, for example, on the point that Jews had to ride in the last car of trains. Truffaut's contention that "this film is not concerned merely with anti-Semitism but intolerance in general" is evidenced by the fact that *The Last Metro* encompasses a homosexual director (Poiret) and a lesbian designer (Andréa Ferréol) with great ease.[2] Why include these characters whose sexual orientation is not an issue? In Truffaut's words,

Suzanne Schiffman [co-screenwriter and assistant director] and I observed that the collaborationist, extreme-right press condemned Jews and homosexuals in the same breath. The French pro-Nazis had a very naïve image of Germany—virile male strength. It's absurd to look only at films like Visconti's *The Damned:* sure, there were lots of homosexuals in the SS. But for the Nazis, the weak were "female" in a pejorative sense. Hence, the phobia against homosexuals. It always pops up in reviews of the collaborationist newspaper *Je Suis Partout* ["I Am Everywhere"]: you read, for instance, "a play that reeks of Jewishness and effeminacy."[3]

In *The Last Metro,* this accusation is leveled by Daxiat at the Steiners' productions, and many of the film's lines and details come from actors' memoirs and research. The film has an extremely realistic specificity of background, décor, and costumes (right down to the women's dark-toned legs— make-up rather than stockings!); the first shots are archival photographs and footage, accompanied by a male voice-over narration that roots the story in a precise time and place. Nevertheless, *The Last Metro* is closer to Lubitsch's *To Be or Not to Be* than to Marcel Ophuls' *The Sorrow and the Pity,* for Truffaut's affectionate tale puts his actors rather than the Occupation in the foreground. As he explained at the press conference of the 1980 New York Film Festival (where his film was the closing-night selection), "It's an invented story nourished by real details but deliberately outside my reality. The Occupation is the echo chamber for the actors. My intention was to make a dramatic comedy with true or plausible elements."

By the last part of the film, the director's relationship to the audience and material is downright playful. "Our story awaits its epilogue," announces the narrator, and locates us in the summer of 1944. Marion enters a hospital room, approaches a wounded and sullen Bernard, and says, "He's dead now." We assume the reference to be to Lucas, especially when she asks Bernard to make a new start with her. As the scene progresses, the window behind them (showing people moving) is suddenly a painted backdrop; their faces seem more heavily made up; and the eruption of applause reveals that this has been a play. Truffaut suggests how easy it is to confuse "theater" with "reality," and then elicits a sigh of relief when Lucas is spotted. He moves, symbolically enough, from shadow into light to accept the applause, and then joins Marion and Bernard onstage to take a bow.[4] He is back where he belongs, a survivor of claustrophobia, loneliness, and the pernicious if abstract intolerance of the French.

As Peter Pappas wrote in his perceptive review of *The Last Metro,* the most extraordinary performance of the film, the one true revelatory appearance, belongs to Heinz Bennent, playing the role of Lucas Steiner. Bennent's performance is evocative in the most Proustian sense of the word; it is the madeleine which pulls us into the obscurely remembered past. Through Bennent's portrayal of Steiner, which is to say, through Steiner's every delicate movement of his body, every aristocratic nuance of his hands, every measured step of his feet, we are swallowed into a Paris that no longer exists: the city of Sacha Guitry, Alain Cuny, the young Jean-Louis Barrault, and, of course, Louis Jouvet.[5]

Although more screen time is devoted to Marion and Bernard, it is Lucas who towers over the other characters—even from the basement. (Bennent's performance is all the more remarkable when we recall his Nazi-linked incarnations in *The Serpent's Egg* and *The Tin Drum.*) Through Lucas' bitter acknowledgement, for example, of a children's crossword puzzle that posits, "You can never trust one" for a four-letter word beginning with J ("juif"), Truffaut creates a muted but unflinching depiction of the French anti-Semitism that the Nazis inflamed. *The Last Metro* is certainly idealized and tame in its imagery, but cinematically vital in its juxtaposition of stage and cellar, resister and performer.

The protagonists of *The Boat Is Full* ("Das Boot Ist Voll"), on the other hand, are *not* actors—except when forced to improvise in order to survive. This restrained and moving 1981 film by Swiss director Markus Imhoof was a co-production of Switzerland, West Germany, and Austria. While Imhoof's *Boat* moves quite differently from Truffaut's *Metro,* both lead us to comprehend and identify with an endangered group held together by strong women. Because its focus is on life as theater rather than theater as life, *The Boat Is Full* is ultimately more successful at re-creating the real terms and textures of Jews in hiding. These victims of Nazism are neither wealthy nor famous: when they escape, they take almost nothing with them.

Like Lucas' pipeline in *The Last Metro, The Boat Is Full* is structured by open areas becoming blocked and vice versa, whether spaces or emotions. This tension is announced in the first shot, when the camera tracks forward to a tunnel that workers are filling with bricks. We learn that this is to stop the train from bringing more Jewish refugees into Switzerland from Germany. The camera then positions itself within the tunnel (a subtle hint that it is on the train's side and will assume its point of view), preparing for the next shot— a cut to night and the refugees being forced to leave the train.

Only a few of these victims escape into Switzerland, thrown together by chance: "Being Jewish isn't enough," declares a Protestant minister—only political refugees are allowed to remain in Switzerland. However, an exception for families with children under the age of six prompts the group to pretend to be a family. Accordingly, Judith (Tina Engel), who is trying to find her non-Jewish husband in a Swiss prison, passes herself off as the wife of Karl (Gerd David), a Nazi deserter. The elderly Ostrowskij (Curt Bois) becomes her father and claims that a French orphan named Maurice is his grandson; because the child speaks no German, they say that he is deaf and dumb. Another young child, Gitty, becomes Maurice's sister, and Judith's brother

Olaf (Martin Walz) assumes the uniform of the Nazi deserter. Together, they take refuge in a shed that turns out to belong to a middle-aged Swiss couple. The initial reaction of the wife Anna Flückinger (Renate Steiger) upon discovering these "visitors" is fear and distaste; nevertheless, she gives them food (for which they try to pay with silverware) and gradually begins to feel more responsible for them. Her coarse husband Franz (Mathias Gnaedinger) was originally even more anxious to get rid of them, but he too comes to realize that if they are on the run, it is not because they are criminals. Flouting Swiss law, which does not permit refugees to remain unless they are political, the Flückingers help them in increasingly more risk-defying ways.

When the district policeman questions them, he is initially pleased to accept the refugees' jewelry in exchange for needed papers. But like the Flückingers —as well as most of the characters in the film—he is unpredictably subject to change. If the couple shifts from an initial reluctance to be implicated to finally sympathetic action, the policeman swerves from a readiness to help to later bureaucratic steeliness. A soldier who watches over Judith's husband (Hans Diehl) in prison abruptly offers him a chance to escape on his bicycle. Some of the people want their town rid of these foreigners. Others shelter them, offer them food, and even accompany them when they are forced back to the border. The film's focus is therefore personal, suggesting that the Swiss persecutors of the Jewish refugees were less "evil" than callously indifferent. Or are these terms synonymous?

The Jewish refugees in *The Boat Is Full.* **A QUARTET/FILMS INCORPORATED RELEASE**

Being forced back to the border was the fate of ten thousand Jews who were returned by Swiss authorities to Germany—in other words, to concentration camps. As is true of the Holocaust in general, inhuman policies were implemented at least in part by ordinarily decent people, willingly blind to atrocities. According to Imhoof, the crux of the problem is "the half-heartedness of people who came into contact with the refugees—their complicity."[6] Imhoof's direction is sober, perhaps reflecting his immersion in Brecht's writings (the subject of his dissertation at the University of Zurich). His refusal of facile emotion can be seen in the film's total lack of music and in its understated acting. Rather than manipulating the audience, *The Boat Is Full* reveals the spectrum of human response to persecuted people: like the spectators watching this film, some will accommodate them—whether under one's roof or in one's sympathy—and some will not. Moreover, the film shifts constantly from danger to relief, from drama to comedy, from brutality to hope, forcing the viewer to be mentally alert and aware that easy expectations—about narrative or human behavior—cannot hold. As Imhoof explained,

Here I tried to accept more emotion, but not soap opera. I want to lead the spectator not only to have feelings like in the circus, but to think. For example, there is no music in the film at all so as not to put "ketchup" on the scenes.[7]

Imhoof maintains a formal distance from the action, permitting the inherent drama of the situation to assert its quiet power. At the end, for instance, he does not indulge in a violent climax; rather, as Wolfram Knorr's eloquent review in *Die Weltwoche* put it,

One haze-covered morning, four Jews are driven by Swiss soldiers in a truck to the German border. They have to get out in front of a bridge; their luggage is examined; the deportation order correctly stamped. An officer finds two bars of Swiss chocolate, which he confiscates because rationed Swiss products are not allowed to be exported. But since there are two children among the group, the Swiss display their marked sense of humanity: an officer pushes the already confiscated chocolate into their mouths: "There, eat as much as you can." This bitter, sharp sequence captures the whole paradox of bureaucratic procedure and the wish to be human.[8]

Titles inform us that Judith and Gitty were gassed at Treblinka; Olaf was deported and disappeared; Franz Flückinger received a Swiss prison sentence.

If the film's first shot tracked into a tunnel being clogged to prevent movement, the movie ends symmetrically with a long shot of a bridge in the rain —another narrow track on which the victims are forced to return to Germany. Like the train that was halted at the beginning, the camera is an immobilized witness. "I didn't want to go into Germany with the camera, so we remained outside," the director admitted simply. The conflicts within *The Boat Is Full* —and perhaps the film's tone—are particularly Swiss. With 8,300 refugees in Switzerland by July 1942, the Parliament considered the maximum level to have been reached and coined the term, "the boat is full." For Imhoof, this decision, and especially the way many people enforced it, should not be interpreted

Tina Engel (Judith) in *The Boat Is Full,* above;
and Swiss police stop the refugees in the same film.
A QUARTET/FILMS INCORPORATED RELEASE

as an alibi for the Germans. It's important that the film does not remain only a historical fresco: that's why the focus is on a few people with strangers. I accuse the Swiss people because if Switzerland was really a democracy, it wasn't necessary to let things happen as they did. . . . As always, everything is a little bit restrained in Switzerland, but perhaps that is only our talent for hypocrisy: the creeping anti-Semitism, the almost friendly, argumentative brutality, the selfishness which we idolize.[9]

Imhoof's rationale for making *The Boat Is Full* included a desire to "correct the way things are taught in school—half the children never heard about this Swiss law or World War Two events—and to question a film that had become a national myth: *The Last Chance* ("Die letzte Chance"), directed by Austrian refugee Leopold Lindtberg in 1945, was a prize-winning story of refugees coming from Italy to the mountains of Switzerland. Lindtberg was Imhoof's first teacher and he confessed to his student that he had made a mistake in adding a happy ending, but it was the only way at the time to get the film made. "To criticize *The Last Chance* was forbidden," Imhoof explained, and indeed he found himself deprived of a $100,000 government subsidy for filmmaking "because they said my film lacks the critical respect for the problems Switzerland had."

Imhoof was obviously thinking of another film about crossing frontiers—Jean Renoir's *Grand Illusion.* It is not simply that this drama about World War I also stops at the Swiss border, but that Renoir's tolerant and complex vision of people also can be felt here. Like the French master's work, *The Boat Is Full* is less concerned with labeling "heroes" or "villains" than with accommodating a spectrum that ranges from Nazi deserters to callow bureaucrats. Some characters act nobly, others act selfishly, and some change in the course of the film—as if asking the audience how we might have acted in their place. Indeed, acting in someone's place ultimately connotes both the role-playing forced upon the characters and the sympathetic capabilities of those confronted by their plight. After she begins to care for the refugees, Anna Flückinger complains, "I feel like a fugitive myself," and her husband later states, "I feel locked up in my own house." By the act of caring, they—and we—are paradoxically "taken over" as much as the hidden characters. This empathy is rendered more powerful by the conditions of film-viewing, whereby spectators are immobilized in darkness, forbidden to speak or make a sound, waiting for "The End" as the signal to emerge into the light. Since it is inherently easy to thus induce identification with the characters in hiding, filmmakers must be as careful as Imhoof was in guarding against sentimentality. As Renoir so succinctly put it, "The more emotional the material, the less emotional the treatment."

CHAPTER 7

BEAUTIFUL EVASIONS?

The casting of Dominique Sanda and Helmut Berger as the blond and blue-eyed Jews of *The Garden of the Finzi-Continis* requires an initial suspension of disbelief—particularly if one has just seen Berger as the decadent Nazi in *The Damned* (made the same year). In *Les Violons du Bal* and *Lacombe, Lucien* as well, the Jewish characters are gorgeous, assimilated, and wealthy. These three European films of the seventies are unquestionably beautiful, but there is a sense in which they evade the specifically Jewish identity of the Holocaust victims by defining them primarily in terms of class. While this type of characterization is partly a strategy for attracting a mass audience, and is in fact faithful to a certain segment of Europe's Jewish population, it is questionable because the reason they're being hounded in the first place is qualified or neutralized by their upper-class status. This is also the case with Visconti's *Sandra,* as will be developed in Chapter 8, and with the two Jewish characters of *Cabaret.* Natalia's aristocratic family is described as "stinking rich" and Marisa Berenson's delicate features are the exact opposite of the gorilla with which a cabaret number counterpoints her; and as far as Fritz is concerned, he has been passing himself off as a Protestant: he confesses that he is Jewish only minutes before the film's end. Once again, Judaism is secondary to status and social acceptability. Apart from potentially reinforcing the cliché that fuels anti-Semitism—that all Jews are rich—this narrative strategy renders the characters' loss painful *not* because they are Jews but because they are dispossessed, stripped of class. Rainer Werner Fassbinder's *Lili Marleen* is a less beautiful variation on the same theme.

The Garden of the Finzi-Continis ("Il Giardino dei Finzi-Contini") does acknowledge the uniquely anti-Semitic reasons for the characters' deportation. Vittorio De Sica's 1970 film is adapted from Giorgio Bassani's autobiographical novel of the same title. An introductory note informs us that the period

Dominique Sanda (Micol) in *The Garden of the Finzi-Continis.* CINEMA 5

is 1938–1943, when Italy is applying "racial laws." All Jews have been expelled from Ferrara's country club; therefore, the beautiful young Micol Finzi-Contini (Sanda) invites her attractive friends to play tennis on the family's massive estate. She and her brother Alberto (Berger) live in an idyllic world of natural expanse and sumptuous architecture, underscored by a lyrical tracking camera that often pans up into the dappled sky. Nevertheless, even this aristocratic family will not find itself exempt from implacable racial laws and ultimate deportation.

The capricious Micol is worshipped by Giorgio (Lino Capolicchio), her friend since childhood days when they would exchange furtive smiles in synagogue. Giorgio's parents are well-to-do, but clearly not in the same league as Micol's blue-blooded ancestors. His father (Romolo Valli) says disparagingly that the Finzi-Continis "don't even seem like Jews," but is quite willing to adapt to the racial laws while considering himself assimilated: "So there aren't any more public schools for Jews, no mixed marriages, no phone listings, no obituaries in the newspaper . . . at least a Jew can still be a citizen," he rationalizes to Giorgio. As the voice of accommodation, he even pretends that Mussolini is better than Hitler, and Fascism better than Nazism—willfully blind to the connections between the two.

The situation worsens as Giorgio is evicted from the library where he is writing his thesis. He continues his work in the massive Finzi-Contini library, but soon thereafter, Micol's rejection of him on a personal level mirrors Ferrara's rejection of Jews on a public scale. Visually, De Sica expresses Giorgio's eviction when, in the foreground, he leaves Micol's house on his bicycle: with the sudden approach of the Fascist parade behind him, he is forced outside the frame which is then filled by the crowd; Giorgio is expelled from an image—and a world—in which there is no room left for individual consideration. His identity as an outsider is most painfully rendered when he sees Micol in bed with her brother's handsome friend Malnate (Fabio Testi). Peering through a window, he is forced to behold what he cannot become, a voyeur yearning to be a participant. The brother Alberto's physical deterioration mirrors Giorgio's spiritual state, and Alberto finally dies of lymphogranuloma. Six months later, the Finzi-Continis are taken from their home by the police, and rounded up with all the other Jews at the school where Micol was once a privileged student. Their fate is deftly implied by the soundtrack, a Hebrew prayer for the dead that substitutes the names Auschwitz, Treblinka, and Majdanek for those of departed loved ones.

The wailing cantorial voice accompanying the film's last images underscores how even this aristocratic family must accept its fate as Jews. Their demise is subtly suggested by the last of the still photographs that close the film: from a close-up of desolate ground seen through a fence, the camera moves back to reveal that it is the Finzi-Continis' abandoned tennis court. The initial image, however, links this spot to the barbed wire and barren ground of the concentration camps whose names are cried out by the male voice. Moreover, this is not the first time that a camp is mentioned in *The Garden of the Finzi-Continis:* when Giorgio visits his brother who is studying in Grenoble, he encounters a tall blond man with a number tattooed on his arm. He inquires about its origin, and the blond man responds that he got it at Dachau, a hotel in the woods, 100 chalets, no room with a bath—just a single latrine surrounded by barbed wire—service provided by the SS with the tattoo as a souvenir of their hospitality. The guests at Dachau are Jews, Communists, Socialists like myself . . . what the Nazis call the dregs of the human race.

Significantly enough, this is the only major scene that does not exist in the original novel.

The elegance of this response is in keeping with the tone of the film, which neutralizes horror and even strong emotions through high style. For instance, it is noteworthy that we see Passover celebrations at the homes of both Giorgio and Micol. It is even more noteworthy, or perhaps memorable, that the Finzi-Continis greet the holiday in black tie, embodying a genteel Judaism that contrasts with the unrestrained singing of Giorgio's family. In this sense, their identity as Jews is played down. Whereas the novel tells us that Professor Finzi-Contini "had asked permission to restore, at his own expense, 'for the use of his family and of anyone interested,' the ancient, little Spanish synagogue on Via Mazzini,"[1] the film does not convey this kind of concern. Micol defines herself according to class rather than religion, as in the scene where she tells Malnate she doesn't like him because he's "too industrious, too Communist, and too hairy"—all of which point to the lower-class origins symbolized by his name (badly or lowly born).[2]

Fascist parade in *The Garden of the Finzi-Continis*. CINEMA 5

When the Finzi-Continis are taken from their home, the image is truly aristocratic: they take nothing with them, unlike the other Jews rounded up for deportation. It is this image of dispossession that haunts the viewer, as they are forced to abandon all their beautiful things. Indeed, when a clumsy policeman accidentally knocks over a small statue, the gasp usually heard in the audience at this moment is revealing: the film has led us to identify with a respect for beauty, a care for possessions, an appreciation of objects. The delicacy of the characters is mirrored in De Sica's cinematic style with its aristocratic love of textures. In the latter part of the film, the camera moves into a close-up of rose petals that have fallen from their stems—a shot that expresses the situation and exquisite sensibility of the Finzi-Continis with a lushness of its own.

Ultimately, it is gratuitous and even incorrect to fault *The Garden of the Finzi-Continis* because its central characters hardly seem or act Jewish—for they say as much themselves. Already in Bassani's novel, the narrator admits,

That we were Jews . . . still counted fairly little in our case. For what on earth did the word "Jew" mean, basically? What meaning could there be, for us, in terms like "community" or "Hebrew university," for they were totally distinct from the existence of that further intimacy—secret, its value calculable only by those who shared it— derived from the fact that our two families, not through choice, but thanks to a tradition older than any possible memory, belonged to the same religious rite, or rather to the same "school"?[3]

De Sica is in a sense as true to his subject here—the crème de la crème of Italian Jewry—as he was to the impoverished Italians that he depicted in postwar neorealist classics like *The Bicycle Thief* and *Shoeshine.* This is a different kind of realism that records the fragile and vulnerable beauty of a particular world just as it is about to disappear forever.

Michel Drach's *Les Violons du Bal,* previously discussed in Chapter 2, is a Proustian exercise in that everything the director (playing himself) sees in the present serves as a visual "madeleine" to conjure up his childhood in occupied France. We therefore view the past through the child's eyes or, more exactly, through an artist's idealizing memory which selects only that which looks beautiful onscreen. Pauline Kael's review in 1975 focused on this problem:

Les Violons du Bal—the title is Drach's private slang for "The others call the tune" —is a romantic memoir about the efforts of Drach's gracious and beautiful mother to save the family from the Nazis. Drach re-creates the Nazi period as he remembers it —in terms of what his vision was when he was a little boy. And his memory seems to burnish everything: everyone in the family is tender, cultivated, and exquisitely groomed. . . . The smartly tailored hat that Marie-José Nat wears for the flight across the border and the fine gloves with which she parts the strands of barbed wire are the height of refugee chic.[4]

During the final escape through the woods to Switzerland, the mists convey less terror than scenery, and when the mother's hat falls off during her run across a field, it is hardly believable that their accomplice runs back into danger to retrieve it.

Questions of realism aside, *Les Violons du Bal*'s definition of Judaism—the ostensible reason for the family's persecution—is sketchy. After one of his schoolmates wonders if Michel is Jewish, Michel asks his mother, "What's a Jew?" Instead of answering, she continues to chop vegetables with a smile. His grandmother tries to explain that it all began with Jesus "who was good, but then trouble started." The boy inquires why they never told him before. "We never talk about it," says his unperturbed mother. The insubstantiality of their answer is brought home in the next scene for, unaware that being Jewish has become the cause for ostracization, Michel cheerfully tells his friends at school, "I'm a Jew." They hit and taunt him. He runs into an ornate church, where the only person praying turns out to be his grandmother. Michel is surprised to see her there, to which the smiling old lady responds, "So what? I felt like saying a prayer." The casual substitution of houses of worship seems hardly more problematic to this family than learning the new names on their forged papers. A delightful scene toward the end of the film does little to particularize the identity for which they are being hunted. When Michel is sheltered in the country, the little girl he "romances" gives him a religious medal from her neck. "But I'm Jewish," he blurts out. "So what,"

Jean-Louis Trintignant as Michel Drach directing *Les Violons du Bal.* CARLOS CLARENS

says the girl. "My father's a Communist!" A child's equation, an adult's evasion.

It is, of course, beside the point to reproach Drach for not including a religious dimension to which he himself was never exposed. And he does acknowledge stylistically that the film is a personal exorcism rather than a historical document. For example, the first sequence in the past shows the family reading about evacuation procedures. Visually, they are crowded into a narrow area of light in the center of the frame, surrounded by brown wood. Moments later, it turns out that they were being viewed in a thin mirror— which the movers suddenly take away. Drach thus implies that what we are watching is a reflection rather than "the real thing," and that the characters are enclosed within the frame of his own recollections. For a less romanticized chronicle of escape into Switzerland, one must wait eight years until *The Boat Is Full*—a stark drama of what happened to some Jewish refugees *after* they had made it to the border.

Les Violons du Bal does not show any nasty Nazis—a decision that seems less like an evasion than a redefinition of the enemy. As in *The Last Metro,* the villains are not German, but French, and their cruelty is less physical than verbal or indirect. The only German we really see in the film is a kindly soldier seated behind Michel at a fashion show that features his sister. By contrast, the mother of her rich Gentile fiancé tells the pregnant girl that marriage is out of the question because she is "an Israelite"; the French policemen who

Aurore Clément (France)
in *Lacombe, Lucien.*
CARLOS CLARENS COLLECTION

raid the apartment steal their money; Monsieur Robert, who seemed to be helping the refugees, deceives them and runs off with all their money. These Parisian Jews live more in the fear of French denunciations and greed than of German bullets.

Lacombe, Lucien also redefines the concept of the enemy—perhaps at the expense of the victim's ethnic identity. Director Louis Malle's focus in this masterful film of 1974 is a French peasant (Pierre Blaise) who joins the fascist collaborationists in 1944—after the Resistance turns him down. The amoral youth meets a Parisian tailor, Albert Horn (Holger Löwenadler), who is now hiding in southwestern France because he is Jewish. With a sense of dignity bordering on snobbery, this former king of Paris haute couture must now accept the venal visitors who exploit him. After Horn makes him a suit, Lucien develops a bizarre relationship with the tailor and his beautiful daughter France (Aurore Clément): this illiterate, young gun-toting agent for the German police visits them regularly, bringing stolen goods from various fascist raids. Horn grows increasingly exasperated with his situation, and with his daughter's sexual relationship with Lucien. He goes to the fascist enclave to see the boy, and is arrested by a rabidly xenophobic Frenchman. Lucien rescues France and her taciturn grandmother (Thérèse Giehse) from a Nazi roundup; when he tries to drive them to Spain, the car breaks down—leaving them to pass the time in an abandoned house in the French countryside. A title informs us that Lucien was arrested, court-martialed, and executed on April 12, 1944.

Lacombe, Lucien's references to Judaism contain no positive resonance. "Monsieur is a rich and stingy Jew" is how the easy-going fascist Jean-Bernard (Stéphane Bouy) introduces Horn to Lucien (while taking money from the tailor). When Lucien asks Horn, "Aren't the Jews the enemies of France?" Horn answers, "No, I'm not" (as opposed to *we're* not). His identity is rooted in having been the best tailor on Paris' chic Avenue Pierre-Ier-de-Serbie, an assimilated individual of exquisite taste. Dressed in his dressing gown and ascot, Horn conveys a certain disdain—the haughtiness of having once been high on the social scale. And the blond, blue-eyed France cries, "I'm fed up with being a Jew," before throwing herself tearfully into Lucien's open arms.

Once again, the interest of the film lies elsewhere, for the racial identity of the victims is incidental to the carefully etched portrait of a casual young fascist and his group. There are almost no Germans in the film (a rather pleasant Nazi visits the collaborators at the beginning, and Lucien shoots the one who arrests the Horn family), for it is against the French who are being placed under the microscope. Malle faithfully captures the spirit of obedient collaboration that characterized much of French life. "What they teach French children about the Occupation period is a bunch of lies," he told an audience at Yale University in 1978, referring to the collective amnesia about collaboration, and in *Lacombe, Lucien* he demythologizes the France of "active resisters." The Nazi sympathizer Mlle. Chauvelot says of the Germans, "They're so obliging and punctual. Had we been like them, we'd have won the war." As she reads letters from informers, the coldly efficient woman acknowl-

Lucien (played by Pierre Blaise) receives a warning in *Lacombe, Lucien.* CARLOS CLARENS

edges, "We get two hundred a day. One even wrote to denounce himself. It's like a disease." The sickness is presented objectively, with no directorial judgment expressed by self-conscious camera angles or editing. With the exception of the credits and the last scene, the only music we hear comes from within the story (such as France's piano playing) and is never used to manipulate the viewer. *Lacombe, Lucien* portrays the collaborators as creatures of amoral impulse. Lucien's first action in the film is to shoot a bird with a slingshot; later he shoots rabbits, poaches other animals, smacks a hen's head off—wanton killing that may be unpleasant to watch, but that seems natural to the farm boy. But by the time he catches animals in the last sequence—in order to feed France and the grandmother—the hunting is redefined into necessity for survival.

Shot on location in southwestern France, *Lacombe, Lucien* often "feels" like a documentary: its first and last sequences chronicle simple daily existence with little dialogue. Lucien is played by a non-professional, a peasant who looks and sounds authentic in his uncomplicated relationship to things and people. His accent is palpably different from that of the displaced Parisians, and his straightforwardness gives the film a unique flavor. (A few years later, Pierre Blaise was killed in an auto accident, without ever having made another film.) Lucien is an uncalculating and spontaneous animal. Everything he is and does is externalized in action: his lack of worldliness is even manifested by the clumsy way he smokes cigarettes. When he sees France standing in a long line for groceries, he pulls her up to the front in order to look important, flashing his "German Police" card. When he shoots the Nazi who comes to collect France for roundup, it seems like an unpremeditated action, sparked by the German's attempt to pocket the gold watch that Lucien originally gave to Horn. Lucien is drawn to the fascists because they accept him and make him feel important, but he is equally drawn to Horn's exquisite sensibility and to France's porcelain beauty. As Horn tells him, "I can't bring myself to really hate you," for Lucien seems too naïve to be labeled evil.

Malle's direction allows for deep ambiguity about why certain people become fascists. Some of the individuals in the posh hotel headquarters admittedly have axes to grind: the boss was fired from the police in 1936 as an "undesirable"; the unattractive maid who screams "Dirty Jew!" hysterically at France is jealous of the woman's attractiveness to Lucien; and Lucien himself was told by the Resistance leader that he was not serious or old enough to join their group. In general, these are ordinary people, with recognizable impulses, fears, and needs. *This* is what we're up against, Malle seems to be saying: people who believe what they hear on the radio (the first broadcaster announces "we hear nothing but Communist lies") or from a bicycle champion (one of Lucien's heroes). Like many shortsighted people in the forties, Lucien does not question the ludicrous fascist position articulated in the scene where the "French Gestapo" group arrest a doctor. "Do you want Bolshevism in France?" they ask him. "But I'm a Gaullist," he responds. "De Gaulle is surrounded by Jews and Communists," they retort.

It seems hardly coincidental that *Lacombe, Lucien, Les Violons du Bal, Black Thursday,* and *Mr. Klein*—implicit indictments of the French population—were all made in the mid-seventies. The French philosopher Bernard Henri-Lévy suggests that

until 1969, nobody knew there was something in their history called *pétainisme.* There was a taboo during De Gaulle's era—an image of collective heroism. The people believed fascism came from the *outside,* not that the virus was French. The only country in occupied Europe that didn't try to "de-fascize" itself was France.[5]

Filmmakers in the seventies—following the stirring example of Marcel Ophuls' *The Sorrow and the Pity*—finally addressed themselves to the fatal indifference and complicity of the French, but only with Jewish characters assimilated (or classy) enough to appeal to an audience still subject to anti-Semitism. This is not to say that the more "authentic" Jewish characters are or should look unattractive; but rather that the predominance of characters who bear neither external nor internal acknowledgement of their Judaism can offer only a fraction of the historical picture. When physical beauty or social class eclipses all other roots of identity, there is a danger that the aesthetic can become an anesthetic; in such cases, the specificity of the Holocaust victim is lost.

Rainer Werner Fassbinder's *Lili Marleen* (1981) is the most insidious of the recent cinematic revisions of the Nazi era, a fairy tale that gives a new twist to Hannah Arendt's term, "the banality of evil." Shot primarily in English and

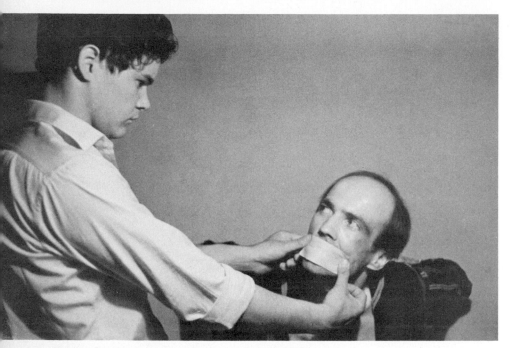

Above, Lucien assumes authority in *Lacombe, Lucien*.
Below, Pierre Blaise (Lucien) and Aurore Clément (France)
in *Lacombe, Lucien*. CARLOS CLARENS

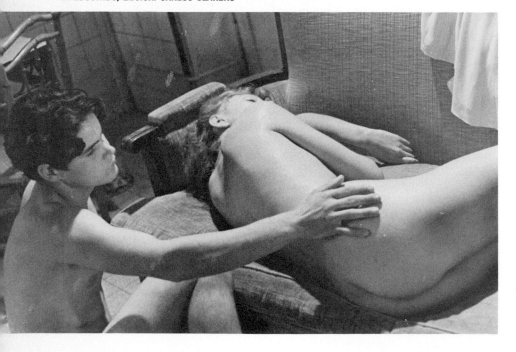

then presented on American screens dubbed into German with English subtitles, it is an exercise in displacement: the Nazis are either benign, ineffectual, or secretly good guys; the Jews are wealthy and comparatively safe, while the most deceitfully manipulative character in the film is the Jewish father. "Money, he's got plenty," says his son. Beyond what some viewers construe as the film's obvious irony, it is no wonder that *Lili Marleen* was the number one box-office hit in Germany: it offers a myth about the late thirties that is comforting for those who prefer to avoid guilt and responsibility. "It's not as bad here as some people might think," says a Nazi official to the heroine in Gestapo headquarters.

Lacking a coherent point of view, the film offers a love story between Robert Mendelsson (Giancarlo Giannini, looking and sounding less convincing than in *Seven Beauties*), a rich Swiss-Jewish conductor who helps obtain false passports for endangered Jews, and Willie (Hanna Schygulla), a wide-eyed cabaret singer of dubious talent. Robert's father (Mel Ferrer) suspects the Aryan Willie might foul up their operation, and maneuvers her expulsion from Switzerland. Back in Germany, Willie's career is guided by the influential Nazi Henkel (Karl-Heinz von Hassel), and her recording during the early months of World War II of the tune "Lili Marleen" turns her into a celebrity. Even Hitler wants to meet Willie, and her rendezvous with the Führer is presented as her disappearing through a massive door into a heavenly blast of white. She and her pianist Taschner (Hark Bohm) are given a sumptuously vulgar apartment, as Willie continues to perform the song so beloved of German soldiers.

Despite her status as a Nazi icon, Willie helps Robert's Jewish resistance organization in its attempt to obtain proof of what is happening in Poland. During a tour of the German front, she smuggles out accusatory film of concentration camps—a fact Mendelsson keeps secret from his son lest Robert return to this *shiksa* rather than marry the nice Jewess that Papa picked out for him. When Robert is captured, Mendelsson makes a deal with the Gestapo for seventy-eight people plus his son to be returned across a bridge into Switzerland, presumably in exchange for the film. After the war, Willie and a leading Nazi (Erik Schumann), who was really helping the Resistance all along, are on the run, having no witnesses to testify to their good deeds. Willie sneaks into a concert hall where Robert is conducting: seeing his wife and cozy family, she conveniently disappears into the night.

It is significant that *Lili Marleen*'s opening and closing locale is Switzerland, where the Jew is unthreatened if he stays put: Robert's difficulties arise only when he is in Germany. And even there, the worst torture inflicted on this Jew is to be locked in a cell plastered with posters of Willie, forced to listen to the same few bars of "Lili Marleen" without end. The Nazis never do anything particularly vicious onscreen, and during the big party sequence, they are more interested in hearing Willie sing than in acknowledging Hitler's birthday. This sequence is quite long and colorful, laced with a kind of nostalgia for the boisterous camaraderie of the "good old thirties." The quintessential German is perhaps Willie, naïve but decent as she claims, "I'm only singing a song," when Robert tells her that cruel things are happening.

It is really the Germans who are portrayed as victims, for every time Willie performs "Lili Marleen" in a radio broadcast, there are intercuts of sad young

Above, Hanna Schygulla (Willie) in *Lili Marleen.*

Left, Willie and Henkel (played by Karl-Heinz von Hassel) visiting the Führer in *Lili Marleen.* UNITED ARTISTS CORPORATION

German soldiers. (The bomb footage and the faces tend to be identical in every scene, as if Fassbinder ran out of film.) The displacement becomes evident when Henkel informs her that she is heard by six million soldiers. "Six million?" she repeats incredulously. A loaded number indeed. And Fassbinder reserves his sympathy for Taschner, who is dispatched to the Eastern Front when he talks back to the SS. This particular action serves to reinforce the complacency of "But what could we do?" The Jewish resistance organization is likewise depicted as a relatively ineffectual clan: one of its members, Aaron (Gottfried John), abruptly blows up the bridge after Robert is returned to his father. "I don't like that kind of deal" is his feeble explanation.

Fassbinder casts himself as Günther Weisenborn, the head of the resistance organization. (Whether consciously or not, he appropriates the name of a German director who made *Memorial,* a documentary celebrating Gentiles who resisted the Nazis.) With dark glasses, thick beard, and paunch, he becomes a caricature with far more fidelity to forties movies than to wartime realities. Similarly, the music of *Lili Marleen* distances the viewer from potential identification with the Jewish characters: almost every time they are shown, the melodramatic and heavily percussive score roars in. One is reminded of Volker Schlöndorff's remark in an interview, "It's really quite difficult to give credence to the action in a Fassbinder film. The excessive melodrama tries to conceal the failure of imagination."[6]

The only self-consciously masterful touch in *Lili Marleen* is the name given to Willie's Nazi patron: Henkel. For those who have seen *The Great Dictator,* it is difficult to forget the parodic Hynkel and not to view Fassbinder's Nazi as little more than a joke. This is especially the case when Henkel toys with a globe in his office—a visual echo of Chaplin's delirious dance. Apart from the knowing wink this scene might constitute, *Lili Marleen* is as flat as the globe balloon at the end of Chaplin's ballet.

Finally, since the Mendelssons are the only Jewish protagonists in a film about the Nazi era, Fassbinder would have us believe, once again, that Judaism is tantamount to wealth, lack of solidarity, and clever calculation. *Lili Marleen* allows the viewer to assume that a Jew could always buy his way out of real danger. Ferrer's soulless characterization of the despotic patriarch and the Jewish victim in one is more ruthless than religious (the same kind of Jew that Fassbinder presents in his earlier [1979] film, *In a Year of Thirteen Moons*— a former Bergen-Belsen inmate who becomes a fiercely powerful businessman). When it is difficult to accept responsibility—so you don't have to think about your own role—how convenient to project onto the victims the despicable characteristics of the oppressors.

CHAPTER 8

THE CONDEMNED AND DOOMED

Among the Italian films that deal with the postwar legacy of the Holocaust, at least three explore guilt in an upper-class family eroded and ultimately doomed by its accumulated ghosts. The major elaborators of this theme are Luchino Visconti *(Sandra* and *The Damned)* and Vittorio De Sica *(The Condemned of Altona* and *The Garden of the Finzi-Continis),* directors particularly sensitive to history's weight on individuals. For these two filmmakers who began their careers as neorealists, shooting nonprofessional actors in the street, and ended with sumptuous period adaptations *(The Innocent* and *The Voyage),* the past is often a burden that individuals must comprehend and then surrender—lest they become prisoners of history. Liliana Cavani's *The Night Porter* presents a variation on this theme of imprisonment by the past. In Visconti's *Sandra* ("Vaghe Stelle dell'Orsa"), for example, the heroine maintains, "We have no ghosts." The 1965 film itself illustrates the contrary, denying her claim with an abundance of both literal and figurative shadows.

Sandra (Claudia Cardinale), a beautiful young Italian Jewess married to the American Andrew (Michael Craig), returns from a chic modern environment in Geneva to her family home in the crumbling hill town of Volterra for a dedication ceremony: the statue of her father—who died in Auschwitz—is to be unveiled. Her brother Gianni (Jean Sorel) also returns, a troubling and troubled erotic presence vis-à-vis his sister. Sandra believes that her Gentile mother (Marie Bell) and the lawyer Gilardini (Renzo Ricci) denounced her father during the war, and eventually confronts each of these characters. In this tense environment, Sandra searches for her distinct identity in terms of class, sexuality, Judaism, and her American husband, but it is ultimately in terms of her father and his legacy that she defines herself. Whereas Andrew wants her to leave the patrimonial home, claiming that "the past is but a time for choosing the future," Sandra says she will remain, "unable to forget, doing penance."

Dirk Bogarde (Max) and Charlotte Rampling (Lucia) in *The Night Porter.*
MUSEUM OF MODERN ART/FILM STILLS ARCHIVE

Sandra's guilt over being alive while her father was murdered in a concentration camp is heightened by her mother's screams, "You have your father's Jewish blood in your veins." (Having been spared his suffering, Sandra actually went to Auschwitz after the war to work as an interpreter during survivor investigations.) Visconti's heroine seeks lucidity about her relationship to her family, but the film's stark contrasts between darkness and light and its doubling of figures suggest the difficulty of clear perception. As Bertolucci, heavily influenced by Visconti, would develop through the self-conscious style and obtrusive lighting of *The Conformist, what* one sees depends on how it is illuminated (whether by a lamp or a mentor—or a film). Part of Sandra's home is sealed off, perhaps like an area of her mind that remains in darkness. When she meets Gianni in the water tower where they used to hide as children, leading to a flashback of their mother, the high-contrast lighting turns Sandra's face into a mask. And when the camera pulls back from the siblings to their reflected images in the water, it expresses the split within the characters: a part of them exists in a submerged union. Moreover, Sandra's departure at this moment makes her ascent (up the twisting stairs) look like a simultaneous descent into the water—a contradictory movement in space that represents her confusion in time.

A subsequent scene in which their past appears, bathed in rich firelight,

Claudia Cardinale as *Sandra.* CORINTH FILMS

clarifies that Sandra and Gianni are awash in memories. A harsh corollary is provided by their lighting in the present that consists, in the scene that follows, of a naked bulb suspended under a dark chandelier. Beneath this emblem of the upper class that is more ornamental than functional, the simple light bulb is the agent of vision—and it is Gianni who turns it on. Throughout the film, he moves in and out of light, alternating between hiding and revelation until his definitive merging with darkness at the end of the film: Gianni's suicide is crosscut, significantly enough, with the unveiling of their father's image.

This is not the first occasion of visual rhyming between father and son in *Sandra*. In an early sequence, Gianni covers his face with his sister's white shawl just after we see the statue of the father covered with a white sheet. The reason for this kind of doubling is not merely symmetry, but to suggest that Sandra's ambiguous relationship with her brother derives its meaning from— and is in a sense a substitute for—unresolved feelings about her lost father. Indeed, the behavior of Gianni and Sandra seems less like that of lovers than of children pretending to be concentration camp inmates: they feel persecuted; they leave notes for each other in secret places; and Gianni finally writes to her in fear and despair, "I don't want to die"—before taking his life. Andrew understands that Sandra "went to the concentration camp to relive [her] father's Calvary," but other elements of the film seem to place a disproportionate emphasis on incest rather than on the Holocaust legacy.

The lawyer Gilardini, perhaps like the film itself, evades questions of denunciation, concentration camps, and Jewish identity to focus on the perverse romance of the children. *Sandra* does not really explore the more basic Oedipal (rather than brother-sister) underpinning of the film—namely, that Sandra's fundamental relationship is to her Jewish father killed in Auschwitz. For the unveiling of his statue, she dresses in white, like an expectant bride. Perhaps incest was a more commercially provocative theme than post-Holocaust Jewish identity. Perhaps Visconti was more interested in extending the patterns of betrayal, denunciation, and accusation, moving from the Holocaust to an allusive treatment of the transmission of a family curse. Or perhaps, as in *The Garden of the Finzi-Continis,* the suggestion of incest is a complex metaphor for the "racial bonds" that tie *Sandra* together. In both cases, the death of the brother allows for the image of a new couple created by the Holocaust—a father-daughter union (even though Micol embraces Giorgio's father as a substitute for her own lost one).

In *The Garden of the Finzi-Continis,* it is no coincidence that the book Micol reads when she is sick in bed is *Les Enfants Terribles*—*"molto chic,"* as she says to Giorgio. Jean Cocteau's novel has deep connections with aspects of this film: through the ambiguous brother-sister relationship; the attraction the siblings hold for the young man (Gérard/Giorgio) enamored of the strong sister; the fourth party who disrupts the situation (Agathe/Malnate); the possible homosexual impulses of the brother; and the enclosure from which the siblings refuse to go out ("the room"/"the garden"). Micol tells Giorgio that the reason she can't love him is that they are too similar, "like two drops of water. It would be like making love with my brother."

Both Paul in Cocteau's work and Alberto in De Sica's are sickly, mothered by the sister, tormented by her absence, and perhaps romantically attached to

Micol (Dominique Sanda) comforts her grandmother in
The Garden of the Finzi-Continis. CARLOS CLARENS

her. As artists in the former and as Italian aristocrats in the latter, the siblings do not go out and mix with ordinary people. (The hermetic enclosure of the Finzi-Continis against the outside world is particularly visible during Alberto's funeral: as they walk behind the hearse, an air-raid signal is heard. They remain oblivious to the sound, quietly following the coffin.) This suggests that the family, by being too close for comfort, is doomed to die out. Such a theme is not unconnected to the Holocaust, for the enforced insularity of the Jewish family can be seen as a response to an increasingly hostile environment. At the end of *The Garden of the Finzi-Continis,* the painful truth is that the family can survive only through separation. At the beginning of *Kapo* and at the end of *Black Thursday,* for instance, the young women jump onto the transports bearing their mothers away. By contrast, De Sica implies that both the aristocratic Finzi-Continis and the middle-class family of Giorgio have to accept dispersal: Giorgio's father has sent his wife and sons far away; Micol silently enters one room during the roundup as her parents are led into another. Only when Micol is separated from her family and Signor Bassani from his, can these divergent characters come together: when they hug in the classroom, class is finally obliterated and only their common bond as Jews from Ferrara remains.

Incest could thus be seen as an extreme symbol for family bonds so tight that they ultimately choke its members. But when the families are German rather than Jewish, they seem to derive their meaning from the "cursed house" motif prevalent in Greek mythology. Both De Sica and Visconti present aristocratic families doomed to extinction, less by an external threat than by the indifference of the patriarch to anything but the family's success. As *The Damned*'s Baron von Essenbeck puts it, his one objective has been "to hold on to the unity and prestige of our firm."

The Condemned of Altona, like *Sandra,* is about a wealthy family that contains itself within a large house that has a hidden part. The shipping magnate Gerlach learns that he has only six months left to live. He wants to leave his empire to his reluctant son Werner, an upstanding lawyer whom we see accusing four thugs in 1959 Hamburg of desecrating a Jewish cemetery (implying a sizable inheritance of anti-Semitism by present-day Germany). He and his actress wife Johanna return to the family home where she discovers one of the Gerlachs' secrets: the elder son Franz who was tried in Nuremberg for war crimes is not dead, as reported. He is locked upstairs, seen only by his sister Leni, about whom Werner laments, "It's a relationship I don't like to think about." Johanna penetrates the refuge and tries to unify the family. She learns that Gerlach's empire is the result of his collaboration with the Nazis during the war, including the use of his land for a concentration camp where 30,000 Jews died. And she realizes that all his children are dominated by his legacy of guilt, from Franz who yells at his father, "It's because you're an informer that I'm a torturer," to Werner whose integrity melts at the fiery touch of power. Gerlach's response when Werner says he can't give orders— "Wait until after I die; then you'll think you're me"—functions as a self-fulfilling prophecy.

Like Andrew in *Sandra,* Johanna is an outsider who tries to undo the burden of the past: however, she is no more successful than Andrew in liberating these prisoners of history. Rather, a similar triangle of sexual tension emerges through the initially happy couple and the forbidden brother (in-law), Franz. As it becomes increasingly clear that Werner's motive is personal aggrandizement, while Franz's is blindness stemming from guilt, Johanna beckons Franz into the "real world"—inseparable from the world of theater. Unable to come to terms with his past (as a torturer whose entire company was killed in Smolensk in 1941), present (an abrupt end to his conviction that the war is not over), or future (inheriting his father's dynasty), Franz jumps to his death—taking his father with him. Under the high-angle camera, his body assumes the form of a broken swastika.

"Franz has a memory that will doom us all," proclaims Gerlach—a fact borne out by the film's events. Both men die because they are unable to let go of their past actions, the father through pride and the son through guilt. They therefore incarnate vestiges of Nazism that must self-destruct before a new society can flourish. Gerlach can even be seen as a Hitler figure, guilty not of direct killing but of indirect mass murder. He is a veritable patriarch, a despot who demands obedience from his "children." In the Brecht play performed by Johanna's company, the Hitler figure, Arturo Ui, is seen on a pedestal, much like Gerlach when he surveys his empire from above. Symmetrically, then, Gerlach must fall at the end.

Maximilian Schell (Franz) and Françoise Prévost (Leni) in *The Condemned of Altona*.
MUSEUM OF MODERN ART/FILM STILLS ARCHIVE

De Sica's own appraisal of *The Condemned of Altona* supports the notion that his focus is wider than the film's immediate conflict; as he told the New York *Times,*

A critic once described me as "the poet of suffering." Certainly the horror, the pain and suffering of the war years brought profound changes into my approach to life and I suppose, therefore, it was natural that when I saw Jean-Paul Sartre's play, "The Condemned of Altona," I was immediately filled with a burning desire to translate this indictment of oppression into cinematic terms. Set in post-war Germany as a study of fanatical Nazism, it remains an accusation against all dictatorships.[1]

Gerlach himself becomes the paradoxical mouthpiece for the awareness of postwar oppression when he reveals to Franz the existence of Joseph McCarthy's red-baiting witch hunts, Russian denial of personal freedom, and torture in Algeria.

The themes of guilt, incest, and postwar Nazi legacy are given a more perverse treatment in Liliana Cavani's 1974 film *The Night Porter,* shot in English by the Italian director. Here, two "families" are created by the Holocaust: an organization of neo-Nazis who meet periodically in Austria and "eliminate" dangerous witnesses; and a sexual union between Max (Dirk Bogarde), a former SS officer, and his "little girl" Lucia (Charlotte Rampling), whom he knew as a concentration camp inmate. In the Vienna of 1957, Max is a night porter in an elegant hotel. When Lucia enters the lobby with her conductor husband (Marino Mase), there is a tense exchange of looks whose significance is fleshed out in flashbacks: Lucia was one of a group of naked prisoners being filmed by an officer—who is revealed in a subsequent flashback to be Max. These past images punctuate the present narrative with urgent frequency and suggest that Lucia survived by being his plaything.

Amid the growing tension of their mutual anxiety over being alone together, Max "eliminates" a former prisoner who had been his friend. He and Lucia are finally reunited in a scene of violent passion, the more steamy for their accumulated repression. Rather than "file her away," as he is told to do, he locks his willing partner in his apartment where they replay their concentration camp scenes. *The Night Porter* thus depicts not only the political continuity between the Holocaust and 1957 Austria, where Nazism is alive and well, but the psychological grip of a past that locks characters into repetition compulsion. Lucia is not the only former prisoner who seeks to re-create the

Charlotte Rampling (Lucia) in *The Night Porter.*
MUSEUM OF MODERN ART/FILM STILLS ARCHIVE

conditions of intense sensation: there is also the young male dancer who used to perform seminude for the SS, and who now has Max arrange lights in his hotel room so that he can do his number once more.

On one level, the obscene instances of replay constitute a role reversal, for one flashback presents Lucia as a Nazi emblem: in the requisite smoky cabaret scene (of which variations can be found in *The Damned, Cabaret, Just a Gigolo, The Serpent's Egg, Lili Marleen,* and John G. Avildsen's 1980 *The Formula,* where a particularly distasteful nightclub projects concentration camp footage as the background for nude dancers and rock music), Lucia sings in German, wearing only pants, suspenders, and an SS cap. (Redolent of *Salomé*-like decadence, the scene ends with the opening of a gift: inside the package is the head of a prisoner.) In the present tense of *The Night Porter,* Max chains Lucia, and at the end, their obsessive love re-creates a concentration camp situation in which both are victims. They experience paranoia because they are being pursued; they no longer go out; finally, hunger and lack of air make them regress to an animal level. Max and his "little girl" move inexorably toward a consummation in death. One can see this merely as perversion and exploitation of the Holocaust for the sake of sensationalism. Or one can take seriously Max's confession that he works at night because during the day, in the light, he is ashamed. His repressed guilt is perhaps as great as his initially repressed lust, and Max's ultimate action is to turn himself into a physically degraded and emotionally shattered prisoner.

The characters incarnated by Bogarde and Rampling in *The Night Porter* carry associations with the roles they played five years earlier in Visconti's *The Damned* ("La Caduta degli Dei"): here he is Friedrich, a German businessman who ruthlessly rises to power—aided, manipulated, and ultimately undone by the Nazis—and she is Elisabeth, daughter of the aristocratic Von Essenbeck family, who dies in Dachau because of her husband's anti-Nazi activities. Bogarde's potential for sleek savagery and Rampling's skeletal beauty are well-suited to these demonic films where the only exit is death. Visconti's film is clearly the more rich and complex, exploring a powerful family à la Krupp/Thyssen as a microcosm of German society in the thirties.

At his birthday party, the magnate Baron Joachim von Essenbeck (Albrecht Schönhals) announces his retirement from the steel works and the transfer of power to one of the family members. He begrudgingly appoints the Nazi Konstantin (René Kolldehoff) because he realizes that the steel works will become increasingly interdependent with the state. This choice rejects his antifascist son-in-law Herbert (Umberto Orsini) and his depraved grandson Martin (Helmut Berger). Martin's mother Sophie (Ingrid Thulin) is the mistress of an outsider to the family, Friedrich Bruckmann (Bogarde); this businessman is appointed managing director of the firm, largely through the support of Aschenbach (Helmut Griem), an SS officer and cousin of the Von Essenbecks. This manipulative Nazi plays the other characters off against one another—first urging Friedrich to kill Joachim and Konstantin, and then Martin to kill Friedrich and Sophie—until all the power remains with Martin, who can easily be controlled by the SS.

Despite *The Damned*'s numerous scenes of murder and sexual perversion (rape, incest, pedophilia, transvestism), it constitutes a historically faithful tapestry of the rise of Nazism. The tensions within the Von Essenbeck family parallel the larger struggles of German society. For example, Konstantin is a member of the SA, the brown-shirts who established Hitler's power on the popular level and were then eliminated by the military faction, the black-shirted SS. Konstantin wants the steel works to provide arms for the SA, but Friedrich—puppet of the SS—refuses. This conflict culminates in the "Night of the Long Knives," with the SS wiping out the unprepared fascists.

Visconti frames the characters' demise with actual incidents such as the Reichstag fire, to which the film's opening refers; the book-burning at the universities; and the Night of the Long Knives. Through the mouthpiece of the liberal Herbert, he acknowledges the complicity of German capitalists: "Nazism was born in our factories, nourished by our money." And the director points to class structure and division by introducing Friedrich into the family. As the outsider who wants to get inside—the bourgeois who yearns for the power of the elite—Friedrich is ultimately the agent of disorder. It is not any of the aristocrats but the bourgeois who shoots both the father and his surrogate, Konstantin.

The convoluted plot of this melodrama has mythic, biographical, and aesthetic resonances. As in *Sandra* and *The Condemned of Altona,* the aristocratic family of the thirties is cursed through internal blindness, ambition, lust, and—perhaps most significantly—complicity with an immoral state. That Visconti views this family as doomed is implied in the film's original title— *La Caduta degli Dei* ("The Fall of the Gods"). In its German version, *Götterdämmerung,* the title derives from the last part of Wagner's *Ring Cycle,* in which the fate of the gods is sealed. The very structure of *The Damned* reinforces an implacable destiny, for the first and last images are identical— the demonic fire of the steel works. And the Wagnerian strain returns when a drunk Konstantin sings from *Tristan und Isolde* during a boozy SA gathering. It is provocatively placed between a Nazi drag show and the bloody massacre of the brown-shirts by the SS.

Visconti's juxtaposition of Wagner's music and transvestism illustrates a problematic aspect of *The Damned.* Visconti often indulges in gratuitous shots of handsome male faces in make-up, or a group of young male bodies frolicking in the nude. Not unlike the character of Von Aschenbach in Visconti's next film, *Death in Venice,* the director is drawn to the beauty of young boys—albeit in a more refined manner than the coarse fumblings in the SA scene. There is a certain ambivalence in his work, not only vis-à-vis the decadence whose very stylization is close to his heart, but with respect to the doomed aristocrats. Visconti himself came from an upper-class family, against which he chafed in his Marxist youth. The love of opulence, however, remained, as evidenced by the glistening surfaces from *Senso* to *The Innocent* (not to mention his numerous opera productions starring Maria Callas at La Scala).

A comment recently made by a French filmmaker seems applicable to Visconti. Pascal Thomas, director of *Heart to Heart,* said in the New York *Times* that "directors say they make a film about a brutal character in order to denounce him, but that's not true. They experience a certain voluptuousness in the character's presence."[2] Given Helmut Berger's striking appearance, it is not such a shock that Martin triumphs: in Visconti's enclosed cinematic universe, there is always an attraction for the rebellious son of aristocrats, drawn to forbidden sexual practices.

Like much of *The Damned,* Martin's introduction elicits a response of perverse fascination. Onstage for Joachim's birthday celebration, he cavorts in Dietrich drag while singing one of her numbers from *The Blue Angel.* The scene functions on at least three levels: it symbolizes Martin's rebellion against the Von Essenbeck clan, his own decadence (subsequently developed in scenes with little girls), and the decadence of Germany in the thirties. While Martin sings, shots of a woman watching from the wings are intercut. The deep red filter adds to the ambiguity of her expression: is she smiling? embarrassed? proud? enamored? malicious? She is subsequently revealed as Sophie, Martin's mother. The red tone in which she was bathed will continue to surround her, as discomfiting as it is rich.

Martin (Helmut Berger) oversees the marriage of Friedrich (Dirk Bogarde) and Sophie (Ingrid Thulin) in *The Damned.*
MUSEUM OF MODERN ART/FILM STILLS ARCHIVE

Containing few natural outdoor shots, *The Damned* relies heavily upon heightened lighting and carefully worked-over color to express the turbulence of its characters. The morbidly compelling red returns after Joachim's blood-spattered body is found in bed. The central characters convene in the room where the performance took place a few hours earlier, and the red light remains visible on the stage in the background. Konstantin, Sophie, Friedrich, and Martin drink, sweat, and plot, accentuated by theatrical lighting. Under his mother's influence, Martin nominates Friedrich to run the steelworks, thus opposing himself to Konstantin. It is the lighting that tells us who the real manipulators are: shots of Konstantin or Sophie reveal only half their faces. The other half is in darkness, as if the character were showing only half his cards. By bathing them once again in a red glow, Visconti associates these characters with blood and fire.

The flames that recur in *The Damned* suggest the hell on earth that Nazism became. Whereas we hear about the burning of the Reichstag, we actually see the burning of books in the universities. (Among the writers reduced to ashes are Thomas Mann, Helen Keller, Marcel Proust, Jack London, George Bernard Shaw, and Émile Zola. The attitude of a venerable professor who watches the conflagration is neatly summed up in his remark, "I don't want to know anything.") As mentioned before, the film opens and closes with the fire of the steelworks which, by the end, bears a relation to the destructive flames set by the SS. The red glow that surrounds Sophie as well as some of the other "damned" reflects these fires and the red background of the Nazi flag. This family of imagery, combining blood, passion, and flames, pulsates throughout the film.

Another work of art that begins with an image of fire and a premonition of doom had been of great interest to Visconti: *Macbeth*. In 1945 the director had tried unsuccessfully to find a producer for a film version of Shakespeare's play. *Macbeth* can be invoked as an antecedent to *The Damned* if one looks closely at the characterization of Sophie. She gives Friedrich the malevolent strength to kill the patriarch, urging him to prove himself. And Visconti's close-ups of her naked breast, hard and angular as she stretches out upon her bed, are more comprehensible if one recalls Lady Macbeth's "Unsex me here,/And fill me from the crown to the toe top full/Of direst cruelty! . . . Come to my woman's breasts,/And take my milk for gall." Sophie's breast has more of a defiant tautness than a maternal curve as she stokes Friedrich's ambition. By the end of the film, she lies in a drugged daze—fingering incestuous relics of her son's youth—a pale ghost not unlike the Lady who cannot wash the blood clean from her hands. In contrast to earlier scenes filtered with almost lurid color, Sophie's face is now so ashen that it looks no different once she is dead.

Both works are structured by an implacable destiny that destroys the ruthless power-seekers. They are initially undone by the return of someone supposedly eliminated: when Friedrich plays the new lord at the dinner table, the reaction shots of shock that precede Herbert's entrance make it seem that they've seen a ghost. Like Banquo, Herbert has returned to haunt his tormentors with guilt. And as with Banquo, his offspring survive—potential adversaries for the murderers of their parents. The sense of fulfilling a legacy, which once again recalls the "cursed house" theme, is conveyed through Martin and the young Günther (Renaud Verley). In the opening sequence, the Baron pounds on the dinner table three times for everyone's attention. When Friedrich assumes responsibility for the Von Essenbecks, a close-up of his hand pounding twice on the same spot expresses his sense of control. Instead of the third thump, his hand clenches into a fist, unable to fulfill the Baron's pattern; a cut to Martin's hand clenching playfully foreshadows the next stage of succession. Likewise, Konstantin predicts that, in ten years, his son Günther will be in command. The sensitive young man (an ally of Herbert) refuses. But when Martin informs him that Friedrich killed his father, Günther becomes a perfect target for SS manipulation: Aschenbach channels his *hate* and thus draws him into the Nazi mentality. Because his desire for vengeance will be used by those in command, Günther may very well inherit power himself, as his father predicted.

All these characters are ultimately pawns in the hands of the state, as incarnated by the smooth Aschenbach. If Martin seems triumphant at the end, it is because he is the weakest and most easily manipulated. Aschenbach, the literal link between the family and the state, is able to pull all the strings because he believes that "personal morals are dead." In his first conversation with Friedrich, Aschenbach speaks in the first person plural and this "we" establishes his symbolic nature. (He is also driving an impressive Mercedes at the time, which—as in *The Conformist*—suggests a control of situations beyond the vehicle.) When the family members verbally assault one another, Aschenbach sits calmly at a distance, eating grapes. His ability to shape the violent impulses of both sons says a good deal about Nazism. Aschenbach allows for two needs that Freud saw as pre-eminent in civilized man: aggression and obedience. In *Group Psychology and the Analysis of the Ego,* Freud described the group as "an obedient herd, which could never live without a master" and concluded,

The leader of the group is still the dreaded primal father; the group has an extreme passion for authority; in Le Bon's phrase, it has a thirst for obedience.[3]

Aschenbach urges the murder of established fathers (Joachim by Friedrich, Friedrich by Martin) and the adoration of a new one (Adolf Hitler). The killing of the patriarchs is pushed to an extreme by Martin, who rapes his mother before forcing her and his stepfather to commit suicide. Upon satisfactorily examining their dead bodies, he raises his arm in the Nazi salute, identifying himself with the new state—and a more demanding father. This last image of Martin is superimposed on the fire of the steel works, now raging with the accumulated presence of Aschenbach's victims. From the hell of this "heil" comes the ammunition of the Nazis.

The endings of these post-Holocaust films, focusing on the demise or rebirth of the father, go beyond the concept of family. When the father is a Jewish victim, as in *Sandra* and *The Garden of the Finzi-Continis,* he represents a severed link in historical continuity, and the responsibility for reforging the chain falls on the child. But when the head of the family imposes his will and rules with an iron hand, he can represent the head of state who likewise "protects," frightens, and dominates the people. Gerlach's motto is "serve the government in power." Those who inherit this thirst for obedience—either demanding submission or offering it—are doomed to repeat the mistakes of the fathers.

PART III
RESPONSES TO NAZI ATROCITY

In extremity life depends on
solidarity. Nothing can be done or
kept going without organizing,
and inevitably, when the social basis
of existence becomes self-conscious
and disciplined, it becomes "political"—
political in the elementary human sense.
— Terrence Des Pres, *The Survivor*

CHAPTER 9

POLITICAL RESISTANCE

Why do most of the films that present political resistance to the Nazis during the Holocaust—such as *The Gold of Rome, Jacob, the Liar, The Fiancée, The Last Stop, Kapo, Samson, Landscape After Battle, Kanal, Ashes and Diamonds,* and *Professor Mamlock*—come from Eastern Europe? Is it because most of the organized resistance during World War II came from the left, and its survivors prevailed in Communist countries?[1] Political resistance certainly does not mean only organized activity by the left; however, there have been very few feature films dealing with issues like Zionism, the political role of the Church in Poland, or the ambiguous political resistance of rightists who applauded (silently) the extermination of Jews while fighting against Nazi invaders of their homeland. Part of the problem is that it was precisely a sense of Jewish solidarity that prevented Jews from openly revolting: knowing that any aggressive act against the Nazis would result in retaliation against Jews elsewhere, these martyrs submitted to death. Would it be worth killing one Nazi if that meant an entire Jewish community would be wiped out—as was the case in Lublin? Their sacrifice was political to the extent that they knew it would protect fellow victims and ensure that Judaism would not perish.

As far as organized resistance during World War II is concerned, there are three major obstacles to overcoming ignorance, especially about the Jewish component:

1) active resisters risked their lives as a matter of course, and few survived. There is consequently a lack of written or photographic records of their work. Moreover, as Terrence Des Pres notes, "Certainly it is not true that they did not revolt; to live was to resist, every day, all the time, and in addition to dramatic events like the burning of Treblinka and Sobibor there were many small revolts in which all perished";[2]

2) countless Jewish survivors of Auschwitz admit to having had no knowledge of the organized political network that existed in the camp. Indeed,

political prisoners enjoyed comparatively more mobility and access to information than Jews, who were programmed for extermination. Accounts of *individual* survival have therefore paid scant attention to group solidarity;

3) almost all the existing photos and newsreels of the ghettos and camps were taken by German cameras. A documentary like Frédéric Rossif's *The Witnesses* (1962) is thus able to trace with poignancy the destruction of the Jews in the Warsaw Ghetto by re-cutting original Nazi footage, but it cannot show what those cameras would not, or could not, record. How can one reconstruct images or activities that were secret even to the Ghetto inhabitants? Thus, we see thousands of starving and humiliated Jewish faces that elicit sympathy, but few defiant ones to command respect.

Lucy Dawidowicz has called attention to this problem in an article about *The Warsaw Ghetto,* produced in 1968 by BBC Television as a "documentary" film. How faithful could this film be to historical reality if it was assembled from photos and film footage produced by Nazi propaganda teams?

When the Germans undertook to photograph the Warsaw ghetto in 1941 and 1942, they intended to use the film to justify their anti-Jewish policies and atrocities. From the records left by the Jewish diarists in the Warsaw ghetto (Adam Czerniakow, Emanuel Ringelblum, and Chaim Kaplan) showing how the Nazis staged the scenes to be filmed, the propaganda objectives of the Nazis become quite transparent. The film would graphically illustrate how generous the Germans were in providing the Jews with a place of their own in which to live. The ghetto would then be shown as a place of pleasure and plenty, where the Jews, looking like the hook-nosed monsters of racist stereotypes and the bloated capitalists of Streicher's *Stürmer* caricatures, gorged themselves on food and drink and reveled in vulgar, even depraved, entertainments. Indeed, the faces of the Jews we see during most of the film definitely conform to those racist stereotypes.[3]

Although the British film was clearly intended to condemn German treatment of the Jews, "the images of the Jews which persist in our minds . . . are the very images which the Nazi propagandists originally wished to impress on the minds of *their* viewers."[4] Dawidowicz offers the crucial reminder that

no photographs were made of the schools which the Jews operated for their children, sometimes legally, more often clandestine institutions.[5] . . . The Germans made no films of Jewish cultural activities, of the secret lending libraries, . . . of the political parties and their youth organizations, of the valiant men and women, boys and girls, who conceived, planned, and carried out the ghetto uprising.[6]

A variation on this problem can be found in documentary films that include footage from Leni Riefenstahl's *Triumph of the Will* (1935), such as *Genocide* (1975), also made by the BBC in their "World at War" series. We see crowds that signify the swelling of support for Hitler, but this footage was filmed precisely to buttress that support—grandiosely displaying the numbers already on the Führer's side. The voice-over that explains the development of Hitler's popularity thus turns propaganda into history. Such prevalent distortion must be demystified.

Few motion pictures are as successful as Carlo Lizzani's *The Gold of Rome* ("L'Oro di Roma") in sympathetically exploring both political and religious self-definition. This Italian production of 1961 is based on real events and was shot in the actual places where they occurred. The Gestapo demands from the Jewish community of Rome one hundred pounds of gold—or two hundred families will be taken hostage. These primarily poor Jews (the rich have already fled to less menacing locales) try frantically to come up with the gold, while David (Gérard Blain), a young Jewish shoemaker, insists that they must not give in to such demands. He urges them to prepare for armed resistance, but the frightened crowd wants to believe that the Germans will be appeased by the gold.

As the collection grows (including the offerings of non-Jews), the well-meaning president of the Jewish community goes to David for advice. Here, Lizzani judiciously chooses to frame the young dissenter in a manner that expresses solidarity: rather than isolate David in a close-up, he includes in the shot a window that reveals his comrades outside. These comrades, however, abandon David when the one-hundred-pound level is reached. In a shot rendered excruciating by hindsight, Jewish women steal and dump the group's arms in the river, for fear of provoking the Germans. The gold collection proves to have been in vain: Rome's Jews are rounded up and deported. Only David manages to escape, joining the partisans "to be not just a Jew fighting the Germans but an Italian fighting them."

The Goliaths that David must struggle against are not merely the Nazis, but the other Jews who believe they will be saved if they yield their gold. David acknowledges that it is not easy to overcome centuries of indoctrination that Jews should not kill. This pacifist streak, inherent in the faith, has been internalized even by David, so that when he must kill a German for the first time, he can't pull the trigger. A partisan yells "Shoot!" to the paralyzed novice, and only at the last moment does David kill the soldier. To emphasize the moral price David pays for his first murder, the German's death is presented in slow motion, drawing out his agony.

A contrasting image of solidarity is suggested through Giulia (Anna Maria Ferrero), a beautiful Jewess who is protected by Massimo (Jean Sorel), a Christian medical student in love with her. Like her other admirer, David, Giulia ultimately abandons the community and is baptized—but when she realizes that the Germans have arrived to seize the Jews, she decides she must go with them. Despite her love for Massimo and fears for her person, Giulia reassumes the burden of Jewish communal identity in the penultimate scene. Subsequent shots imply the extinction of Rome's Jews, for we see a montage of the now-empty ghetto, accompanied by the sound of Massimo's hollow footsteps as he searches vainly for Giulia. Like Nicole in *Kapo* and Jeanne in *Black Thursday,* Giulia chooses to die as a Jew. While *The Gold of Rome* does not condemn her for this decision, the film valorizes David's resistance over Giulia's martyrdom.

David's polar opposite can be found in *Jacob, the Liar* ("Jacob, der Lügner"), a 1978 East German film directed by Frank Beyer from Jurek Becker's script and original novel. In a ghetto, Jacob (Vlastimil Brodsky) maintains everyone's morale with optimistic newscasts from his hidden radio. Through this

Vlastimil Brodsky as *Jacob, the Liar*.
MUSEUM OF MODERN ART/FILM STILLS ARCHIVE

sole contact with the outside world, the inhabitants are told that the Russians are advancing. Jacob refuses to show his radio to anyone and when a little girl (Manuela Simon) begs to listen to it, the reason becomes apparent: from behind a wall, it is Jacob's voice that becomes the radio announcer's for this child. The "voice box" does not exist, and the news bulletins are merely Jacob's wishful fabrications. When he finally admits to his friend Kowalski (Erwin Geschonneck) that he never had a radio, Kowalski hangs himself. The film thus raises the question of whether Jacob was not in fact wrong: though well-meaning, he offered illusions that kept the Jews from banding together and fighting. His lies prevented not only suicides (he tells the doctor that no one tried to kill himself since he began reporting the "news") but also the will to organize and resist.

Jacob, the Liar begins with an invitation to question what we believe and to believe what we question. A title states, "The story of Jacob never really happened this way." There is a cut to Jacob. "Really it didn't," continues the written narration. And after another shot of Jacob comes the line, "But maybe it did." (Indeed, the film presents a rather benign version of events, for the Nazis are depicted as humane in two instances: a kindly German policeman sends Jacob home after a guard claims it is past curfew, and another soldier passes him two cigarettes.) A flashback reveals that our hero used to be a cook in a restaurant, flipping potato pancakes in the air. His nourishment of the ghetto community, however, is verbal and plentiful: when he says the Russians have advanced three kilometers, his friends' subsequent version to others makes it five kilometers. The truth is that deportation is imminent, and *Jacob, the Liar* ends with the entire ghetto crowded into a transport. Jacob imagines a scene in the snow, hiding from brutal reality in dreams that halt in a freeze frame. The final credits superimposed on stills of the faces in the train suggest, through stopped images, arrested lives.

Jacob, the Liar does not really grapple with the danger of its protagonist's stories. Jacob tells the little girl Lena that things will be better when the Russians come: she won't have to wear an identifying star and will have as much as she wants to eat. When Lena then imagines being a waitress in a café, we see her fantasy. Later in the film, Jacob tells Lena a story about a princess, which a slow-motion dream sequence literalizes. Lena is the princess in a beautiful dress, but the fact that a Jewish badge is still attached to it conveys the poignant subjectivity of the image. On an individual level, the escape into imagination might be a means to survive. For the survival of a group, however, Jacob's lies are pernicious.

Another film from East Germany offers one of the most inspiring visions of solidarity and integrity ever put on film: *The Fiancée* ("Die Verlobte"), co-directed by Günter Reisch and Gunther Rücker in 1980, is based on Eva Lippold's three-part autobiographical novel, *The House with the Heavy Doors.* The author—who was in a Nazi prison from 1935 until 1945—served as adviser on the film, which is set in the thirties. Hella (Jutta Wachowiak), a young Communist, is sentenced to ten years in prison for distributing anti-Nazi propaganda. Two things keep her alive in this debasing environment: love for the man who was her accomplice, and commitment to a cause. These spiritual life lines enable her to be generous with the other women, and to be respected by murderesses and political prisoners alike. Much like Fania Fenelon in *Playing for Time,* she acts with an authority born of innate dignity, refusing to allow the other inmates to fall into self-pity or aimless bickering. Wachowiak plays the courageous heroine with such conviction that the film remains a stinging experience—even for those who do not agree with the political cause for which she is struggling.

Hella is the spiritual sister of the resisters in *The Last Stop* ("Ostatni Etap"), one of the only Holocaust films directed by a woman—Wanda Jakubowska. The 1948 Polish production, from a script by Jakubowska and Gerda Schneider, is also one of the most powerful and historically accurate feature films made about (and in) Auschwitz. *The Last Stop* celebrates female solidarity: as is true of the women in *The Fiancée, Passenger, Kanal* (whose most heroic figure is Daisy), *Playing for Time,* and *The Wall,* their survival is predicated upon this solidarity. Since *The Last Stop*'s first dramatic scene is the birth of a baby followed by its immediate murder, the film suggests that the shared identity of childless mother was the source for many women's relationships in the concentration camps. Mothers whose children were taken from them (or even women who realized they might remain childless because they had stopped menstruating[7]) channeled their frustrated maternal instincts into caring for their fellow inmates. It is possible that the conditioning of women as nurturers made them better suited to social survival.[8]

The Last Stop has tremendous authenticity because the film was made *where* it happened; by and with people *to whom* it happened; and in the native languages. The Poles speak Polish, the Russians Russian, the Germans German, and the French French. The filmmaker, who was herself imprisoned in Auschwitz, re-created an unrelenting portrait of the brutality of the Nazis (as well as of some Kapos and *blochowas*) on the one hand, and of the saving solidarity of the female prisoners on the other. (Since the only existing print in the United States is at the Museum of Modern Art in New York, the following plot summary will be more exhaustive than that of other films discussed in these pages.)

We are introduced to Auschwitz through shots of hundreds of women standing in the cold, mutely accepting the vicious insults and blows of the *blochowa,* the prisoner responsible for maintaining order in her block. (Such women receive special privileges for their usually harsh treatment of others.) Because one Polish woman in labor sinks to the ground, the *blochowa* punishes the entire group, ordering them to continue standing in the cold. Her attempt at divisiveness ("Tell the Russians and French they're suffering for the Pole") does not have its intended effect, since most of the prisoners in *The Last Stop* are united against the Nazis: on an immediate level, each woman around the pregnant one comforts her; on a visual level, a high-angle shot of the group embraces how they weave together, rocking gently in place as one body.

The baby is born, delivered by the Russian doctor Eugenia (Tatiana Gorecka), a figure of dignity and purpose. But the German chief doctor takes the infant away, makes out a report, and proceeds to "inoculate" the baby—presumably murdering it. The mother joins the group of politically active women in the hospital, a privileged locale that retains contact with the outside world.[9] They try to smuggle information out of the camp, and their dreams are crosscut with the realities of German officers who are trying to reduce the time and cost of gassing. (When a man suggests that it would make more economic sense to use the prisoners as labor, a woman officer insists that the priority of the camp is the destruction of "racially non-desirable elements." With cold-blooded calm, they establish a goal of killing fifty thousand per day.)

The realization of their goal is demonstrated in the film's next sequence, as a train pulls into Auschwitz in the night. The camp commandant, speaking only German, and his armed soldiers brutally separate the 2,500 Polish Jews from each other and take their luggage away. He notices that Marta (Barbara Drapinska), a young woman from the transport, is translating his orders into Polish and consequently he makes her his interpreter—thereby sparing her life. The rest of the group is herded off, leaving the space empty except for a child's abandoned doll. In close-up, a German's boot steps on it, symbolizing the fate of its young owner. Each woman is methodically stripped of all her jewels, possessions, clothes, hair, and then is tattooed on the left arm. Like the audience, Marta is a newcomer to this incomprehensible hell, forced to translate not only German into Polish, but apprehension into comprehension, or the act of seeing into an awareness of evil. She asks another prisoner about the emaciated body she sees on the barbed wire and thus learns about "the Moslems"—a nickname for the skeletal inmates "who can't take it any more" and succumb to death. Marta (and the audience) are then informed that the rising

Above, the women prisoners in *The Fiancée,* and below,
Jutta Wachowiak (left) as Hella in *The Fiancée.* KEN WLASCHIN

smoke she sees comes from the cremated bodies of her entire transport. As with the woman in labor at the beginning, Marta's sudden loss of family will turn her into a defiant member of the resistance, replacing blood ties with those of active solidarity.

Jakubowska shows both the brave opposition to the Nazis, and the cowardly acquiescence. A group of elegant women arrive at Auschwitz still in their furs; by the next shot, they are in prison garb. Class tensions arise as the coarse *blochowa* lords it over these socialite Poles—this is her one chance in life to act superior to them. However, as some of these ladies come to realize her power, they connive to become her "friend," bringing her little gifts and thereby enjoying the warmth of her private room. The most pernicious member of this group is Lalunia, a profoundly silly woman who, upon the death of Eugenia, pretends to be a doctor to save her own skin. The wife of a pharmacist, she is appointed by the chief doctor to replace Eugenia—who is tortured and killed for telling the truth to the commission of neutral countries formed to investigate Auschwitz. (The Nazis have suddenly improved the look of the hospital, but Eugenia blurts out *in German* to the visitors, "It's all a lie. Innocent people are being killed!") Lalunia steals things from the hospital to give to the *blochowa,* and this group of selfish prisoners side with their oppressors.

Nazi guards in *The Fiancée.*
KEN WLASCHIN

These ladies remain ignorant of how the women are being organized through the hospital. In particular, a group of Russian female officers, arrested as prisoners of war, instill more spirit into the Auschwitz community. The resistance arranges for Marta and Tadek, a male prisoner, to escape in order to get to the Allies the Nazi plans to liquidate Auschwitz. They succeed in publicizing the Germans' strategy to hide the traces of their death factory—but are then captured. Marta is to be hanged publicly, although a knife slipped into her hands by one of the prisoners, followed by a shot of a trickle of blood, suggests to the viewer that she takes her own life. She declares that the liberators are coming, and suddenly there are indeed planes flying overhead. Her dying words to a woman who cradles her are "You must not allow Auschwitz to be repeated"—the informing impulse of *The Last Stop,* from its first image to its last.

In the course of this film, most of the major characters die; and yet the central character, which is the Cause, remains—a whole greater than the sum of its parts. From the opening scene, in which prisoners comfort each other, the emphasis is on unifying in the face of the enemy. Those who speak Russian understand Polish and vice versa, whereas a point is always made of translating whatever is said in German. In fact, the precise cause of Eugenia's torture (and death) is that she refuses to divulge who taught her the damning German words she had uttered to the commission. This older Russian woman is the most noble of the prisoners, while her replacement Lalunia seems the most despicable. Between the two exists a spectrum ranging from the savage *blochowa* to the self-sacrificing inmates. As in *Samson, Passenger,* and countless other Polish films, hope lies in (presumably) Communist resistance.

Stylistically, *The Last Stop* is straightforward, presenting overwhelming events with effective simplicity. The music is less noticeable than in other films on this subject, except when it has narrative significance. From a truckload of French Jews bound for the gas chambers, a woman yells to one who has survived the selection, "You must live to tell everyone what happened to us." Understanding French, the German in charge orders the survivor to board the truck as well. When the young Estelle does so, she begins singing the "Marseillaise," and is soon joined by other voices as the truck approaches the chimney. The use of the French anthem is deeply moving here, for these women (and the audience) know it is the last song they will ever sing. Jakubowska also uses music as ironic counterpoint: when the inmates are being beaten and forced into the gas chambers, the women's orchestra plays Beethoven and Brahms (a historical fact); while Eugenia is being tortured, the German officer puts on a dance record of a Russian song. Contrapuntal music was appropriate to Auschwitz—and therefore, perhaps, to the films about it.

It is unfortunate that Gillo Pontecorvo did not think along these lines when he made *Kapo.* This Italian/French co-production released in 1960 offers not only an American star, Susan Strasberg (who had originated the role of Anne Frank on Broadway), but a musical score that seems American in its conception: like that of *The Diary of Anne Frank* and *Judgment at Nuremberg,* it is relentless and often maudlin. For example, the heroine screaming at the sight of naked people being marched off to the gas chamber—an already horrifying image—is cheapened by the accompaniment of hysterical music. As well as directing, Pontecorvo also collaborated with Carlo Rustichelli on the score with far less impressive results than in his later masterpiece, *The Battle of Algiers* (where he worked with Ennio Morricone). In *Kapo,* we see the transformation of a delicate Parisian adolescent, Edith (Strasberg), into Nicole, a hardened concentration camp prisoner put in charge of other inmates. She is introduced playing the harpsichord—a musical connection that will be repeated throughout the film: whenever the past is invoked, the sentimental harpsichord theme returns.

During a Nazi roundup, Edith jumps onto a transport bearing her mother away. Once inside the chaotic darkness of Auschwitz, she is spared by a doctor who gives her the clothes of a dead prisoner. She becomes Nicole, number 10099—a new identity for a new system of being. "You're not a Jew any more," the doctor tells her. She is taken to a labor camp where the kind interpreter Teresa (Emmanuelle Riva) establishes that half the prisoners are political, including many Russians. Nicole's adjustment is difficult for, like Marianne in *Playing for Time,* she is not in control of her physical needs: when she puts her frozen hands on a stove, she not only burns them badly but the Kapo also beats her and gives her fifteen days in solitary. Hunger subsequently leads her to steal Teresa's potato. When another woman is killed, Nicole quickly takes the socks off her feet. And when she realizes that food can be obtained for sexual favors, she complies. By the next scene, Nicole's long hair —which had been shaved off—has returned and she is playing cards with Carl, the Nazi who killed her friend.

Nicole assumes the mentality of a fierce and isolated survivor: she becomes a Kapo, content to be eating and sleeping well—even if it means beating other women. When a Russian prisoner, Sasha (Laurent Terzieff), accuses her of being like the Nazis, she has him punished. However, when he is forced to stand by a high-tension barbed-wire fence all night (if he moves he dies), Nicole's first glimmer of humanity emerges. They eventually fall in love and plan an escape that, for the politically minded Sasha, must include other prisoners as well. Romance and social commitment conflict when Sasha learns that everyone will get out *except* Nicole, since to arrange the escape she must remain behind the others to turn off the electric power of the fence. They go through with the plan nevertheless, and enjoy only a Pyrrhic victory in which many prisoners are shot. The wounded Nicole asks Carl to remove her Nazi badge, and before dying reassumes her Jewish identity by reciting a Hebrew prayer.

The last shot of Sasha emerging from a mass grave suggests that survival means stepping over dead bodies. *Kapo* thus questions the price of individual safety and celebrates collective spirit as the means to heroism. When Nicole tells Sasha to escape, he worries about friends suffering possible reprisals. And toward the end, everyone but Sasha is willing to sacrifice one person—Nicole —for the sake of many. He admits to Nicole that she will be killed if she turns off the electric power and concludes, "I ask you to do it all the same." Will she choose self-sacrifice over selfishness? Even the Nazi Carl questions the survivor mentality when Nicole declares of camp life, "Now I like it: I eat well,

Above, Prisoners arrive at Auschwitz in *Kapo.*
Susan Strasberg (below left) as Nicole in *Kapo.*
MUSEUM OF MODERN ART/FILM STILLS ARCHIVE

sleep well. . . ." (Carl is indeed linked to Nicole in visual terms for he has only one hand—a bond with Nicole's burned hands from touching the heater.)

It is Nicole's connection to Teresa that provides the film with its greatest resonance, for the translator mediates between the two sides of Nicole's nature. Like Marta in *The Last Stop* and Marta in *Passenger* (all three characters based on an actual interpreter at Auschwitz), Teresa is a Resistance figure of truly heroic proportions. As in *Passenger,* the translator is put to a test in a public action and, refusing to give information, is punished. In *Kapo,* the high-tension fence is the place that measures integrity: Teresa purposely jumps onto it when she realizes her life has no more dignity—and dies; Sasha is forced to stand beside it an entire night without moving; and Nicole's act of solidarity is to turn off its electric power. As Nicole grows stronger—mirroring her oppressors—Teresa grows weaker. This transfer is made literal by the repetition of food-stealing: first Nicole steals Teresa's potato, appropriating her source of nourishment; later, after fifteen days in solitary, Teresa steals another woman's bread. Once Teresa is dead, Nicole begins to reassume that part of herself that Teresa represented.

Kapo traces Nicole's transformation from a frightened, orphaned, and selfish victim into a political heroine who ultimately embraces her heritage and sacrifices herself. She is therefore similar to Samson in Wajda's portrait, who also moves from passivity to meaningful political action. *Samson* focuses on a young man in the process of shaping his values through loss, as he is stripped

Liberation of camp prisoners in *Landscape After Battle.* NEW YORKER FILMS

of rights, freedom, family, and the sense of his own manhood. In prison for accidentally killing a fellow student, he meets Malina, a kindly, apolitical humanist, and Pankrat, an inspiring Communist professor. Malina says of Pankrat, "He's a man of steel, but I'm not sure that a man should be made of steel" (thus paving the way for Wajda's 1977 *Man of Marble* and 1981 *Man of Iron*). Because Malina represents individualism and the refusal of political action, he is quickly disposed of by the narrative. Similarly, Samson's sense of Judaism is diminished, while his political identity—fueled by Pankrat—grows. For example, he tells the actress who hides him that he wants to return to his people in the ghetto. Her response to his idea that no individual survival is possible within the concept of Jewish destiny is: "That's false solidarity." The film supports the argument that abstract sentiment for the Jewish ghetto is less tenable than concrete solidarity with the Communist Resistance. Wajda intensifies his thesis by having the camera pan between Samson and Pankrat in prison, unifying them within the frame a number of times. And if Samson's assumed name suggests that his strength derives from his Jewish identity, Kazia (the second woman who hides him) destroys this when she cuts his hair, cuts him off from the world, and removes the Jewish star from his sweater. His strength, Wajda seems to propose, can exist only in terms of a larger political struggle: at the end, the hero's own voice urges him to show his strength by killing the German persecutors. He smiles, throws a grenade, and dies in the rubble.

The inadequacy of individual survival and the denial of positive Jewish identity are also explored in Wajda's *Landscape After Battle* ("Krajobraz Po Bitwie"). Based on the autobiographical stories of Tadeusz Borowski—the Polish writer who survived Auschwitz, Dachau, and the postwar displaced-persons camps, only to commit suicide in 1951 at the age of 29—this 1970 film returns to the themes and stylistic devices of Wajda's masterful World War II trilogy. It begins with the liberation of a men's concentration camp, expressed—without recourse to dialogue—by a breathlessly mobile camera, jubilant Vivaldi music ("The Four Seasons"), and the men's physical explosion of energy. The only diffident character is Tadeusz (Daniel Olbrychski), a bespectacled young writer who is more interested in reading than in taking revenge on a German guard. For all their exhilaration, the men realize they have nowhere to go: in the film's first dialogue, they are told by the American officer in command that they must remain in the former SS barracks, now a DP camp.

These Poles are technically free, but psychologically still at war. A Polish sublieutenant continually insults a Communist; American soldiers make fun of a Polish priest; and the food-obsessed Tadeusz is punished for cooking on the sly. Before he is thrown into a hole, however, the former prisoners try to protect Tadeusz from the authorities—even without knowing what he has done. When some American women come to see the camp, Tadeusz accosts one and asks her with bitter humor, "Do you know the crematory tango?" This loner meets another person branded by the war, Nina (Stanislawa Celinska), a young Jewish woman who was hidden as a Catholic. After arriving at the DP camp in a truck with other women, Nina tries to convince Tadeusz to run away with her, but he is even more passive than Samson in Kazia's cellar. His memories are like the number tattooed on his arm: "You can't kiss that off," he warns Nina. "It's expert German craftsmanship, indelible." Chained to these memories, Tadeusz refuses to leave the gutted landscape of postwar Poland. He insists that he can't erase his Polishness, for "a country isn't just a landscape; it's the people, the traditions, the language."

Tadeusz's ties to Poland are less nationalist than mythic, for he takes refuge in the written word rather than seeing the people around him. Nina, on the other hand, declares "I'm neither Polish nor Jewish." In her acknowledgement that "Jews disgust me" and "Israel terrifies me," she is as rootless as Tadeusz. Having first seen each other when Tadeusz was distributing wafers for the Mass, they seem linked by a false communion: the wafer passed from the hand of a disbeliever into the mouth of a Jewess. After roaming outside the camp, they decide to return, but an American soldier accidentally shoots Nina. Tadeusz takes this in stride, telling the American in command that "the Germans have been shooting us for six years, and now you. What's the difference?" After a fight with the priest beside Nina's dead body, Tadeusz finally leaves the camp, on a train dotted with red flags.

Tadeusz's psychic self-enclosure during the first part of the film is made tangible by the solitary confinement that he seems to enjoy: he can read in the hole and not be bothered by the others. Although Wajda elicits sympathy for this tortured loner through close-ups, he also invites criticism of Tadeusz's disconnected artist's soul. Tadeusz is thus closely linked to the musician in *Kanal,* an outsider who joins the Resistance even though he is less a fighter than an artist. Once in the sewers, he loses his mind in the labyrinth, quotes Dante, and plays an ocarina while the others search for an exit. Wajda's entire war trilogy—*A Generation* (1955), *Kanal* (1957), *Ashes and Diamonds* (1958) —devalues the lone hero in favor of collective consciousness. The tension in *A Generation* ("Pokolenie") is between Stach (Tadeusz Lomnicki) and Janek (Tadeusz Janczar)—the committed hero and the agonized martyr. Like the anti-hero of *Landscape After Battle,* Janek is a victim of Polish history, an indecisive and unconnected young man. Stach, on the other hand, is an embryonic version of the men of marble and iron that would form the center of Wajda's later work: he is a laborer and a resister (perhaps reflecting the fact that Wajda himself joined the Resistance at the age of sixteen). As Boleslaw Sulik's introduction to the war-trilogy screenplays proposes,

A Generation presents a positive hero of working-class descent, and it idealizes his social environment and his own experience. The plot, a story of a boy's growth to maturity through contacts with revolutionary resistance groups, showing the development of political awareness and a gradual assumption of responsibility for his own and others' actions, has been the socialist-realist favourite ever since Maxim Gorky.[10]

In *Kanal,* the solidarity of the Polish Home Army fighters in the sewers is emphasized by a constantly panning and tracking camera that literally binds them together and insists on the flexibility (and subservience) of the camera vis-à-vis the characters. The famous four-minute tracking shot that introduces us to the protagonists acknowledges each one but only within the visual/political context of the group. *Ashes and Diamonds* ("Popiol i Diament"), on the other hand, synthesizes *A Generation* and *Kanal* by focusing on the dilemma

Above, Daniel Olbrychski (Tadeusz) and Stanislawa Celinska (Nina), and below, Tadeusz and his books in *Landscape After Battle*.
NEW YORKER FILMS

of Maciek (Zbigniew Cybulski), a former Home Army fighter, on the day World War II ends. He is given the assignment to assassinate Szczuka (Waclaw Zastrzezynski), the representative of the new order—the Communist party. (It is important to know here that the Polish Nationalist Home Army had been as forcefully anti-Communist as anti-Nazi.) The central tension of the film is the existential hero versus the cause, the individual who sees no reason to kill a sympathetic old man versus the political dictum that takes little account of private morality. Wajda masterfully expresses this tension through the use of deep-focus photography, which maintains Maciek and Szczuka in a charged spatial proximity. In addition, his frequent use of a low-angle camera perspective results in a feeling of entrapment, as the ceilings seem to continually bear down upon the characters' heads.

Sulik sees Wajda's work as "animated by a true heroic impulse, desperately frustrated . . . made absurd by its context, its nobility corrupted by the modern Polish experience. . . . In *Ashes and Diamonds* this ever-present nostalgia for heroic action found an additional, direct channel in the performance of Zbigniew Cybulski."[11] This actor—like his character—could not sustain the feverish romanticism of his turbulent life, and died while trying to jump onto a moving train in 1967. Maciek, too, dies a useless and drawn-out death— suggesting perhaps that the new Poland has no place for the romantic individualist. It is clear, nevertheless, that Wajda is attracted to this fiery spirit, even as he questions it. What gives his work its complexity is that—despite the hopeful message of political solidarity—his characters have the courage of their confusion. Samson, Tadeusz, Stach, and Maciek all struggle to comprehend politics and are often sacrificed to or comprehended by the struggle.

In Wajda's films, the Jews and the self-centered characters die, paving the way for the Communist order. The paradigm for this treatment can be found in what may be the first fiction film made about the Holocaust, *Professor Mamlock* (1937), from the Soviet Union. Hailed by New York critics as timely, it was banned in Chicago in November 1938 as "purely Jewish and Communist propaganda against Germany"; Ohio and Rhode Island followed suit; Massachusetts banned it for Sunday showings in March 1939 "because it might incite a riot on the Sabbath." *Professor Mamlock* was the first film to tell Americans that Nazis were killing Jews; however, what must have made the censors really nervous was that it is a political film that places its faith in Communism. The story of *Professor Mamlock* is by Friedrich Wolf, the German playwright and friend of Brecht who was forced to flee his country in 1933. Wolf's play, *Dr. Mamlock's Way Out,* was suppressed in Germany but had a two-year run in Moscow. There, it was seen by Herbert Rappaport, who had fled from Austria after being an assistant to G. W. Pabst. He met with Wolf, suggested the film version, and went to work with him and co-director Adolph Minkin on a screenplay (which was first written in German).

Shot in Leningrad on sets that are redolent of German "atmosphere," *Professor Mamlock* begins on February 27, 1933, as an agent provocateur yells to German workers, "Destroy the Reds and drive the Jews out of the country." In a hospital, the respected surgeon-scientist Professor Mamlock (S. Mezhinsky) says, "I don't care much for politics." His son Rolf (O. Zhakov) is in love with Mamlock's assistant Inge (N. Shaternikova), who believes in Nazism as a way of "cleansing French and Asiatic elements out of science." The peaceful doctor is against Rolf's political sympathies, and forbids him to return home if he goes to Communist meetings. After the Reichstag fire, Nazi attacks escalate, the slogans always blending "Communists" and "Jews" as if it were an equation: storm troopers barge into apartments; books are burned; men are brutally taken away. Dr. Hellpach (V. Chesnokov), a rival, enlists the aid of storm troopers to expel Mamlock from his operating room, and the professor is paraded through the streets with the word *Jude* scrawled across his white doctor's smock. Hellpach wants to operate on the Nazis' chief of staff —but the officer himself insists on the more experienced Mamlock! True to his Hippocratic oath, Mamlock returns to the clinic and performs the operation. Hellpach's sleazy tactics include forcing patients to sign a petition to rid the clinic of Mamlock, and warning the other doctors that they will lose their jobs if they don't sign as well. As symbolic cross shapes and shadows become more and more noticeable around the Jewish doctor, he suddenly falls (off-screen) after we hear a shot. Later, while Mamlock recovers from what might have been a suicide attempt, all he wants is to see his son.

In the meantime, Rolf has become actively engaged in "the People's Front." When he and a friend are jailed and refuse to give information, they are ordered to a concentration camp. Resistance comrades and Inge help Rolf escape, and the camera points up the spontaneous solidarity of nameless people. Mamlock is killed—but not before declaring to the Nazi soldiers, "You are doomed." The film ends on Rolf and his comrades, expressing a hope for the future. *Professor Mamlock* implies that the doctor dies not simply because he is a Jew, but because he never allowed politics to touch his life. Blinded by his love for abstract science, Mamlock did not realize what the Nazis were plotting, and would not even permit Rolf to consort with the underground. By the end, it has been made clear that science, culture, respect, and integrity are no bulwark against the Nazis, and that the only answer is organized resistance. Unfortunately, the assumption implicit in *Professor Mamlock* and other East European films is that Judaism can inhibit resistance. The message from Communist countries—derived from Marx's own pronouncements on "the Jewish Question"—is that Jewish identity must be subsumed into larger political realities. For compelling examples to the contrary, with Jewish characters standing up for themselves and organizing others *as Jews,* one would have to wait for *Playing for Time* and *The Wall*—both made, ironically enough, for American television. Whether it's Fania in the women's orchestra of Auschwitz, or Berson and Rachel in the Warsaw Ghetto, their generous actions redefine politics from the sphere of factions to the radical domain of daily interchange.

CHAPTER 10
THE AMBIGUITY OF IDENTITY

George Steiner has argued persuasively that the context of the Holocaust goes beyond politics to metaphysics—that the deep anti-Semitic loathing built up in the social subconscious was rooted in Judaism's "claims of the ideal," to use Ibsen's phrase. Given that "some political scientists put at roughly 80 percent the proportion of Jews in the ideological development of messianic socialism and communism,"

when it turned on the Jew, Christianity and European civilization turned on the incarnation—albeit an incarnation often wayward and unaware—of its own best hopes. . . . The secular, materialist, warlike community of modern Europe sought to extirpate from itself . . . the carriers of the ideal.[1]

Steiner sees the Holocaust not as a political or socio-economic phenomenon, but as the enactment of a suicidal impulse in Western civilization:

It was an attempt to level the future—or, more precisely, to make history commensurate with the natural savageries, intellectual torpor, and material instincts of unextended man. Using theological metaphors, and there is no need to apologize for them in an essay on culture, the holocaust may be said to mark a second Fall. We can interpret it as a voluntary exit from the Garden and a programmatic attempt to burn the Garden behind us. Lest its remembrance continue to infect the health of barbarism with debilitating dreams or with remorse.

This suicidal impulse can be seen in films that focus on *individual* responsibility vis-à-vis Nazi domination—such as *The Shop on Main Street, Mr. Klein, General Della Rovere,* and *The Man in the Glass Booth.* They depict the breakdown or transfer of identity among bystander, survivor, and victim, and locate the drama within the self, where a Jewish or Nazi identity is gradually assumed.

Klaus Maria Brandauer as Hendrik Höfgen in *Mephisto.*
ANALYSIS FILMS

Mephisto (1981) is a striking cinematic exploration of Nazism as devil's work. István Szabó, the Hungarian director who already probed the Nazi era through the haunting flashbacks and dreams of *25 Fireman's Street* (1973) and the urgent role-playing in *Confidence* (1979), turns here to the story of an intelligent German actor whose accommodation of Nazi rule constitutes a selling of his soul in exchange for success. The Prime Minister sees "perfect evil in the mask" that the actor wears as Mephistopheles in Goethe's *Faust*, adding with approval, "Mephisto is also a German national hero." The film is adapted from the novel by Klaus Mann (son of Thomas) who fled Germany in 1933, wrote the prophetic book in 1936, and found no one to publish it because of its obvious parallels between the protagonist Hendrik Höfgen and the German actor Gustaf Gründgens. (Although imprisoned at the end of the war, this personal friend of Göring returned to prominence in postwar Germany, and publishers told Mann that the book would be seen as a defamation.) After a second publisher's refusal in 1948, less than a year later Mann committed suicide.[2]

The German-language film traces the external rise and internal fall of Hendrik, played with flamboyant verve by the Austrian actor Klaus Maria Brandauer. In Hamburg of the thirties, this talented actor desperately wants to move up in the theatrical world, and charms various women to this end. As a stepping-stone to success, he marries the aristocratic Barbara (Krystyna Janda), and is then made a member of the State Theater in Berlin. After playing the role of his dreams, Mephisto, Hendrik accepts a film offer in Budapest—where he learns of the Nazi takeover in Germany. Instead of remaining in exile, he is lured back to Berlin by the promise of favor with the actress Lotte Lindenthal (Christine Harbort), mistress of a powerful Nazi General (Rolf Hoppe). Hendrik plays Mephisto once again, acclaimed not only by the public but also by the diabolical General. Under the Nazis' aegis, Hendrik becomes Germany's most celebrated actor and, finally, director of the State Theater. Stripped of wife, mistress, principles, and self-respect, he ultimately becomes a mouthpiece for the General, acting at every public (and private) occasion. Despite his second marriage to a similarly ambitious and compromising actress (Ildiko Bansagi), at the end he is alone and aware of the price he has paid for his empty success.

Hendrik's first appearance on screen is vivid: as the applause for Dora Martin (Ildiko Kishonti) swells, we see a man backstage screaming, crying, and covering his head with histrionic abandon. This actor is so jealous of Dora's applause that he raves like a spoiled child. That his crazy energy lacks a channel (and is thus potentially dangerous) is implied in the next sequence where his black mistress Juliette (Karin Boyd) declares, "You love only yourself, and even then, not enough." This lithe dancer realizes that his face is a mask: Hendrik changes expressions (and positions) with suspicious versatility. Although he and his friend Otto (Peter Andorai) agitate for populist theater and openly despise the troupe's Nazi sympathizer Miklas (Gyorgy Cserhalmi), Hendrik already manifests a willed blindness: when he sees a group of Nazis yelling "Jew, out of here" while beating up a man, he merely thinks they're drunk. Increasingly, he retreats into the theater as a shelter from the world's turmoil, especially after coming back to Germany from Hungary.

Hendrik Höfgen playing the role of his life in *Mephisto*. ANALYSIS FILMS

In the second half of the film, a new relationship takes shape: the General is to Hendrik as Mephisto is to Faust, a parallel that is heightened by the openness of both manipulators. Although the Nazi official insists on calling the actor "Mephisto" offstage, it is really his own name that he utters. The un-named General (at least partially modeled on Göring, since he declares the famous line, "When I hear the word 'culture,' I reach for my revolver") feeds Hendrik's vanity in order to control him; when the actor fulfills the Nazi design, he rewards Hendrik with the post of director of the State Theater. That this is merely another role for Hendrik to play is expressed by the glasses he suddenly begins wearing—a new prop for a new part. He rationalizes that freedom is not a prerequisite to his art, but soon learns that *Kunst* (art) is not immune from the taint of Nazi doctrine: his own playing of Mephisto grows more diabolical in its precision and control via surprise; the Arno Breker kind of sculpture encouraged by the State is inhumanly immense and perfect; and even the version of *Hamlet* Hendrik directs has been re-interpreted as a saga of "Nordic man" who is "not weak."

Hendrik's transformation is enacted through the inextricable blend of life and theater that characterized the growth of Nazism. This is particularly well expressed by the intercutting of a "political" rehearsal with scenes of Hendrik's performances; Miklas leads a large Hitler Youth Group, teaching them to speak their lines louder and with more vigor. This kind of life *is* theater: Dora Martin puts it well when she says of Germany, "Here, the curtain is gradually descending," before leaving for America. And when the General congratulates Hendrik in his balcony box during the intermission of *Faust,* Szabó masterfully cuts from their meeting to a long shot of the theater, as the crowd below slowly turns to gaze upward at the box. They watch the two men on this new stage, dazzled by the spectacle of Mephisto in make-up alongside the General in uniform. Szabó acknowledged in an interview that "these are two actors in love, speaking about the problems of their craft. The General even tells Hendrik that he learned a lot from him, especially the element of surprise."[3] Appropriately enough, the General's birthday party at the end is held inside the theater, which has been taken over for the lavish ball.

In the final sequence, the General squires Hendrik away to an empty stadium, where he teases him with the idea that it would make a great theater. Bellowing the actor's echoing name and pushing him into the center of the arena, the General directs his little *mise en scène* with malevolent mirth, and demonstrates how powerless the performer is. Hendrik is caught in the inescapable light, a theatrical device that now blinds him. The stark white light gives his face the cast of the Mephisto mask; we see that even this supposed engineer of evil is trapped by his device, unable to control the lunacy of Nazism. "What do they want of me? I'm only an actor," he whispers to the camera in close-up, his pale face fading into the glare that surrounds him.

As Brandauer pointed out in an interview, "After World War Two, everyone said, 'I was only an artist; I was only a professor; I was only a policeman.' . . . The big question is responsibility. Everyone must be a member of society and take a position vis-à-vis their society."[4] If, as the General declares, "there's a little Mephisto in everyone," it is even more true that there's a little Faust in everyone. Szabó leads us to identify with the latter by using a subjective camera at two key moments: from the point of view of the General and his mistress Lotte as they acknowledge the bowing spectators at the theater; and near the end, from Hendrik's point of view, greeting the guests at the birthday party. In both cases, the camera identifies itself with power and records how people humble themselves to its gaze. According to the director,

If the spectators find something in the film, in a character, which ties into their personal problems, you have won. Cinema means identification—to live and feel something together—and to meet yourself in a mirror. This actor who works with the Nazis is us during the film.[5]

The one who understands this process best is Juliette, for she perceives that Hendrik likes to be a "well-behaved boy," enjoying his rewards for obedience.

Hendrik is hardly an "evil" character; after all, he hides an old Jewish friend in his home even when he is working for the Nazis, and he risks the General's displeasure by pleading for his politically suspect friend Otto. He is, quite simply, weak—and so obsessed with his career that he jumps into the spotlight, even when he knows that he is hiding in the glare. The last image reinforces how the light of spectacle can blind as well as illuminate, if the actor and spectator are not aware of who controls the stage, and to what purpose.

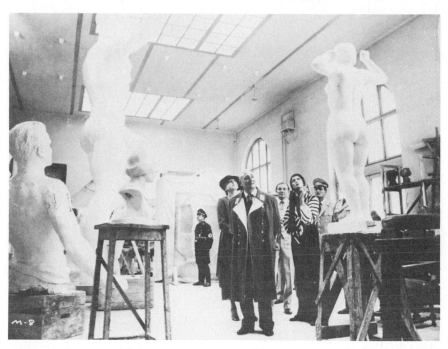

Above, the General (Rolf Hoppe) surveys Nazi art in *Mephisto;*
and below, a Nazi show in *Mephisto.* ANALYSIS FILMS

The Shop on Main Street ("Obchod na Korze") traces the wartime transformation of Tono Britko (Josef Kroner)—a simple peasant who enjoys nothing
more than soaking his tired feet in a bowl of water—into a number of other
identities. In this 1965 Czech film co-directed by Jan Kadár and Elmar Klos,
it is 1942 in Slovakia, and Tono is designated the Aryan Controller of the
button shop owned by the elderly widow Rosalie Lautmann (Ida Kaminska).
The half-deaf Jewish woman does not understand that they are living under
Nazi occupation, nor that Tono is to "occupy" her little store. This occupation
is paradoxical: he should be taking over her shop, but it is she (through
goodness) who takes him over. When Tono's brother-in-law (Frantisek Zva-
rik) gave him this job, Tono lost his true occupation, for he was no longer able
to be a carpenter. But Mrs. Lautmann gives him back his occupation, and
Tono works behind the store. He arranges with the leaders of the Jewish
community to be paid a wage in return for helping Mrs. Lautmann. Like Sol
Nazerman in *The Pawnbroker,* Tono gives the illusion of power but has none:
both men play with meaningless objects. He thus becomes a "white Jew"—
a Christian who helps the victim of anti-Semitism.

Tono is often seen in mirrors or reflected in windows, graphically suggesting
his dual personality of Aryan Controller and "white Jew." Moreover, each side
is doubled or externalized by another character: his brother-in-law Marcus is

**Ida Kaminska (Mrs.
Lautmann) and Josef Kroner
(Tono) in *The Shop on Main
Street.* MUSEUM OF MODERN
ART/FILM STILLS ARCHIVE**

the "good fascist" who says to Tono, "We have to become rich; it's our duty, for God and for the Führer." (He also gives Tono a cigarette case with a mirror inside it.) Kuchar (Martin Holly), the old fisherman who helps Mrs. Laut- mann, is ostracized for his sympathy: Marcus calls him "worse than a Yid because he helps them," and Kuchar is dumped into the street with a sign, "White Jew." The mirrors in *The Shop on Main Street* imply that Tono is also a reflection of what is happening in this small Slovak city.

When the Jews are rounded up for deportation, Tono wants to protect the Widow Lautmann but is terrified of the consequences. Her deafness is symbolic of the Jewish victims who are either unable or refuse to comprehend what is happening to them. (Mrs. Lautmann even believes the police will protect her.) Tono drinks himself into a stupor and shoves the old widow into the back room. Although he intends to save her, his push accidentally kills her. Tono's remorse and inebriation lead him to hang himself. The last scene is a reprise of a slow-motion dream sequence shown earlier, in which Tono and Mrs. Lautmann stroll together in an idyllic street scene. The sound of a male choir implies a heavenly ascent, and they are dressed in white. Drunken fear over- came his good instincts, but Tono finally achieves transcendence, redeeming himself, as it were, by joining the Jews in death.

A complex variation on the theme of rejecting and then assuming a Jewish identity can be found in *Mr. Klein* (1976). Directed by Joseph Losey from a script by Franco Solinas, this French-Italian co-production is haunting, diffi- cult, and appropriate to the director's claim, "I don't see why serious films shouldn't be viewed two or three times, just as books are read and reread."[6] Alain Delon, superbly restrained in the role of a wealthy and egotistical French art dealer in Paris during the Occupation, produced as well as starred in *Mr. Klein.* We initially see Robert Klein in his opulent home, bartering with a Jew (Jean Bouise) who must sell his precious possessions before fleeing. It is Janu- ary 16, 1942, and upon ushering his client out, Klein finds a Jewish newspaper *(Informations Juives)* on his doorstep. Angry at such a "joke," Klein goes to the newspaper bureau to report the mistaken delivery. In an ostensible attempt to clear his name, he also obtains Robert Klein's previous address and visits the man's seedy Pigalle apartment. The concierge (Suzanne Flon) takes him for her absent tenant; while inspecting the apartment, Klein pockets a photo- studio envelope—and when he goes to pick up the pictures, the photographer seems to recognize him as the fuzzy person in one of the badly taken snapshots. The art dealer returns home to find the police waiting, as there is now some suspicion that he may be Jewish.

A letter from an unknown woman named Florence invites Klein to a châ- teau outside Paris where it is finally acknowledged that he is not the other Robert Klein: the aristocratic Charles-Xavier (Massimo Girotti) asserts that they are not the same person, and Florence (Jeanne Moreau) admits, "He never spoke to me about you." (She likens the other Klein to a serpent, reading in our hero's face that he is more of a vulture.) Nevertheless, he takes the other Klein's place at dinner. We are still uncertain of whom we can trust, as a mysterious man on a motorcycle leads Florence to run out. (The murky

Jeanne Moreau (Florence) and Alain Delon (Robert) in *Mr. Klein*. QUARTET FILMS

snapshot of Klein had also included a motorcycle, a girl, and a dog.) Klein then journeys to Strasbourg to question his father, who affirms: "We've been French and Catholic since Louis XIV!" He returns to the Pigalle apartment, where he continues to seek traces of the absent tenant. He begins a search for his namesake's mistress, while the Paris police makes preparations to round up Jews for deportation. A dog attaches itself to him (the other Klein's dog in the picture?) while his own mistress Janine (Juliet Berto) decides to leave him. A newspaper article leads Klein to a morgue and the bodies of five men who tried to blow up Gestapo headquarters: Is the other Klein dead? He telephones Klein's Pigalle apartment, and a man answers, who may or may not be the other Klein. The two agree to meet. But when Klein arrives before the Pigalle building, he is just in time to see the police leading out a man by force.

Klein gives himself up, ostensibly to follow his namesake and have a confrontation. He is taken to the Vélodrome d'Hiver, where thousands of Jews are already being segregated in alphabetically designated areas. Klein's lawyer (Michel Lonsdale) tries to save him, showing him a certificate proving that he is not a Jew, but Klein insists on following the man who just raised his hand in response to the voice over a loudspeaker calling out "Robert Klein." He jumps onto the transport—inches away from the Jewish client who sold him the painting at the film's opening—headed for the camps.

The fictitious story of Robert Klein is thus constantly juxtaposed with the real background of French anti-Semitism, and includes a symbolic or metaphysical dimension. Although Pauline Kael dismissed *Mr. Klein* by claiming "the atmosphere is heavily pregnant, with no delivery,"[7] the film's richness can be discovered through close analysis. For example, the credits unfold over a tapestry of a vulture with an arrow through its heart—an image whose meaning will be revealed at an auction a few scenes later, and whose import permeates the film. The auctioneer interprets the canvas as representing indifference, followed by cruelty, arrogance, greed, and finally remorse, and he points out the Cabalistic origin of the signs. By invoking Jewish mysticism, the film suggests not only the concrete aesthetic significance of the tapestry, but the symbolic component of these attributes: they describe France—incarnated at the outset by Klein—in its movement from indifference to remorse vis-à-vis the Jews.

On the one hand, Losey situates Klein's quest for his "double" within the historical reality of the Occupation. The introductory titles acknowledge that the central character is fictitious—or a composite of the experiences of several individuals—but the facts "are a matter of history. They took place in France in 1942."[8] The film begins not with Klein, but with the cold medical examination of a naked, middle-aged Jewish woman: the doctor measures her features to ascertain if they might be "Semitic." Later, the camera pans quickly from Klein leaving a café to the sign "No Jews Allowed." In a cabaret whose wealthy patrons include Germans, a transvestite singer does a German song. Along comes a long-nosed caricature of a Jew who takes her jewelry; a poster from the viciously anti-Semitic film *Le Juif Süss* is visible behind them. The performer removes his mask and says, "I'm going to do what *they* should do —leave before being thrown out!" This distasteful theater scene is followed by a kind of "rehearsal" in which the French police practice for the day when they will round up the Jews. This culminates in the last segment, as massive crowds of Jews are herded into the sports arena. That French citizens did little to prevent the roundup is shown when Klein is in a bus filled with Jews under arrest: he throws a scribbled note out the window, but the people in the street make no protest. As in *The Last Metro,* we see very few Germans, for Losey's indictment is aimed at the French.

At other times, *Mr. Klein* enters a truly Kafkaesque realm, more hallucinatory than historical. It seems no coincidence that the title brings to mind "Mr. K." for Losey depicts an absurd universe of paranoia where the antagonists remain nameless and faceless. Indeed, the casting—and occasionally the visual construction—specifically invoke Orson Welles' film of Kafka's *The Trial* (1962): Jeanne Moreau's role as Florence amounts to a cameo part and functions partly as an allusion to her role of Miss Burstner, the neighbor of Joseph K. (Anthony Perkins). Moreover, Suzanne Flon as the concierge is the same actress who played Miss Pittl in Welles' film. A shot in the police bureau presents an enormous room with high ceilings, the walls filled with files. In the center is a long table where people consult these dossiers—reminiscent of the inhuman office in *The Trial.* The German Occupation takes on the look of Kafka's dark visions.

As one of Losey's later films, *Don Giovanni* (1979), would illustrate, this director is no stranger to stylization. For all its realism of detail, *Mr. Klein* is also structured through a dense pattern of imagery. In particular, the film implies the bestiality of people during the Occupation through animal symbolism: a long shot of the black-caped police against the white walls of the station makes them look like bats; *Moby Dick* is a recurring allusion, first when Janine reads from it in bed, and later when Klein finds a copy of it in the Pigalle apartment (could Klein's obsessive pursuit of his nemesis be a variation on Captain Ahab?); Florence speaks of the invisible Klein as a snake who has gone into hibernation, and of the man before her as a vulture. This brings us back to the vulture of the tapestry, to the vulture handle on Klein's lawyer's cane, and to Klein's initial activity of preying on the misfortune of clients.

From the first scene of *Mr. Klein* to the last, we view his gradual transformation from elegant opportunism to an ultimately inexplicable self-sacrifice. Klein is introduced after the humiliating objectification of the Jewish woman by the doctor, and the art dealer then measures the Dutch painting for sale in a clinical manner that seems to rhyme with the preceding scene. Klein's treatment of the unnamed Jewish client is clearly more polite than the doctor's with his chilling feature-measurements, but Klein shows no real sympathy for the Jew before him. That he might have another side (or identity) is suggested by the mirrors prevalent in the film: we see him together with his reflection when he first receives the Jewish newspaper; when he phones the newspaper from a café; and when he is paged by an unidentified man in another café. This doubling of Klein's image prepares us for the ambiguity central to the story. At the outset, and especially on first viewing, one might assume that he is indeed *both* Kleins; as the Commissioner (Fred Personne) puts it, after Klein reports the newspaper mistake to the police, "A man comes forward, the better to hide." Isn't his pursuit of the other an example of "the lady doth protest too much"?

Once he becomes the potential victim of racial prejudice, we are led to identify with Klein: for example, Losey draws out the moments when our hero is waiting for the mailman, forcing us to experience the wait with him. And when Klein goes to the château, we enter through his point of view (along with a hand-held camera that conveys uncertainty). We see only as much of the "enemy" as the protagonist, perhaps because the other Klein is a composite figure: he fits into all milieus—collaborator, gangster, aristocrat, resister (a piece of music found in his apartment turns out to be "L'Internationale," the Communist anthem). We are never really sure why Klein I sacrifices everything to pursue the other—is Klein II's life simply more interesting than the art dealer's?—but the film suggests that spiritual redemption might be the reason.

When Klein is supposed to leave France with a false passport, he laments to his lawyer that the French have become "too civilized, well-mannered, processed," having perhaps realized that his own life was the epitome of indifferent leisure. But like the dog that follows him—which he initially kicks, but finally accepts—Klein's second identity sticks to him, and he finally makes it his own: he gets off the train leading him south to safety and calls his nemesis on the phone. The tapestry remains the key to the film, its pattern offering remorse as the central emotion. When Klein's father decries indifference as "a still, flat sea around a drowning man" and asks his son if he knows what remorse is, Klein responds, "Yes. It's like a vulture pierced by an arrow, but which continues to fly." One could even say that remorse is the key for France, or at least for the producers of this film (which officially represented France at the 1976 Cannes Film Festival), as well as for Klein. The last image reinforces this sentiment as we see the same strip of film—men's faces in the transport—repeated, to the voice-over accompaniment of the film's opening conversation between Klein and the Jewish man. The film slows down and fades out, suggesting not only the slow death in store for these travelers, but the auctioneer's line about remorse: "A vulture, its heart pierced by an arrow, which continues to fly." Among the persecuted Jews, Klein achieves a measure of transcendence by merging his destiny with theirs.[9]

Klein's psychological transformation into the person for whom he is erroneously taken is comparable to that of Grimaldi (Vittorio De Sica) in Roberto Rossellini's 1959 film, *General Della Rovere* ("Il Generale della Rovere"). This shady character in wartime Italy is arrested by the Germans for taking money from families of imprisoned Italians. Müller (Hannes Messemer), the German in command, makes him a proposition: Grimaldi will be spared if he pretends

Vittorio De Sica (Grimaldi) and Hannes Messemer (Müller) in *General Della Rovere.* IMAGES FILMS ARCHIVE

to be General della Rovere, a recently killed partisan leader. Through this impersonation, the Nazis hope to learn the identity of the prison Resistance chief. Grimaldi gradually turns into the noble General for whom he is mistaken, and finally chooses to be executed with other partisans instead of revealing the Resistance chief's name.

The focus of this magnificent black-and-white study of guilt and redemption is the process by which Grimaldi's second self emerges to confront the Nazis. Rossellini, who had already explored wartime Italy in the Rome of films like *Open City,* locates this story in Genoa, where black-shirted Fascists march and sing. He establishes the self-indulgent character of Vittorio Emanuele Bardone, alias Grimaldi, from his first gesture: he takes a piece of sugar from his pocket, unwraps it, throws away the wrapper, and eats. His acquiescence (bordering on obsequiousness) toward the Germans is then indicated as he helps Colonel Müller, whose car has a flat tire. When this German asks where he's from, Grimaldi answers, "Naples." But when Müller counters by complaining the Germans weren't liked in Naples, Grimaldi smiles accommodatingly and says he's "not from there exactly." Grimaldi begins to understand something beyond personal comfort only after he is imprisoned: confronted by the graffiti on the cell wall—scratched out by its inhabitants just before they were to be shot—he shivers with a new awareness.

A letter from the General's wife moves Grimaldi to tears, especially when she quotes the real General's words: "When a man doesn't know which course to take, he must choose the more difficult." Müller announces that he must execute ten men as retribution for a Resistance attack in Milan. Grimaldi/Della Rovere assumes the burden of his adopted identity and chooses to die with the patriots—even though Müller tries to stop him. He writes his last comforting words to the Countess della Rovere, as her husband, and then addresses the ten victims, as their General. Grimaldi finds a new truth in playing his role: he discovers within himself the resources of courage and sympathy that enable him to die as a real hero.

When one was stripped of possessions, status, and external self-definition by Nazi brutality, the question of "who am I?" became problematic. And if one lost family or friends, the isolated self was all the more vulnerable to remorse, guilt, internalized aggression, and the assumption of other identities. A remarkable film in this regard is *The Man in the Glass Booth* (1975), adapted from Robert Shaw's play and directed by Arthur Hiller for the American Film Theatre series. Maximilian Schell is even more compelling as the quick-tempered, quicksilver Goldman than in his previous Holocaust-related roles, including *Judgment at Nuremberg* and *The Condemned of Altona.* The film opens in contemporary New York, where Arthur Goldman is a wealthy, charismatic, and rather manic Jew who constantly harps on the Holocaust (especially that "the Pope forgave the Jews"). From the telescope of his penthouse, he glimpses a Jewish peddler in the street and (the camera suddenly becoming subjective) Nazi soldiers. The sound of marching feet also locates us within Goldman's distorted perspective, and he utters the crucial but ambiguous words: *"Mea culpa."*

**Maximilian Schell
(Goldman/Dorf) in *The
Man in the Glass Booth*.**
CARLOS CLARENS

In this extremely literate script by Edward Anhalt, Goldman then remi-
nisces about his father who died in a concentration camp, bids farewell to his
five mistresses seated around the dinner table, and claims, "A Christian is just
a nervous Jew who thinks he bought himself an A-1 insurance policy." The
verbal bravado winds down and Goldman begins to disintegrate before our
eyes: wearing a yarmulke, he takes photos of tortured victims from a trunk,
lights candles, beats his chest, and singes his arm. The soundtrack establishes
the origin of this bizarre rite as we again hear marching feet, this time followed
by Hitler's voice, sirens, screams, and gunfire. When armed men suddenly
break in, it turns out that he was burning off an SS insignia. This man is not
Goldman, but Dorf—a former Nazi officer.

The scene shifts to his trial where witnesses offer harrowing testimony about
Dorf's savagery during World War II. Berger, who had been a cinematographer in the Polish ghetto, tells about mutilated corpses that were returned to
the ghetto where relatives were forced to assemble the parts; Dorf had made
him shoot extreme hand-held close-ups of this. Samuel Weinberg, a former

concentration camp inmate, testifies how he dreamt of revenge. "Not in the camp," Dorf insists, embarking on his insidious line of defense—attacking Jewish meekness. He boasts that the Jews were sheep who didn't believe what was happening, and the Judge (Luther Adler) even asks Weinberg why there was no revolt if there were hundreds of prisoners and only twenty guards. "Our fate was beyond our imagination," responds the witness (without, however, dwelling on the crucial point that Jews in the camps were subject not to mass cowardice but to a loss of the very desire to live—or resist dying—after witnessing daily atrocity).

Dorf's other line of defense is the insistence on collective rather than personal guilt: "If I'm psychotic, eighty million Germans were psychotic." (His net for guilt-trapping is so wide that he calls the My Lai massacre a classic example of Nazi work. The Judge snaps, "Irrelevant.") Dorf declares, "You will love me because I have done what you all want to do . . . murder," as Hans-Jürgen Syberberg's Hitler-figure would paraphrase five years later. Dorf's demented reasoning insists that all this happened out of love, not hate:

The Führer who rescued us from our fears and made us believe in ourselves . . . that Jews had to be destroyed because he—and we—were afraid of Jews. . . . If we only had someone now to lead us, a father to kill for, and in killing, live.

It therefore seems downright silly when Charlie Cohen (Lawrence Pressman), loyal assistant to Dorf's previous self Goldman, testifies that the man in the glass booth *has* to be a Jew—because of his sense of humor and perfect Yiddish! "No Gentile could be as anti-Semitic as Goldman," he claims in defense of his former employer.

As it turns out, Charlie may not be as naïvely mistaken as he seems. When the doctors are called in to identify Dorf through X-rays, Dr. Alvarez goes back on his previous testimony and confesses, "That is not Dorf"—and that he was paid to replace the X-rays. The camera moves in to a close-up of Goldman/Dorf/? as he becomes catatonic. We are once again led to identify with his being overtaken by the past: through subjective camera and sound, the Judge appears out of focus, and the soundtrack repeats the memories of marching feet, sirens, and screams. "Dorf" removes his shirt and falls amid the imagined sound of gunfire, frozen in a Christ-like pose. We are given no explanation, merely a final close-up of his enigmatic face.

Who is the man in the glass booth? The film suggests that he *is* a Jew, and a dramatic emblem of survivor guilt. All stems from the *mea culpa* we hear at the beginning—guilt over having survived, leading to identification with the enemy ("I killed them"). His testimony also reveals a streak of Jewish self-hatred, especially for the "meekness" of those who died without revolt. In this sense, Goldman/Dorf is related to the protagonists of *Kapo, The Gold of Rome,* and *Mr. Klein,* for all these films posit Jewish identity in the context of the Holocaust as inseparable from going to one's death. The ultimate ambiguity—or distortion—of these films is that to assert yourself as a Jew is also to embrace your own death.

The man in the glass booth is like the pawnbroker of Sidney Lumet's film, encased both literally and figuratively. Goldman (whose flashbacks are aural where Nazerman's are visual) is isolated by his memories, branded by what he has seen and been. As in the last shot of *Mephisto,* the protagonist's spatial entrapment signifies guilt, with the self fragmenting into roles. These films support George Steiner's speculation about the Holocaust, for Jews are depicted in them as "carriers of the ideal," or that which the Christian characters need in order to achieve their own redemption. That Hendrik in *Mephisto* hides a Jewish friend in his apartment even while mouthing Nazi rhetoric adds a humanizing—and self-justifying—dimension to his character. That Tono, Klein, and Grimaldi choose death in solidarity with another identity revalorizes them. Finally, Goldman's conscience dramatizes the haunting bond between those who felt compelled to die and those who were condemned to live.

CHAPTER 11

THE NEW GERMAN GUILT

The New German Cinema created a stir in the seventies comparable to that of the French New Wave a decade earlier: the work of talented young filmmakers like Werner Herzog, Rainer Werner Fassbinder, Wim Wenders, and Volker Schlöndorff impressed itself upon American filmgoers, especially for its richness of cinematic expression. The Holocaust was hardly their main theme, but one could argue that it was in the background of such disparate films as Herzog's *Aguirre, the Wrath of God* and Fassbinder's *The Marriage of Maria Braun:* the demented demagogue who leads his soldiers on a death trip is a Spanish conquistador in Peru, but his incarnation by the German-speaking Klaus Kinski suggests an image of Hitler (especially when he says, "We need a *Führer*"). And Fassbinder's resilient heroine (Hanna Schygulla) is a product of her culture, indeed an incarnation of postwar Germany—a survivor of sorts.

In the late seventies, however, a growing number of German films began to confront the Holocaust, revealing and eliciting responses ranging from profound guilt to perverse fascination. Sparked perhaps by the televising of *Holocaust,* many filmmakers made the long-overdue attempt to assess a suppressed past. Among the most notable results were *Auschwitz Street, The Children from Number 67* (both shown in the Museum of Modern Art's New German Cinema series, January 1981), *The Tin Drum, Our Hitler,* and *The Confessions of Winifred Wagner.* By the early eighties, the work of three women directors—Helma Sanders-Brahms *(Germany, Pale Mother),* Margarethe von Trotta *(Sisters* and *Marianne and Juliane),* and Jeanine Meerapfel *(Malou)*—suggested that film was becoming a sharp instrument for dissecting the German past. All three filmmakers explored family relationships in the attempt to pierce the collective amnesia that characterized postwar Germany.

Germany, Pale Mother ("Deutschland, Bleiche Mütter"), released in 1980, is Helma Sanders-Brahms' story of a German couple transformed by the war, told from the point of view of their now-grown daughter Anna on the sound-track. This narration (by Helma Sanders-Brahms herself) permits both the initial nostalgia and ultimate questioning that constitute the film's backward glance. Anna's parents are not Nazis, but they want Germany to win the war. The father Hans (Ernst Jacobi) is one of the first soldiers mobilized to Poland precisely because he is not a member of the Party. The mother Lene (Eva Mattes) gives birth to her daughter in a gripping scene that crosscuts her labor with bombs falling: the child born of war is extremely bloody in close-up, as if marked by the external as well as internal violence. Expulsion will become the norm for both mother and child as their house is reduced to rubble. Lene carries Anna (Anna Sanders) and their meager possessions on her back, seek-ing shelter in the gutted landscape. By the end of the war, this exhausted survivor is reunited with her husband, whose closest friend Ulrich (Rainer Friedrichsen) is a Nazi who now—conveniently—denounces the Party. One side of Lene's face swells and stiffens, externalizing an ugly infection and inner hardening that could be interpreted as both personal and national. Although the ostensible source of the disease is removed (all her teeth), the effects remain to torture Lene. Mother Germany—even purged of Nazis—continues to suffer quietly.

Von Trotta's *Marianne and Juliane* (winner of the 1981 Chicago Film Festival's Golden Hugo Award under the title *German Sisters*) contains a scene where the sisters, upon seeing *Night and Fog* for the first time, become ill. Similarly, in her previous film *Sisters* (1979), there are nightmares and eerie symbols about which the director admitted, "It's always going back to the past, to the suppression of our Nazi past. In the fifties, parents wouldn't talk about the war, the guilt, the burden of awareness."[1] Consequently, a new generation of filmmakers has begun to do "the enlightenment work," in their words.

Meerapfel's *Malou,* (1982), for example, is a partly autobiographical ac-count of a young German-Jewish woman trying to learn about her mother Malou (Ingrid Caven). Like the director, Hannah (Grischa Huber) was born in Argentina after her parents had fled Nazi Germany. Hannah's search for her dead mother's life is really an attempt to shape her own identity, as she grows obsessed with photos, relics, and the Jewish cemetery. "You'll forget everything one day," observes her exasperated husband Martin (Helmut Griem). "But I have to understand it first," she answers—representing, per-haps, an entire generation of Germans vis-à-vis their Nazi past. For Meerapfel,

That's what the film is about. After the war, there was reconstruction—the German Economic Miracle—but they never really elaborated history. They were ashamed, but this guilt was like a barrier to understanding. It was taboo: children were never able to ask their parents about it. So I had to "give a hand" to help the dialogue.[2]

The "dialogue" has been aided by German television, for which Meerapfel subsequently made *In the Country of My Parents,* a personal documentary about being a Jew in Germany today. And *Auschwitz Street* ("Lagerstrasse Auschwitz") was directed in 1979 by Ebbo Demant for a German television series entitled *People and Streets.* This one-hour documentary is structured by the male narrator's insistence on assuming—and sharing with the audience—

Jeanine Meerapfel directs Grischa Huber (Hannah) in *Malou.* JEANINE MEERAPFEL

the burden of Auschwitz's existence. According to the director, who was born in Berlin in 1943, "no place exists that has moved me so much as Auschwitz . . . a place which must be made visible and palpable to every German who acknowledges his history." Consequently, the narrator's continual reminder that this street in Poland is "our street" includes sobering and complex material: by interviewing three former SS "culprits" (as they are called), Demant gives barbarism an all-too-human incarnation. Looking very unlike a chalk-faced Gregory Peck posing as Dr. Mengele in *The Boys from Brazil,* and very much like familiar and tired old men, each of the three convicted murderers —now imprisoned for life—speaks dispassionately about his crimes. Resisting the stereotype of icy Nazi monsters, these avuncular prisoners suggest not only that Auschwitz is "ours," but how easily the Nazi "I was only following orders" could be ours as well.

In only sixty minutes, Demant offers five effective and integrated approaches to the Holocaust: interviews—not only with three "culprits," but also with two victims, and with a number of German teachers visiting Auschwitz today; devastating black-and-white stills from the forties "to which one can say nothing, but which must be shown"; concrete relics of concentration camp life, such as prisoners' drawings, the hospital death book that meticulously records, at five-minute intervals, the names and medical terms of death, and a mountain of luggage taken from the inmates on arrival, "suitcases like gravestones"; a calm and gently didactic voice-over narration that describes and prods, posing questions like "Have you ever lain bone to bone next to someone with tuberculosis or diarrhea?"; and finally, a visual strategy that (like *Night and Fog*) opposes the fluid camera tracking through present-day Auschwitz in color to the stillness in the gray photos of the past. The comparatively objective camera and subjective voice move back, respectively, in time and space; the result is that past and present, as well as space and time, lose their boundaries in the immensity of this concentration camp. As the narrator informs us, "Between the beginning and end of Auschwitz Street are 270 meters, or five years." Ultimately, Auschwitz extends beyond January 27, 1945, and beyond the individuals who died or killed there.

Auschwitz Street acknowledges at the outset the general climate of indifference to the subject. Its first setting is a German school where, in 1978, teachers continue to present "a better version of Hitler," fascist texts, and the possibility that the gas chambers were a lie. To counteract these distortions, Demant's document moves to the actual place and individuals that gave a form to Nazi atrocity. The first "culprit" interviewed in prison is Josef Erber, found guilty in 1966 of joint murder in seventy cases. In a medium close-up, he describes calmly how, at first, gassed people were buried. "But then the blood serum rose up," so the corpses were dug up and sent to the crematories. The unseen interviewer finally asks Erber if he is still haunted by the smell of burning flesh. His response: "Yes, but we couldn't change anything."

The second interview, which follows color footage of the prison bunks' grotesque sardines-in-a-can design, is more horrifying because the director plays a kind of trick on the audience: by having Josef Klehr describe fatal injections *before* he is introduced as one of the culprits, he allows us to assume that this loquacious old guy was a prisoner himself. The former hospital orderly—convicted of 475 cases of joint murder—even jokes (when the interviewer poses tough questions), "You sure are tormenting me here a lot!" With some self-righteousness, Klehr claims that his injections were less cruel than the gas chambers—which he evocatively describes as a beehive: when the victims entered, one heard a sound like bees, slowly growing silent. What made it simpler for Klehr, he admits, is that his prisoners neither cried out nor resisted; when the questioner pushes him on this point, Klehr acknowledges, "They must have thought, 'my suffering is over.'" Once again, the culprit's explanation does not permit the viewer any easy judgment: "What should I have done? It was ordered," he insists, relying upon the common knowledge that those who did not obey were themselves killed.

In contrast to their tormentors, who are interviewed in prison, the two "victims" we meet are both photographed outside on Auschwitz Street. Dr. Stanislav Klodzinski, a prisoner orderly, offers sentiments surprisingly similar to those voiced by the culprits: manifestations of sympathy were forbidden, requiring orderlies to look dispassionately on the other inmates' suffering. The second survivor emerges out of what seems to be an arbitrary selection among an interminable row of camp photos. One man's road to Auschwitz—sending letters and medicine to friends in Cracow—is presented by the narrator, aided by photos: "He had a life" is the understated conclusion. Bearing witness to this life is the task of his son, who is interviewed not far from the spot where he watched his father's murder. Mieczlav Kieta recounts in his native Polish how he was forced to observe the humiliation and the blows; "the worst thing," he says quietly, "is that I couldn't say anything to my father." The narrative spine of this documentary snaps into place when Kieta specifies that the SS man who selected his father for death was Josef Klehr.

The third culprit, Oswald Kaduk—sentenced for joint murder in one thousand cases—seems to feel little remorse that he used to crush prisoners underfoot. As a kind of antidote to this image of heartlessness, Demant then presents a group of Hessian teachers visiting Auschwitz: "For these Germans, this street in Auschwitz is our street." Nevertheless, the group is hardly consistent in its responses. Some express shock, some guilt, some numbness. One young woman refuses the guilt and replies, "For us, it's terribly far away." To bring the experience closer—to the spectator, at least—the film moves to a mountain of prisoners' abandoned luggage with the urgent admonishment, "Look at these suitcases!"

Finally, the camera tracks outside along the gray street, moving slowly but surely to a spot of sunlight in the middle. Having found a literal glimmer of hope amid the darkness, the camera stops there and, one assumes, the film is over. However, after the credits end, the film continues—like a living presence unable to rest in the sunshine. Through the nervous movement of a hand-held camera, we see abandoned files of the Frankfurt trials. The voice prods, "Should the end of our street be like this?" as a high-angle shot reveals the disarray stemming from neglect. *Auschwitz Street* thus ends not only in the strip of illumination embodied by the film, but with an insistence on action that faces up to the past. Its very strategy of catching the audience unawares—recommencing after it is ostensibly finished—reminds the spectator to be vigilant, both inside and outside of the theater. Given the subject, this suggests an important lesson: just when one thinks something is over, it can easily begin again.

The same "double ending" appears in *The Children from Number 67* ("Die Kinder aus Nº 67"), directed in 1979 by young German filmmakers Usch Barthelmess-Weller and Werner Meyer. Although the film is a fictional reconstruction of life in 1933 Berlin, it offers a surprise similar to that of *Auschwitz Street:* at the end, the action resumes a few moments after the final credits have ended. The directors' motivation might be comparable, since *The Children from Number 67*—while drawing the viewer into sympathetic identification with its characters—yields a sobering lesson on the rise of fascism and the need for resistance. The film opens with a band of kids who furtively pull down a Nazi flag at night. An angry man yells that they need the firm hand of discipline—the film's first acknowledgement of the connections between rigid patriarchal rule and totalitarianism. This stiff order of father and state is undercut by a liberating laugh when the credits appear with the second part of the title, *Heil Hitler, Give Me Some Horseshit* ("Heil Hitler, ich hätt gern'n paar Pferdeäppel"). The film reveals not only the value of such a debunking rejoinder to the salute, but the economic necessity that assisted the growth of Nazism: the children earn money by literally collecting horseshit which they sell to farmers for fertilizer.

The Children from Number 67 revolves around the courtyard of No. 67 and, as in Jean Renoir's explorations of a self-enclosed community in the thirties

René Schaaf (Paul) and Bernd Riedel (Erwin) (far left) in *The Children from Number 67.* ROAD MOVIES FILMPRODUKTION

(such as "la cour" in *Le Crime de Monsieur Lange*), the politics emerge from the interaction among its inhabitants. Erwin (Bernd Riedel) and Paul (René Schaaf) are introduced as best friends, whether they are playing hooky or swiping Nazi flags for shoeshine cloth. There is, however, a fundamental difference between them: Paul's hunger leads him to secretly steal rolls while the more enterprising and ethical Erwin becomes the self-appointed detective for the bakery. The reason for this moral gap can be deduced from the family scenes: Paul's father (Peter Franke) is unemployed and so bitter that he assumes Hitler would have to be better than what he has now. In Erwin's less strict household, they make virtues of necessity, sharing everything from bath water to ideas. The latter spirit tends to animate the courtyard during the first half of the film, culminating in an ebullient outdoor party. Beyond amusement, this fête illustrates concrete solidarity because all the proceeds are offered to Paul's impoverished family so that they can remain in the building. The celebration comes to an abrupt halt when Nazis enter, impervious to the warmth of the inhabitants.

Half a year later, April 1933, finds the families in a less joyous mood. More swastikas are visible in the background, and Paul's parents are already saying that Nazi atrocities are none of their business. Erwin's family, however, makes responsibility its business, to such an extent that the father is arrested. Against the backdrop of growing fear—a Nazi boy learns boxing "so I'll have no one to be afraid of"—Erwin and a few others refuse to follow the fascist flock. The boy's actions may seem slight—he removes the word "Jew" smeared on a sign on a neighbor's door—but they represent the resistance that had to be enacted on the level of daily life. By the end of the film, Paul is sporting a swastika and enjoying the acceptance of his school chums, while Erwin remains alone in his refusal to wear such an armband.

Despite the poor English subtitling (which never explains, for example, that HJ means Hitler Jugend, or Youth Group), *The Children from Number 67* provides profound insights into a prewar Berlin whose high unemployment rate contributed to Nazism. Moreover, it suggests that Hitler was seen as the answer not only to economic problems but to the desire for discipline and the outer trappings of order. At the beginning, the children are morally "correct," using the Nazi flag to wipe their shoes. As they grow up, however, they become subject to fascist parental influence, as illustrated by the Nazi's son who is not allowed to participate in the courtyard party and therefore bullies the others.

Two kinds of group solidarity are presented, the rigid line of saluting Nazis versus the courtyard of dancing individuals, chaotically spilling out of the camera frame. When Erwin's little girlfriend Miriam (May Buschke) offers Paul costumes and shows him how to "walk like Frankenstein," she moves with the stiff gait of a Nazi soldier—an aggressive rigidity linked to "having no one to be afraid of." Opposed to this is the constructive disorder of dance, with its connotations of partnership as well as freely improvised steps. *The Children from Number 67* thus shows that some succumbed to Nazism through the Hitler Youth because they were ostracized even from sports if they refused to salute. And it calls attention to the "good" Germans like Erwin's family and the kind teacher who is dismissed for his lack of zeal in the Nazi cause. The film's focus is both historical and personal, suggesting what it was that might have attracted Germans to Nazism, while celebrating a family that remains resolutely anti-fascist.[3]

The celebration of resistance on a military rather than personal level animates *Top Secret—The History of the German Resistance Against Hitler* ("Geheime Reichssache"). Jochen Bauer's 1979 documentary concentrates on the trial of those who plotted Hitler's assassination in the abortive July 20, 1944, uprising. The remarkable thing about much of the archival footage is that it was shot on the order of Goebbels by hidden cameras and then captured by the Allies. The very same images of which the Gestapo was so proud thirty-five years before become a damning revelation of their kangaroo court. Bauer animates this material with a voice-over narration, occasionally sentimental string music (for example, behind dissolving stills of men who conspired against Hitler and were killed), and cinematic devices such as masking ovals to emphasize noble victims.

Top Secret begins with the German invasion of Poland on September 1, 1939, moving from the dehumanizing ghettos to early attempts to assassinate

Hitler. "This is the beginning of the Holocaust," the verbal accompaniment
states, to splotched documentary footage of poverty in the Warsaw Ghetto. We
see the conditions that fed not only into the uprising but also into the concerted
earlier efforts to remove the Führer: an ordinary carpenter risks his life, as do
the "White Rose" students in Munich—and finally the Wehrmacht officers.
Rather than lament over the fact that hordes "followed orders," *Top Secret*
seeks out the largely forgotten individuals who enacted conscience. The narrator quotes the general who wrote, "I'm ashamed to be a German"—juxtaposed
with concentration camp footage. A conspirator standing before Judge Roland
Freisler's People's Court refuses to say he's ashamed for calling the Nazis' acts
murder—and instructs that, after his death, an iron cross be erected on his
property in Prussia with the inscription, "Here lie fourteen Christians and
Jews. May God have mercy on their souls, and their murderers." The price
for such conviction was not cheap: two hundred conspirators were hanged,
their families arrested, their children kidnapped. The dedication at the end of
the film reads, "To the brave few who tried to end the system in Germany at
the cost of their lives and to the many victims of Nazism everywhere"—
recovered heroes for an era of re-evaluation.

The high cost of questioning Nazism for a German, in World War II or
today, is suggested by *All in Order* ("Ordnung"), Sohrab Shahid Saless' austere
study of a contemporary engineer who becomes increasingly alienated from his
middle-class life. His "disease" is passive resistance. In the constant gray pallor

Erwin and his parents in *The Children from Number 67*. ROAD MOVIES FILMPRODUKTION

of this 1980 black-and-white film, the engineer hardly says a word—except on Sunday mornings. Walking up and down a quiet suburban Frankfurt street, he wakes everyone by yelling *"Aufstehen!"* (Get up!). The literal awakening grows figurative, for by the end of the film, the shout is "Auschwitz!" It is the word that stops sleep, the insistent note that pierces equilibrium, the call that unifies a community in discomfort. Although this film by a Persian exile is not explicitly about the Holocaust, its protagonist seems to be a product of the experience: the grief-stricken conscience, perhaps, of his middle-class neighborhood, he personifies the price and the responsibility of waking up to Auschwitz.

Nothing could be further from the sober starkness of *All in Order* than the stylized symbolism of *The Tin Drum* ("Die Blechtrommel"); nevertheless, both hinge on the protagonist's refusal to assume adulthood in German society. The central character in Volker Schlöndorff's 1979 sumptuous adaptation of Günter Grass's novel is Oskar (David Bennent), who decides at the age of three to stop growing. He is the narrator of his own tale (a point of view dazzlingly reinforced by the use of subjective camera at Oskar's birth, the lens emerging from darkness to unfocused lights and sounds); refusing a more objective frame of reference, the film thus permits a number of interpretations of Oskar's relationship to Nazism.

The boy is born "between faith and disillusion," as he puts it—attitudes that can apply to the Nazi cause as well. On one level, Oskar is the symbol of resistance to fascism, or the debased world of adults. His only activity is playing his drum, aggressively beating his own rhythm. At a Nazi rally, his loud tempo subverts the military band until the scene grows hilarious: the rally becomes a dance as everyone suddenly waltzes to the "Blue Danube." Here, as in numerous other scenes, Oskar seems to undercut the SS, supporting the wise midget Bebra's claim that you must be onstage in order to avoid being controlled. And the keen perception that the Germans were "a credulous people who believed in Santa Claus but Santa Claus was really the gasman" is Oskar's. Finally, it is significant that Oskar chooses to grow again only after Nazism is destroyed.

On another level, Oskar as stunted growth incarnate can be an image of Germany. His agent is noise, specifically a piercing scream that shatters glass. (When storm troopers subsequently destroy a Jewish store, they break glass too.) How can one avoid seeing Oskar's activity as analogous to *Kristallnacht,* the night the Germans burned nearly 200 synagogues, smashed 800 Jewish stores, and arrested 20,000 Jews? Early in the film, his scream is followed by a Nazi parade—the juxtaposition suggesting that the shout engenders the march. In a comprehensive *Film Quarterly* interview with Schlöndorff, John Hughes analyzes Oskar's symbolic value:

for Grass, Oskar represented the destructive infantilism of the Nazis as well as the "scepticism" of the fifties generation. For Schlöndorff, finally coming to terms with the 1959 epic in the late seventies, Oskar also represented the most vitriolic and rage-ridden currents of the post-1968 protest movements.[4]

Schlöndorff elaborates on this question by confessing that the infantile nature of Oskar is what first "hooked me into the book."

> I began to see Oskar as a very wide-ranging metaphor. . . . I did identify with this monster in the most intense way. I was aware of the fact that Oskar was anathema to the puritan mind—a dwarflike, immoral, abnormal child. I was convinced that I had to show how very *normal* he is—neither good nor bad, and certainly not more monstrous than the so-called normal people around him. . . . I wanted to show the monstrous things hiding inside "normal" ones.[5]

The Tin Drum is clearly not a "message" film, but a complex poetic picture bordering on fantasy. Despite the realistic setting—even including titles like "September 1939" or "the first battle of World War II"—its hyperbolic images occasionally heighten horrific events to the point of aesthetic delirium. For instance, following an image of Nazis, we see a decapitated horse's head filled with eels. Again, the juxtaposition creates a visual connection by which Nazism feeds into the revolting head. Is the horse Germany, severed from its living limbs and inhabited by slimy creatures? Or is it resistant to the literalizing imagination?

If the image of Nazism is stylized, that of Judaism is toned down and its attendant persecution assumed by two other groups, the Poles and the Kashubians. The SS never mentions Jews, and its target here is the Polish Post Office in German Danzig. Similarly, Oskar's grandmother says at the end that "the Kashubians weren't Polish or German enough"—a line often applied to the Jews. (Oskar's last word in the film, as he leaves on a train, is *"Babka"* —not the German word for grandmother but the Polish/Kashubian one.) The only direct allusion to the genocide of a race enters through the subplot of Sigismund Markus (Charles Aznavour), the Jewish toy-store owner whose first response to persecution is to become baptized. These elements derive from Grass's novel, whose focus never claims to encompass the Holocaust. Rather, as Schlöndorff articulated,

> Grass shows Nazism deriving from the banality of middle-class life aspiring to become something else. For Grass, these people aren't very innocent. They wanted to feel important, to feel like generals in control of history. And this is a very dangerous energy because it has a certain legitimacy. That's what fascism is built on: *making everybody in the street feel important.*[6]

If *The Tin Drum*'s focus on a willful child constitutes flirtation with the demonic, *Our Hitler*'s kaleidoscopic collage of the Third Reich smacks of relentless obsession with it. Stylistically, Hans-Jürgen Syberberg's audacious 1978 7-hour, four-part extravaganza has little in common with new German documentaries, realistic stories, or even symbol-studded narratives. Nevertheless, its dogged determination to evoke the impulses, development, and aftermath of Nazism suggests a comparable legacy of German guilt, stemming from a shared, suppressed past. Syberberg's point of departure is a refusal of American cinematic convention as exemplified by *Holocaust,* and a return to German romanticism—which Hitler himself tapped. *Our Hitler, A Film from Germany*

David Bennent (Oskar) in *The Tin Drum*. CARLOS CLARENS

("Hitler, ein Film aus Deutschland") is consequently an exploration of both history and cinematic form, opposing spectacle to narrative, theater to realism, and bristling questions to smooth answers. In a New York *Times* interview with Lawrence Van Gelder, the forty-five-year-old director said, "You have to find a new style, a new aesthetic . . . to describe the history of these 50 million people dead. It was not only my task to rebuild the history but to go beyond it."[7] In Susan Sontag's incisive opinion, Syberberg succeeds in this aim:

> To simulate atrocities convincingly is to risk making the audience passive, reinforcing witless stereotypes, confirming distance, and creating meretricious fascination. Convinced that there is a morally (and aesthetically) correct way for a film maker to confront Nazism, Syberberg can make no use of any of the stylistic conventions of fiction known as realism. Neither can he rely on documents to show how it "really" was. Like its simulation as fiction, the display of atrocity in the form of photographic evidence risks being tacitly pornographic.[8]

When *Our Hitler* premiered in New York in 1980, much of the critical response was passionately positive. *The Village Voice*'s J. Hoberman declared, "Part illustrated lecture, part symphony, part circus sideshow, part fever-dream, *Our Hitler* is a prolix, extravagant, staggering work. It is exhilarating, exhausting, infuriating, and devastating."[9] Syberberg's "phantasmagoric medi-

Above, a Hitler-puppet
in *Our Hitler;* and below,
Harry Baer and puppets
in *Our Hitler.*
ZOETROPE STUDIOS

tation" juxtaposes the grotesque with the banal, inundating the spectator with actors, puppets, documentary footage, recorded speeches, Richard Wagner's music, and props that represent Hitler. Blown-up photographs become the background in Syberberg's system of rear-screen projection, permitting the performers to move into and through images of the Third Reich. This cinematic device has its psychological counterpart: *Our Hitler* hinges on the act of projection—a continual play of screen and mind—for Syberberg believes that the Germans projected their darkest impulses onto Adolf Hitler. As one of the characters declares, "Never has so much been projected by so many onto one man."

Our Hitler, A Film from Germany begins as a circus whose ringmaster acknowledges, "We aren't showing the reality or the suffering of victims, arrogance and righteous anger . . . It's about war and genocide, Auschwitz as the battlefield of race war." Different actors incarnate Hitler as Chaplin's "Great Dictator," Hitler as house painter, Hitler as Hamlet meditating on a skull marked "Jew," Hitler as Napoleon with hand tucked in his fly rather than coat, and finally Hitler as a puppet who declares, "I'm the devil incarnate, but a human being who laughed at Mickey Mouse, just as you do." For *Newsweek*'s Jack Kroll, the puppet image is particularly apt:

Using all the techniques of mass culture, Hitler turned his people into puppets. Syberberg reverses this process and shows Hitler himself in the guise of many different puppets, implying that Hitler was really obeying the secret voice of the people whose dark dreams he brought to life.[10]

In reversing the idea that Hitler pulled the strings, Syberberg insists on the collective complicity of the German people. Hitler draped in a toga (played in this incarnation by Heinz Schubert) emerges from the grave of Richard Wagner and states, "I did what they wanted me to do, but dared not do . . . Am I not your secret desires? . . . If you reject me, you reject the masses." This chilling pronouncement was rephrased by Syberberg when he told *The Village Voice* that the German people "elected him and he was the poor guy to do their dirty work."[11] Consequently, the director's desire for "people to realize that we are the inheritors of a certain legacy from Hitler" points to venal ventriloquism—whereby dictators bark what the people want to hear. Hitler's reassuring rantings about the superiority of the Aryan race coexist with "loyalty and obedience—still the substance of the German people," in the words of the Heinrich Himmler character.

With Hitler as a symbol rather than merely a deranged man, Syberberg's style is dizzyingly symbolic, fighting the Führer's image with his own ammunition of irrationality. It places the longing for heroic transcendence that Hitler exploited into the collective psyche of German romanticism, with titles like "The Grail," "A German Dream," "The End of a Winter's Tale," and "We Children of Hell." The effect is twofold: as *New York* magazine's David Denby pointed out,

In Syberberg's view, Hitler is the horrifying climax of German romanticism and the fulfillment of German longings (and, by extension, the longings of the whole world).

This movie, Wagnerian in length and density, and filled with passages of Wagner's most solemnly exalted music (principally from *Parsifal* and *Götterdämmerung*), is a monstrous catalogue of romantic ecstasies—visions of renewal, paradise, extinction—declaimed in language that is frequently as clotted and jargon-ridden as the libretto of the *Ring Cycle*.[12]

Secondarily, Syberberg's densely allusive spectacle distances the viewer from any possibility of emotional identification—the very process that permitted Hitler to manipulate the masses. Reveling in its artifice, the film demands a mental response of alertness, discrimination, skepticism, and tolerance. Even when the soundtrack describes how Ukrainians strip and shave their victims before sending them to the gas chamber, the image keeps us at arm's length: Himmler (again played by Heinz Schubert) lies on a bed in the hands of a masseur. As the voice-over offers horrifying accounts and statistics about the liquidation of Russian Jews, the actor is bathed in an eerie gold light, his unreality balancing the authenticity of the soundtrack's contents.

Shot as a TV film on a single sound stage in twenty days, for under a half-million dollars, *Our Hitler* reveals the influence of Bertolt Brecht (the subject of Syberberg's first films). Far from documentary or narrative, it is alternately didactic, original, boring, vertiginous, obfuscating, and revealing. Especially toward the end, Syberberg seems carried away by the very romanticism that fed into the Third Reich: as his black-caped, twelve-year-old daughter wanders through the set, her hair filled with celluloid, one is reminded that the film is dedicated not to the victims or survivors of the Nazi era, but to Henri Langlois and the Cinémathèque Française of which he was the director. Syberberg's apparent taste for art as salvation leads him to audacious and often forced analogies: in Part I, he lashes out against "enemies of culture," with the suggestion that Erich von Stroheim was a victim of Louis B. Mayer's machinery. The connection between genocide and censorship or mutilation of film is downright silly—almost as cheap a shot as Jean-Luc Godard crosscutting (and thus equating) a picture of Golda Meir with one of Hitler in his film on the Palestinians, *Ici et Ailleurs* (1976). The only time Syberberg's Hitler repents is for aesthetic reasons: he knows he did wrong to ruin UFA—Lang, Lubitsch, Murnau.

At other points, the director's targets seem more justified. In Part II, a porn filmmaker (Harry Baer) tells us that Hitler "sells" now; *"felix culpa"* (happy guilt) is good entertainment and good business. Moreover, Syberberg admitted in an interview, "You see, I can feel guilty and be proud, in spite of it. I am full of energy because I am guilty and my work and thoughts are devoted to exorcising that guilt."[13] (And there is the problematic addition of the word "Our" to the film's title by its American distributor, Francis Ford Coppola.) *Our Hitler* suggests we still have much to be guilty about: a Hitler puppet recognizes his legacy in today's world, as he praises Idi Amin Dada, the death penalty, Yasir Arafat, the United Nations where 110 states disregard human rights, and torture in Latin America. Sontag is right to point out the connections "from Hitler to pornography, from Hitler to the soulless consumer society of the Federal Republic, from Hitler to the rude coercions of the DDR."[14]

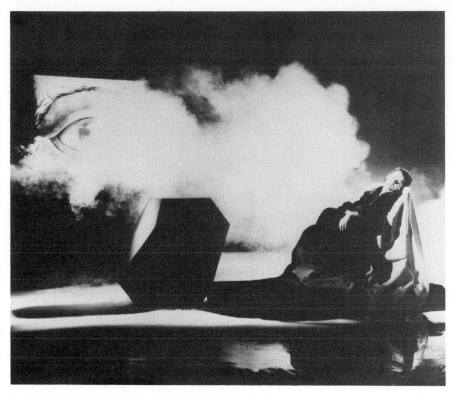

Our Hitler, A Film from Germany. ZOETROPE STUDIOS

The wide-ranging (and often far-fetched) spectacle of *Our Hitler, A Film from Germany* should be evaluated alongside another film by Syberberg, which is its antithesis in style: *The Confessions of Winifred Wagner* ("Winifred Wagner und die Geschichte des Hauses Wahnfried 1914–1975") is indeed a documentary that simply allows the daughter-in-law of Richard Wagner to discourse upon her pleasant friendship with the Führer. Shot entirely in medium close-up, it is nevertheless "cinematic" in capturing the twinkle of her eye or the phlegm of her cough. Perhaps more successfully than *Our Hitler,* this 1975 film presents the paradox of the "decent" people who followed Hitler. Syberberg's presence is palpable not merely as the interviewer, but as an intrusive commentator. Like Godard, he alternates between a documentary presentation of recorded material and the dialectical inclusion of his voice-over and printed words. For example, after Winifred claims that it wasn't really Hitler who wanted to destroy the Jews, there is a quotation from one of Hitler's brutally anti-Semitic speeches. This crosscutting heightens the tension between the woman's honesty and her willful ignorance vis-à-vis seeing Hitler as anything other than a friend. "The banality of evil or the evil of banality?" asks Syberberg, and subsequently warns against facile condemnation: "It's easy not to be a Nazi when there's no Hitler around."

PART IV
SHAPING REALITY

"About seven thousand Germans served in Auschwitz. They must be around me—but where? And who?"
— *Shadow of Doubt*

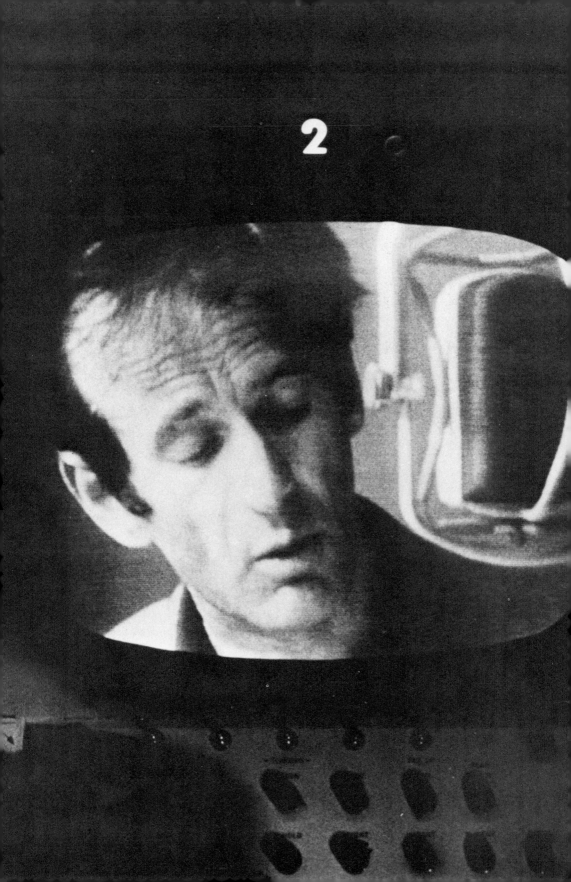

CHAPTER 12

THE PERSONAL DOCUMENTARY

It was once assumed that documentary films were impersonal records of real events or people: you set up the camera, shoot the situation, and it might appear on the TV news. Critics like André Bazin nourished this theory by stressing that the lens (called the *objectif* in French) is "impassive" and that "between the originating object and its reproduction there intervenes only the instrumentality of a nonliving agent."[1] The underlying fallacy here—as anyone who has ever taken a photograph can attest—is that framing, camera angle, lighting, and proximity to subject are "objective." The selection of high-angle versus low-angle, for example, results in a different image: the subject might be the same, but the camera placement determines whether it seems insignificant, threatening, or neutral.

The corollary assumption was that a fiction film is an artificial construct, strongly plotted into a linear narrative progression, using actors, sets, visual tricks, and so on. Such oversimplified categories no longer hold, especially after the advent of Italian neorealism. This film movement in postwar Italy eschewed polished scripts, professional actors, make-up, studios, and addressed itself to the daily problems of impoverished Italians. Films like *The Bicycle Thief, Open City,* and *La Terra Trema* ascribed a new dignity to "reality" and to the notion of the cinema as a sensitizing mirror. The closest analogue in American culture is perhaps *Let Us Now Praise Famous Men* in which Walker Evans' stark photographs of American sharecroppers in the thirties are animated and deepened by the direct perceptions of James Agee's rich prose. The camera-conscious writer acknowledged that his aim was "to recognize the stature of a portion of unimagined existence, and to contrive techniques proper to its recording, communication, analysis, and defense. More essentially, this is an independent inquiry into certain normal predicaments of human divinity."[2]

Particularly when dealing with the overwhelming and still palpable realities of the Holocaust, certain filmmakers have been able to transform the documen-

Elie Wiesel in *Sighet, Sighet.*
MUSEUM OF MODERN ART/FILM STILLS ARCHIVE

tary into a personal genre, closer to the memoir or journal. Most significantly, films like *Night and Fog, Sighet, Sighet,* and *Shadow of Doubt* use "documentary" footage such as newsreels and interviews, but are in fact as formally rich as the best of "fiction" films: they contain a narrative spine, poetic sinews, an edited pulse, and a profoundly personal voice. It is a truism that documentaries depend upon the editing stage for the creative shaping of material, but in the case of films that examine the impact of the Holocaust, montage is the very embodiment of the need for multiple perspectives. Editing can shape the "reality" of newsreels and photographs into personal story-telling—or manipulate these elements (and the viewer) through the imposition of soundtrack. Still photographs constitute raw material, and are often animated by the use of an optical printer: as Chris Marker demonstrated in *La Jetée* (1963), movement can be created by panning across or zooming into static images. Moreover, the very stillness of Holocaust photographs represents the death of its subjects, while the movements of the optical printer embody the filmmaker's examination of the past.[3] Given the degree to which these still frames can be manipulated by filmic technique, directors must be wary of overdramatizing and not allowing the testimony to speak for itself.

For instance, much of the same archival footage appears in *The Witnesses* ("Le Temps du Ghetto"), Frédéric Rossif's chilling French "documentary" of 1962, and *Genocide,* produced by the Simon Wiesenthal Foundation in 1981 (and not to be confused with the 1975 BBC film of the same title mentioned in Chapter 9). *The Witnesses* is structured by the survivors themselves quietly recounting their experiences: each is seen in close-up, speaking out of a black void. By shooting a woman first in close-up and then in profile, the camera suggests a "mug shot" parallel: that the subject is still a prisoner—of her memories. *Genocide* (directed by Arnold Schwartzman) is narrated by Orson Welles, a paternalist voice whose very celebrity tames the material into a cohesive structure. While his tone is generally sober, the film is punctuated by the voice-over of Elizabeth Taylor, speaking—or rather acting—the accounts of individual survivors. With little acknowledgement of the source of the material, Taylor's tearful tales are accompanied by overbearing music as well as screams and gunshots. To what extent is this a truthful depiction of the Holocaust experience? What is the difference between a story told dispassionately by the person who lived it, and a written text performed by a star? And is the former ultimately more "objective" than the latter?

Part of the answer lies in dispensing with the terminology and appreciating the film's composition and effects. As we saw in Chapter 2, *Night and Fog* (1955) is a formally intricate film that both reflects and invites tension. Its director, Alain Resnais, had no direct connection to the concentration camps —and therefore refused the project when it was proposed to him by Argos Films and the Comité d'Histoire de la Seconde Guerre Mondiale. "To make a film about the concentration camps, it seemed to me you had to have been an inmate, or deported for political reasons," the director confessed. "I accepted only on the condition that the commentary would be written by Jean Cayrol because he was himself a survivor. I agreed to make the film with Cayrol as the guarantee of the montage and images."[4]

**Marian Marzynski visits a nun who sheltered him
in** *Return to Poland.* OREN JACOBY

Night and Fog thus contains the dual perspective of the witness—Cayrol/voice—and the visitor—Resnais/image (the identity with which the majority of an audience necessarily identifies)—the survivor and the artist who tries to make sense of survival. Resnais's presence as post-factum investigator rather than participant is expressed by his visual style, especially a tracking camera whose smooth movement actively penetrates the scene. Resnais was well aware that newsreels of crematoria, mountains of women's hair, or rows of headless corpses (the skulls piled in a pail nearby) would challenge audience tolerance. It was partly for this reason that he engaged in "much formalist research," prying *Night and Fog* away from the "documentary" category to what he now calls "something more lyrical—an evocation. The idea that stimulated us in our work was, 'Do we have the right to do formalist research with such a subject?' But maybe with this element, it would have more of an audience. For me, formalism is the only way to communicate." Consequently, Resnais's investigative camera and jarring editing constitute the personal terms by which the concentration camp experience can be perceived and comprehended.

When the survivor himself occupies more of the film's center stage, the style might be less noticeable. *Return to Poland* and *Sighet, Sighet* begin with the same premise—the return of a Jewish survivor to the country from which he was definitely uprooted as a child—but they diverge in style. Marian Marzynski is the director, writer, and constant visual center of the former, a one-hour film made for American public television (WGBH in Boston, aired nationally November 18, 1981). It could be termed a "reportage" in its fearless examination of contemporary Poland. *Sighet, Sighet* (1964), on the other hand, is a poetic meditation written and narrated by the giant of Holocaust literature, Elie Wiesel. This 27-minute film made by Harold Becker is structured by visual juxtaposition, whereas *Return to Poland* continuously follows its director in time and space. Marzynski's film begins in a train that carries the forty-four-year-old director into Poland—for the first time in twelve years. His voice-over establishes that he was born in Warsaw in 1937: "War was my kindergarten . . . my game was survival," explains the accented voice. Hidden by various Poles after surviving the Warsaw Ghetto, he then left at the age of thirty-two —"a disillusioned immigrant"—following experiences of anti-Semitism. The personal meaning of the train is conveyed when he describes how his father cut a hole in the floor of the transport bearing him to a concentration camp, and jumped out to join the partisans. And after the war, his mother rode countless trains looking for her son.

When Marzynski arrives in Warsaw, a neighbor tells him that his house is gone. He walks through the empty space, testifying to the camera, "This was my home." The past exists only in still fragments, as he learns in the subsequent sequences. An exhibition of "forbidden photos" informs crowds of the upheavals of 1956, '68, and '70 and implies a continuity with present-day difficulties. (One gets a sense throughout *Return to Poland* of the importance of images: Marzynski's friends live in a tiny apartment that lacks conveniences, but they do have a TV that is constantly on. And the negotiations between Solidarity and the government that Marzynski sits in upon are a battle over media coverage.) The young faces absorbing brutal images of invasion and repressive retaliation seem hopeful—for politics has become their bread—but the little girls to whom Marzynski speaks reflect a collective amnesia vis-à-vis Jews. They have been assigned to study historical monuments in the area. He asks them what the Warsaw Ghetto was, and what is a Jew. One answers, "Jews are mainly old people." "Do they look different?" "Their eyes are different." The director wonders, "Why were they locked in the Ghetto?" "Um, they did something to Hitler or he did something to them" is the sweetly innocent reply. There are only four thousand Jews left in Warsaw—which had three million before the war—and these children will probably never play with one.

The image Marzynski presents of Catholic Poland is complex. On the one hand, he tells of the sixteen Christian families who, one after the other, accepted him as a "moral duty" after he was smuggled out of the Ghetto in 1942. The Christian orphanage that became his home is presented as a comforting refuge, but one whose pastor says matter-of-factly to Marzynski, "Ninety percent of us Poles are practicing Catholics, and we want you back too." A darker picture is offered when he visits his parents' town, where the central square is paved with gravestones from the Jewish cemetery, "so they would be walked on." It is difficult for this survivor to find the past, but the present thrusts itself upon him: in a high school English class, the young women tell him the situation of Solidarity is good, and he witnesses a demonstration of Polish "hippies" that prompts his remark, "Poland enters the kindergarten of political democracy."

Since Marzynski remained in Poland until the age of thirty-two, he *is* a Pole and ends his tale with the hope that "Poland too will survive." This stance is unavailable to Elie Wiesel whose hometown Sighet is no longer even part of the same country. What was once Hungary is now Rumania; what was once the home of ten thousand Jews is, after their deportation to Auschwitz, now a testament to oblivion: "Nothing has changed—only the Jews had disappeared," he repeats quietly. What was once called "Jewish Street" is now "The Street of the Deported"—ignoring the question of who was deported or why. After twenty years, Wiesel returns for one day to the place "where the world lost its innocence and God lost His mask." Sighet is presented through still photographs rather than moving images, perhaps because the present town is dead to him. The image that accompanies Wiesel's arrival "home" is a photo of him as a child with his mother. Home cannot be a place, only a time; and this time could not be documented by a movie camera, only by photographs. The camera of *Sighet, Sighet* moves across and animates these photos of happy

Elie Wiesel in *Sighet, Sighet.* MUSEUM OF MODERN ART/FILM STILLS ARCHIVE

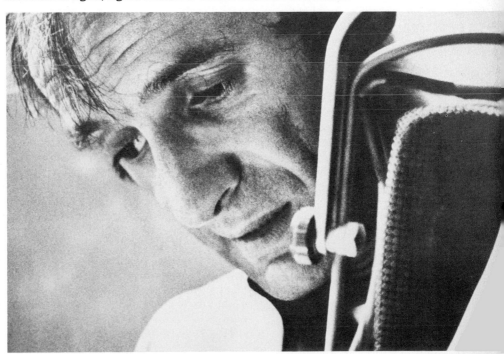

faces; a few sequences later, it pans across the remnants of the Jewish cemetery —the only place Wiesel could feel at home. In hushed slow cadences, Wiesel tells us that he tried to light candles for the dead, but the wind blew them out.

Had *Sighet, Sighet* presented merely this disillusioning return to a Transylvanian town, it would have been a moving meditation. However, its style and concerns extend Wiesel's voyage into an even greater lament and indictment. As the film opens, his voice (and a gentle melody) carry us from the present —expressed by a low-angle tracking camera under skyscrapers—to the past, captured in still photographs. Wiesel finds a town "petrified in its own forgetfulness, and the shame that springs from that forgetfulness." However, as in *Night and Fog,* the images that embody this restrained observation are contrapuntal, both at the film's opening and during the closing reprise. The city looming over the fluid camera is not Sighet but New York, and Wiesel's feeling of isolation exists not merely because of his native village's indifference. For included in this personal documentary are shots of the quiet modern studio in which Wiesel is taping, a slow pan of dials, reels, and two technicians seated beyond the booth, followed by an extremely long take of Wiesel reading his text—a solitary face and voice reaching beyond New York's high-rise buildings. The repetition in the title implies a gap between the city Wiesel remembers and the one he sees: "the town that had once been mine never was." But on another level, Sighet's "double" is quite modern: the film subtly suggests that perhaps New York too is petrified in its forgetfulness.

The poetic meditation of *Sighet, Sighet* can be contrasted with the confrontational aesthetic embodied by *Now . . . After All These Years* ("Jetzt . . . nach so viel Jahren"), made for German television by Harald Lüders and Pavel Schnabel in 1981. They too focus on a town that had a thriving Jewish community of over five hundred in 1928. Today, the only Jewish component of Rhina—150 miles north of Frankfurt—is the cemetery. The one-hour film opens with shots of this graveyard before introducing the Youth Fire Brigade today. On-camera interviews with the townspeople elicit stock responses: "People don't like to talk about the past." "It wasn't me, it was the others." ("Don't ask me, I'm not Hitler," offers one old codger.) And another red-faced citizen defends Nazism because "morally, *they* were a lot better off than people now." The role of the filmmakers grows more investigative as they pore over a book that covers two hundred years of Rhina's history (to the voice-over speech of Alfred Rosenberg, the Nazi Party's "intellectual leader," about ridding German towns of Jews). They find that the pages for November 9–10, 1938 (*Kristallnacht,* which included the burning of Rhina's synagogue) are missing. Despite the mayor's claim that all the records were destroyed during the war, Lüders discovers that a teacher had falsified documents.

Now . . . After All These Years continues its investigation in New York City, which is expressed by jazz, neon, and brisk montage. Lüders and Schnabel track down a few survivors from Rhina and show them photos of how the town and its people look today. The camera offers a poignant commentary when it remains on an old woman seated in a lawn chair in front of her apartment building. She looks alone in a rather alien world—New York with its big radios

Co-director Harald Lüders visits a survivor in New York in
Now . . . After All These Years. ARTHUR CANTOR, INC.

blaring and Hispanic kids staring—after having explained how nineteen members of her family were killed by the Nazis. Subsequent shots of the diamond exchange on 47th Street and the Lower East Side demonstrate quietly that the Jews have not disappeared from New York as they have from Rhina.

The most audacious part of the film is the return to Rhina, where the filmmakers assemble its inhabitants in the same room where the Jews were rounded up some forty years before. Here, they play the New York footage, including the interviews with these long-lost neighbors. As might be expected, the Germans are upset to hear an old Jewish woman answer the question, "Did anyone help you?" with the reply, "Help me? What for?" The townspeople become defensive, antagonistic, and visibly troubled by "all this permanent digging—we want to forget that." The teacher admits, "We didn't want to know," and urges, "Just educate the children and be orderly." The raw footage of the film within the film shakes up the Rhina audience, while the editing of *Now . . . After All These Years* asks us to beware of convenient indifference: a cut to the orderly Youth Fire Brigade we saw at the beginning now confers upon this contemporary group an ominous quality.

When Lüders first came to New York with this film in an attempt to find American distribution, I asked him, "Are you Jewish?" "No," he answered. "Then what led you to make this film?" "I'm German," was the simple reply. The twenty-nine-year-old's confrontation of present with past stemmed from his frustration that the subject was being evaded, that young people know so little about it, and that whenever he asked a German about the Holocaust, the answer was always that someone else had been responsible.

The suggestion that the enemy is not necessarily a monster, or even evil, but perhaps indifference itself—a willed ignorance that allows genocide to sprout unchecked, like weeds choking an untended garden—is also a major concern of Rolf Orthel's *Shadow of Doubt* ("Een schijn van twijfel"). Made in the Netherlands in 1975, its title refers to that self-protective blindness that permitted Germans and Jews alike to ignore the extent of the Final Solution. Closer in tone to the lyrical *Night and Fog* and *Sighet, Sighet* than to the straightforward *Now . . . After All These Years,* this 53-minute inquiry blends interviews of former SS men and survivors with an autobiographical return to the director's blissfully ignorant childhood in The Hague.

Orthel's film begins where *Night and Fog* leaves off, as the director narrates with sober control his personal attempt to comprehend the Holocaust. Still photographs incarnate memories of "suitcases, evacuation, curfew, underground," and he recalls a girl with a Jewish star: "I was told she was special and forgot about her." In 1944, the eight-year-old boy did not know what Auschwitz was, but thirty years later, he hunts for evidence of its existence in the stillness broken only by howling wind. Mozart's Rondo in A Minor mitigates the painful images snatched from aging stills and newsreels of the camps. In addition to some of the stock footage also visible in *Night and Fog* and *The Witnesses, Shadow of Doubt* contains "forbidden footage," purchased by the director from a man who was persecuted for filming the killings in 1941. Mozart also accompanies Orthel's camera tracking through the now-placid Auschwitz and Westerbork. The latter was initially built to house refugee German Jews, but later became the transit point from which they and their Dutch counterparts were deported to the concentration camps.

The place itself can tell him little, so the director collects testimony from a number of witnesses, including a Dutch doctor whom nobody would believe when he told them about Auschwitz, and a French woman who keeps the Holocaust memory alive in her shop: a book on deportation dominates the display window with its frightening photographs. *Shadow of Doubt* intensifies their impact by presenting close-ups of the horrified eyes in the photos. A German with a swastika tattooed on his arm explains that he had the symbol blotted out in 1941 after growing disillusionment with what it represented. A former SS guard, today a doctor, claims his work in the camp was merely "daily routine"; when he is asked, "Did you sleep well?" he responds, "When one is young, one always sleeps well." Another German admits he felt no guilt at the time—"How could one help, alone, among thousands?"—and cautions against facile condemnation: "It's easy nowadays to worry, 'would you help' . . . but at the time, [we] had no experience of that." The prisoners looked like a gray mass to him, so ill that they were unrecognizable. Occasionally, he gave them a bite of bread, but more would have gotten him into trouble with the SS.

The film's title comes from an interview with Primo Levi who recalls that in his camp (Monowitz), there was an Italian who refused to understand German and Polish so as to avoid knowing what was happening. Like this prisoner, people gratefully exploited their silence and "the shadow of doubt" —unsure exactly what awaited them. The title can be extended to all those who chose not to grasp and react against the enormity of extermination. The final interview is with the curator of Auschwitz, a former inmate who never really left—an embodiment, perhaps like all survivors, of memory. When the film ends on the dark space between two monuments, Orthel's exemplary quest serves as a reminder to keep one's eyes open rather than hiding in the "shadow."

With its kindred title, *In Dark Places* (1978) is an even more personal document since the director, Gina Blumenfeld, is the child of Holocaust survivors. The subtitle of this one-hour film, "Remembering the Holocaust," underscores the act of vigorous and vigilant recall that informs Blumenfeld's work. In her own words, "As a filmmaker and the daughter of Holocaust survivors, my primary goal was to make a film about the memory of this historical tragedy—about how we remember such an experience—and why we might try to forget." Her concern is less to reconstruct the event than to comprehend its legacy, especially upon what has come to be known as "the second generation." The first insight is provided by an interview with Armand Volkas, director of the New Artef Players, a theater group. He tells of growing up in an area where he was the only Jew: "I felt I had this burden, this historical inheritance." His mother's concentration camp stories marked him deeply, especially those about the emotional and moral support the women gave each other. And the burden is rendered more specific when he admits about his grandfather, "In a way, I feel I'm living my life for him."

This assumption of a dead relative's identity perhaps provides part of the artistic fuel for Volkas' theatrical productions. In a clip from their theater piece, "Survivors," we see an effective metaphor for concentration camps—a grave game of "Simon says." Blumenfeld intercuts contrapuntal footage from 1934 Nuremberg in which crowds salute Hitler, and she weaves the voices of survivors around the images. Volkas' father attests to constant nightmares, and Nahum Shulman explains that after seeing everyone die around him in the *shtetl,* he can't look back. The director's own identity is invoked when she asks a subject from voice-off, "Mom, who did you lose in the war?" "Everybody" is the simple reply. Shots of the transports are accompanied by both train rumblings and piano music, the harsh sounds of the period combined with the poignant tone of recollection.

Another woman, Genia Schwartz, recounts how her parents and sisters were taken to "selection" in Łódz in 1942. Her sister tried to save her parents as well as her own two children; a nurse told her she had to choose one pair to save. (She took the children and managed to hide her parents with friends.) An intercut of the ghetto suggests the degree to which it continues to exist in Genia Schwartz's mind; after starving there for four and a half years, she wanted to believe the commander who said he'd give them work "in factories." Interspersed shots of cattle cars and barbed wire inform us that these factories turned out to be Auschwitz. An abrupt cut to light music and a photo album offers a different image of remembrance: a young doctor and his family take "A Visit to Mauthausen," as a title puts it. One wonders about the effects of this trip upon his teenage daughter—who said she wanted to see "the gory things." "It was creepy, it was weird!" she remarks after a display of slides of the gas chambers. The reason for placing Susan Sontag's interview at this point becomes clear when the celebrated writer speaks of being twelve years old in 1945 and seeing pictures of Nazi horrors in a book: "I knew I was Jewish but I didn't know it meant what I saw . . . hundreds of bodies stacked like firewood." Sontag was familiar with Hollywood representations of violence and death, and realized that "all those movies I had seen had nothing to do with reality." Her voice returns after the presentation of pictures from the Dachau Memorial Museum, with the crucial phrase that typifies many films about the Holocaust: "Remembering is a moral obligation."

Sontag's participation in the film places Blumenfeld's personal attempt at commemoration into a lucid historical and political perspective. Insisting that history is tantamount to complexity rather than the simplification people desire from it, she perceives, "They want to have their indignation refueled. I think the only thing that's good to learn is how complicated things are." Articulate and low-keyed, Sontag points to the abundance of Nazi symbols today—"the consumerist use of Hitler"—and suggests that the word Holocaust is misleading. "The fire image is unearned, a little bit cheap," she explains, for it was neither spontaneous nor natural—just a "directed and controlled political event." Sontag raises the important issue that the concentration camps were a drain on the economy and military effort, "counterproductive from a military point of view." Her incisive interpretation comprehends the long tradition of anti-Semitism in German-speaking countries: "Hitler said, 'Even if we lose the war, at least we will have killed the Jews.'"

A return to Armand Volkas and his actors counteracts the sentiment of this quotation. They call for resistance to the negative stereotypes of Jews that remain a part of our culture (rendered concrete by a display of caricatures), and to the myth of passivity, which they see as false. Another clip from their play, "Survivors," presents a stylized re-creation of victims on a train headed for death. Using only voice, gesture, dramatic lighting, and locomotive sounds,

Who Shall Live and Who Shall Die? LAURENCE JARVIK

they turn their stage from a dark place to one that pulsates with fearful light. Like the film, their performance is an artful process of testimony and legacy.

An end title tells us that the film is dedicated to "Israel Blumenfeld, Scholar and Warsaw Ghetto Fighter," and it seems appropriate in retrospect that the opening line was Volkas' "I think my father is a hero." *In Dark Places,* if first of all an attempt to validate and commemorate the experiences of parents, is also, however, an effort to shed light on the Holocaust. Like her younger subjects, Blumenfeld has found a way to confront the past, and the film is an act of integration—of history and actuality, intelligence (Sontag) and emotion (Schwartz), newsreel footage and stills, theater and film, survivors and children, a daughter's somewhat perverse fascination in "A Visit to Mauthausen" and Nahum Shulman who "can't look back." As one of the interviewees—clinical social worker Ben Pomerantz—acknowledges, "Involvement with the Holocaust is an attempt to undo the past, the damage done to family and culture. But that's hopeless, mindless." The goal is therefore integration—a coming to terms. The closing epigraphs move from the despair of "dark places" in Isaiah 59:10 to hope, in a quotation from Job. The film thus ends with one possible stance toward the Holocaust—an allusion to being tested and the potential for rebirth.

The personal tone of *In Dark Places* is absent from some of the other films made by the children of survivors. *Who Shall Live and Who Shall Die?* (1981), for example, was directed by the twenty-four-year-old son of a Dutch Jewess: New York-based Laurence Jarvik was clearly out to make a more "objective" document with little acknowledgement of his own identity, yet the film betrays a profound urgency to investigate the action—or lack of it—taken by America (and its Jews) during the Holocaust. Made over a period of three years for a mere $100,000, this black-and-white film looks raw and unsophisticated, but the very poverty of its means allows a devastating political story to recount itself. It is a tale of American shoulder-shrugging and eye-lowering while millions were dying in Nazi concentration camps. Combining interviews with Jewish leaders, American officials, and survivors, as well as newsreels and previously classified information, Jarvik probes the degree to which the Jews of Europe *could* have been saved, had concerted action been taken by the Allies.

The first layer of the 90-minute film locates the problem in official government reaction, beginning with the refusal of the United States to admit refugees during the thirties. "Keep America out of Europe and Europe out of America," declares a spokesman in a newsreel. (A contrasting piece of archival footage offers a glimpse of a Jewish pageant to mobilize government action to save Jews.) *Who Shall Live and Who Shall Die?* shows that the American government knew about the extermination as it was happening, and that it chose political calculation over humanitarian consideration. We then learn of the efforts that led to a reversal of American policy and the establishment in 1944 of a special governmental agency to rescue the Jews.

And what did the American Jewish leadership contribute? Five hundred rabbis organized and marched on the White House . . . while the majority of American rabbis boycotted them. "Don't rock the boat" seemed to be the reigning attitude—especially for Jews who might have felt unsure of their own safety (and status) in the United States. In Jarvik's words, "I originally wanted to make a film which would have shown how the Allied governments were criminally negligent towards the Jews. Instead, I unearthed a story which was more shocking and depressing than the one I originally sought."⁵ What Jarvik found through research and interviews is that the American Jewish establishment thwarted the efforts of the one group that was actively seeking immediate rescue of European Jewry. This group was the Emergency Committee to Save the Jews of Europe, led by Peter Bergson and Samuel Merlin, two Palestinian Jews. A forceful case is presented by the volatile Bergson, as he insists that it was the American Jews who sabotaged his committee's effort. At this point, the second layer of *Who Shall Live and Who Shall Die?*'s historical unraveling comes sharply into view: it is not simply that the War Department rejected the idea to bomb the railway lines leading to Auschwitz, but that well-to-do American Jews did not make much noise about what was happening to their counterparts in Europe. They might have been generous with financial assistance, but were very reticent about pressuring the government into action.⁶

For Jarvik, "the most disturbing thing I came across in my research was a State Department document in which [American Jewish Congress leader] Stephen Wise advocated that Bergson be deported, saying he was worse than Hitler because he would bring anti-Semitism to the U.S." A searing corroboration can be found in Elie Wiesel's *A Jew Today* where he points to the "amazing display of detachment . . . shared, in fact, by the leaders of the free Jewish communities. Why not admit it? Their behavior in those times remains inexplicable, to say the least. . . . For the first time secure Jewish communities took no interest in their distressed brothers' plight.'"⁷

Although Wiesel does not appear in *Who Shall Live and Who Shall Die?*, the questions he raises in this "Plea for Survivors" thicken the film's revelations:

How can one help but wonder what would have happened if . . . if our brothers had shown more compassion, more initiative, more daring . . . if a million Jews had demonstrated in front of the White House . . . if the officials of all Jewish institutions had called for a day of fasting—just one—to express their outrage . . . if Jewish notables had started a hunger strike, as the ghetto fighters had requested . . . if the heads of major schools, if bankers and rabbis, merchants and artists had decided to make a gesture of solidarity, just one . . . Who knows, the enemy might have desisted. For he was cautious, the enemy. Calculating, realistic, pragmatic, he took one step at a time, always waiting to measure the intensity of the reaction. When it failed to materialize altogether, he risked another step. And waited. And when the reaction was still not forthcoming, he threw all caution to the wind.⁸

Bergson's aim was to at least reduce the wholesale slaughter: "If we had made it a retail murder, it couldn't have been done." Requests were made to set up a Jewish Army, purchase Jews, bomb Auschwitz, construct rescue centers, and organize commando raids into the camps. All were turned down. Josiah DuBois, general counsel for the War Refugee Board, explains how he tried to bring two million Jews to America where they would be treated as prisoners of war: only one thousand were taken to Oswego in upstate New York. Jarvik

Concentration camp prisoners in *Who Shall Live and Who Shall Die?* LAURENCE JARVIK

follows these verbal accounts with chilling footage of Buchenwald and of children showing their tattooed arms. The price for American callousness?

Jarvik's program notes claim that *Who Shall Live and Who Shall Die?* "invites the viewer to form his own judgments, and therefore has no narration. It was produced privately, with no partisan, organizational, or governmental support." Nevertheless—and like most good documentaries—*Who Shall Live and Who Shall Die?* develops a point of view, namely an implicit celebration of Bergson's activism and an indictment of governmental as well as personal indifference. The careful arrangement of interviews and newsreel footage results in a profoundly disturbing document that is certain to offend many viewers. For Jarvik, "We all have the responsibility to ask what was the role of our fathers and our organizations. The film tries to look at patterns of responsibility so that in the future, people will look at these moral dilemmas and do the right thing."[9]

Despite his lack of filmmaking experience, the boyish investigator opted for a movie rather than a book because of a

belief that people in positions of authority do have personal responsibility: they're not just puppets of history. When you write a book, people see the title, "Assistant Secretary of War," not the three-dimensional person of flesh and blood. I wanted to show the individual people involved in the political situation of the time.

Given that people are mystified by politics, this film was to demystify. You see someone sitting at a desk: if a certain piece of paper comes his way and he puts it in the *in* box rather than the *out* box, this can mean thousands of lives. Just because you work for the government, or a Jewish organization, doesn't let you off the hook.

Jarvik had personal reasons for delving into this particular issue: his mother managed to get out of Holland in time. "You want to explore why your family survived—who did, who didn't," he admitted. "But there's also the fact that my father is American. What's important is that I'm an *American* Jew: what did my government do? What did my people do?" From the personal foundation of Jarvik's ancestry, *Who Shall Live and Who Shall Die?* is a persistent effort to unearth, comprehend, and prevent the acquiescence behind extermination.[10]

As If It Were Yesterday ("Comme Si C'Était Hier"), on the other hand, is an effort to discover, celebrate, and perpetuate the resistance that saved Jewish children in Belgium. This 90-minute 1980 documentary directed by Myriam Abramowicz and Esther Hoffenberg consists of interviews with some of the Belgians—especially Gentile—whose clandestine efforts saved four thousand children marked for extermination during World War II. Both directors are children of survivors, the former an American photographer, the latter a French artist. Abramowicz began the project after meeting the Belgian woman who had hidden her own parents from the Nazis; Hoffenberg—who narrates the film—felt herself implicated in the stories of survival (her parents were hidden in Poland), and decided to join Abramowicz—despite the fact that neither had ever made a film before.

It seemed obvious to us that all this could not, must not, be lost, and that a book would not suffice. Everything must not only be known, but also seen and heard. And all this was urgent, time was pressing and passing.[11]

They shot the interviews in twenty-two days and spent three years shaping and releasing the film.

As If It Were Yesterday begins with stills and interviews that take us back to 1940. Some of the Belgian "saviors" are interviewed in French, some in Flemish, but three major facts come through in all cases: everyone was well-organized; people from all professions and classes contributed to the salvation of Jewish children; and there was always an emotional price to be paid for separating parents from their offspring. We meet an old priest who provided sanctuary for fifty-four children; the woman who hid at least twenty-three persons, including Abramowicz's parents; Maurice Heiber—former head of the Committee for the Defense of the Jews—who tells the touching story of a Jewish child hidden by Gentiles (at Christmas, he stole the tiny Jesus figure from the crèche, with the explanation that "little Jesus was a Jewish child and so he has to be hidden"); Judith van Monfort, who placed endangered youngsters with families or institutions because "we had to take action against Nazism and Fascism—you can't talk with them"; Yvonne Jospa, who states their three priorities during the war were 1) save the children, 2) save the parents, 3) prepare identity cards; and David Ferdman, a businessman who bought letters of denunciation and bribed informers.

In addition, the directors interview the now-grown children who were saved by these Belgians. The result is an affecting kaleidoscope of day-to-day hero-

A child who was taken prisoner in *Who Shall Live and Who Shall Die?*
LAURENCE JARVIK

ism, with special attention paid to the efforts of women. A majority of the subjects interviewed are female; in Hoffenberg's words,

> Only they could walk on the street holding a child's hand and not attract attention, or hide false identity cards under bunches of leeks in a shopping bag. Their mutual help network was extraordinary.

Even the soundtrack is a predominantly female voice—not only the gentle narration, but the music of "Neige," with her high-pitched incantations. Abramowicz elaborated on this point by confessing, "You see women because women made this film. It's the kind of thing you don't see in Army films, for example. It was *natural* for us to talk to women as well as men."

The effect of the filmmaking experience on Abramowicz was profound:

> I no longer dream about concentration camps, where I could somehow almost imagine a scene as though I'd been there. The film made me understand that people react because it's *in* them to react against injustice; that Jews were not alone; and that it's important to look for positive things, even in something as horrible as the Holocaust.[12]

Amid the grim testimonies from the Nazi era, *As If It Were Yesterday* suggests the glimmer of hope to be found within horrific circumstances; like *Avenue of the Just* (1978, U.S.A.), a documentary about the "Righteous Gentiles" of World War II, it brings to light the generosity and courage of these modest heroes and heroines—by whose graces the filmmakers are alive today.

CHAPTER 13

FROM JUDGMENT TO ILLUMINATION

D ocumentaries tend to do poorly at the box office, where audiences prefer diverting fiction to stark reality. This is unfortunate, because some of the most powerful and important films about the Holocaust are "non-fiction" but not "non-dramatic." Consequently, television has played a significant role in bringing at least two of the following to American audiences: *Kitty: Return to Auschwitz, The Sorrow and the Pity* (both telecast on PBS), and *The Memory of Justice*. All three are compelling personal documents—moving pictures that achieve their greatness through uniquely cinematic means. Brave and often abrasive, they demonstrate that the facts of the Holocaust are richer than the fictions an artist could invent. Particularly in the films of Marcel Ophuls, the montage is the message—namely the juxtaposition of multiple viewpoints which, together, shed light on human response and responsibility.

When *Kitty: Return to Auschwitz* (1980) was aired on American television February 4, 1981, the question raised after *Holocaust*—how much truth can be found in a fictional reconstruction of the Nazi era?—was replaced by the acknowledgement of how much drama could inhere in documentary. This 90-minute film directed by Peter Morley for Yorkshire Television in Great Britain is real "docu-drama"—the simple presentation of one survivor's recollection that yields a profoundly moving and often shattering story. Kitty Felix Hart, a fifty-one-year-old radiologist in Birmingham, returned in 1978 to Auschwitz—where she and her mother had been prisoners for two years—with her son David, a Canadian doctor. Morley had been afraid to take responsibility for her first trip back to the concentration camp, and decided to have the son come along; the film would therefore be Kitty telling him about her experiences "for the sake of continuity."[1] They were accompanied by a small crew and, as the director confided, "Nothing was staged. I just followed her, and didn't even know—when the taxi arrived at Auschwitz—whether

Kitty Hart in *Kitty: Return to Auschwitz.* PBS

she'd turn right back and leave." He used no photographs of the camp or newsreel footage: "The word-pictures this lady paints are more horrific than any photo. But," he added, "children *can* see this."

The film begins in Birmingham where we view Kitty at work and then hear her reminisce about her childhood in the Polish town of Bielsko-Biala, her enforced labor at the Farben plant, and her arrival at Auschwitz in April 1943 at the age of sixteen. The camera rises over Auschwitz-Birkenau in color as the white taxi pulls up, and it simply follows mother and son through the vast ghost town of the concentration camp. Kitty's motivation for returning becomes clear when she explains how people are writing "that it never happened: I owe this to all the people who have died. Everybody's ashes are here." Her desire to bear witness takes methodical and comprehensive form: she recounts gruesome details as if they were engraved in her memory. Kitty is straightforward in her recollection of how prisoners had to lie in their own excrement, wash in their own urine, and cling to their individual bowls that served as both soup plate and toilet pan. A slow and silent tracking shot of the row of holes that constituted the toilet seems endless; the holes begin to look like gaping wounds, or soundless mouths. According to the director, "It was almost unimaginable that twenty thousand women were going to the toilet at once, and we had the problem of giving scale to that ghastly place. We got a dolly at great expense from Warsaw because this was the only way to show how huge it was."

Moving into the barracks, Kitty tells David one of the principles that kept her alive: You had to take things off the dead, but never off the living. She would remove ration cards and clothes from corpses when her work included carrying bodies. Still, Kitty was always cold and she recalls her public flogging of twenty-five strokes because she had gone to get wood to heat the barracks. More significant to her survival than food or warmth, though, was the presence of her mother, who worked in the hospital block. At times, she saved Kitty by hiding her under sick people. And Kitty would occasionally give her mother bread. It becomes clear that what often kept people alive in Auschwitz was having another person to care for. (All this is recounted with a measure of calm, but Kitty breaks down when she remembers how she had to load all her friends' corpses onto a cart.) Finally, she got work in "Canada," the privileged storeroom. This was a focal point for the Resistance, and she explains that when the crematorium was blown up on October 7, 1943, by one of the *Sonderkommando* (Jewish male inmates forced to clean out the gas chambers), it was with ammunition bought by gold hidden in "Canada." Leading her son slowly to the pits where people were burned alive, Kitty—in a shocking moment—digs for . . . and finds . . . ashes. She also recounts how she was taken from Auschwitz in 1944 on a "death march" where, after seeing her friends shot, "obsession for revenge is what kept me going." A male voice-over narration explains what happened to Kitty and the members of her family after the Liberation, and the film ends with her talking about the effects of this experience on her present life.[2]

Morley observed the physical change in Kitty upon their arrival in Auschwitz: "She ignored me. She became like a creature on the prowl. And there was suddenly more of a Polish accent." There was an effect upon the director as well: "I didn't want to pry, intrude, shoot her from the front upon arrival. I tried to be as discreet as possible. But we, the crew, cried. For about three months, I couldn't put my head on the pillow without thinking of that experience." To see Kitty testifying within the physical context of the now-silent death camp results in a uniquely cinematic event, as historically significant as it is emotionally wrenching. The historian John Toland acknowledged, "To my surprise, her oral history turned out to be at least as effective as any written account I've read, if not more so."[3]

If the power of *Kitty* comes from one person's recollection, simply recorded, the impact of *The Sorrow and the Pity* ("Le Chagrin et la Pitié") emerges through kaleidoscopic montage. Marcel Ophuls' 4½-hour 1970 documentary about French collaboration and resistance during World War II is composed of volatile fragments—interviews, newsreels, photographs, film clips, and recorded speeches—that cohere into a revealing "Chronicle of a French Town Under the Occupation," as the subtitle puts it. Like *Night and Fog,* it is the story of a place—Clermont-Ferrand—which, under the filmmakers' scrutiny, yields the story of a time. Clermont-Ferrand is thirty-six miles south of Vichy, capital of France from 1940 to 1944; many of its inhabitants were supporters of Pétain until the area was occupied by the Wehrmacht in November 1942; it was also a pivotal spot for the Resistance, feeding one of the most important underground networks—the Auvergne. The film is wisely rooted in a locale whose resonance is established and extended by the editing. Rather than presenting the interviews as separate segments, Ophuls crosscuts them with one another—for instance, a former German soldier and a former Resistance fighter—and with archival footage. Divided into two parts—"The Collapse" and "The Choice"—*The Sorrow and the Pity* demythologizes France's heroic self-image as a nation of resisters; through interviews with thirty-four witnesses—24 French, 5 English, 5 German—it gives voice to a spectrum that ranged from complicity with the Nazis (a majority of the population) to organized resistance.

The montage of editor Claude Vajda yokes the interviews conducted by Ophuls and co-producer André Harris into a dramatic structure. For example, French anti-Semitism is discussed at intervals by people like former premier Pierre Mendès-France, and then culminates near the end of the film in Dr. Claude Lévy's testimony: he states that Pierre Laval, head of the Vichy government, offered the Germans four thousand Jewish children whose deportation hadn't even been requested. This condemnation of official French policy is judiciously placed after the attempts of Count René de Chambrun, Laval's son-in-law, to whitewash the image of the collaborationist vice-premier: "I am sure today that the French people know that Pierre Laval did everything to defend them," claims his son-in-law. This kind of contrapuntal editing is introduced at the outset of *The Sorrow and the Pity,* with two scenes that precede the credits: a wedding in a small German town in May 1969 and, a month earlier, some remarks by Marcel Verdier (a pharmacist in Clermont-Ferrand) to his children about having been in the Resistance. As the film unfolds, we learn that the bride is the daughter of Helmuth Tausend, former captain in the Wehrmacht, stationed at Clermont-Ferrand from 1942 to 1944. This portly German businessman, cigar in hand, will become one of the central witnesses, discoursing complacently about how the French were "reassured" by their presence: "We didn't loot or rob, so they soon learned that we weren't a wicked enemy." Parts of this interview are juxtaposed with the testimony of Resistance fighters such as Verdier, and newsreels that convey the flavor of the time. As the pharmacist speaks about the devastating lack of food during the war, we see footage of closed markets and signs like "Use saccharin."

The dramatic shaping of this documentary material creates the impression of multiple conversations, or at least complementary appraisals. A record of the eighty-four-year-old Marshal Pétain taking office in 1940—"giving France the gift of my person"—is accompanied by a montage of the people being interviewed in 1969, like Tausend and Mendès-France. And when Mendès-France recounts the trial where he was convicted of desertion, his lawyer's comments about the anti-Semitism that was rampant at the time are interwoven as a supportive commentary. After the champion cyclist of Clermont-Ferrand, Raphaël Géminiani, says, "We never saw the Germans," the film returns to Verdier who claims the opposite. A German soldier who was stationed in Clermont-Ferrand tells the interviewer he had a French girl friend and adds, "a decent girl, mind you." A cut to newsreels of French women whose heads were shaved publicly because they consorted with German men redefines "decency." And the next interview selected within the connective

Marcel Ophuls' *The Sorrow and the Pity.* CINEMA 5

tissue of *The Sorrow and the Pity* is with Madame Solange, a hairdresser who supported Pétain and still doesn't understand why she was tried and imprisoned after the war.

Despite the obvious sympathies of the filmmakers, there is fairness of presentation toward all the subjects. Whether consciously or unconsciously, they reveal themselves to the camera, which maintains the same objective angle for "heroes" and "villians" alike—usually a medium close-up—and presents them in their own environments. (We often see the children of both Verdier and Tausend listening to their fathers. An intercut of the bride when the German speaks of having been ambushed in Clermont-Ferrand underlines that these individuals do not live in a vacuum of either time or space: they have a past and a future, as well as an immediate sphere of influence.) The witnesses are personalized by being in their natural contexts: most of the politicians behind their desks; the Grave brothers (former Resistance fighters) in their Yronde wine cellar; Christian de la Mazière (right-wing volunteer in the Waffen SS) walking through the opulent castle of Sigmaringen. Only in this last sequence is the interviewer obtrusively present (André Harris rather than the retiring Ophuls). In general, the filmmakers' presence is restricted to subtle visual embroidery like an intercut of Mendès-France's hands, gesticulating expressively, or a pan to Mme. Solange's fingers nervously playing with the hem of her dress. Furthermore, the English-language version relies neither on subtitles nor dubbing, but simultaneous voice-over translation. A different voice is used for each subject, thus permitting us to hear both the actual person and an overlapping translation.

By simply asking probing questions, the interviewers elicit telling answers. Mazière, for instance, admits that he was raised in a family steeped in anti-Semitism; that the military French were impressed by the German army: "The French like rank and always turn to a soldier"; and that he knew Jews were being arrested, but never imagined a destination like Auschwitz. Mendès-France acknowledges that anti-Semitism and Anglophobia are always latent and easy to revive in France. (Indeed, he perceived rising anti-Semitism at the beginning of the war as a link between Germany and collaborationist France.) Similarly, "Colonel Gaspar" (wartime head of the Auvergne Maquis) warns against growing neo-Nazism and claims this is the reason he agreed to be interviewed.

In a sense, the most vivid subjects are Louis and Alexis Grave, farmers who were sent to Buchenwald after an anonymous letter denounced them. Looking as if they had stepped out of a Jean Renoir film like *Toni,* they offer Ophuls some of their wine from the barrel and laughingly tell him they sang "L'Internationale" at the beginning of the Resistance "not because we were Communists, but because Pétain sang 'La Marseillaise.'" When he asks them toward the end if they've tried to avenge themselves for the denunciation, their response is a shrug of "what for?" The numerous peasants who instinctively became resisters have a strong presence in *The Sorrow and the Pity;* one

Louis Grave, former Resistance fighter, in
The Sorrow and the Pity. CINEMA 5

complains, "Why do they always put the old at the head of the government?" (pointing to the massive documentary that this film's editor, Claude Vajda, would make ten years later—*The Sick Men Who Govern Us*). Their behavior is illuminated by a remark from Denis Rake, a former British secret agent in occupied France: "The French workers were fantastic . . . they'd give you their last cent if you didn't have money. . . . The middle class didn't help much— they had more to lose—but the common people were marvelous." And Emmanuel d'Astier de la Vigerie, former head of the "Liberation" group, celebrates the Resistance as the only experience he ever had of a "classless society."

The Sorrow and the Pity elicits disturbing realizations rather than quick judgment by the inclusion of propaganda films from the Occupation. We can better comprehend how a Nazi might fight the French after seeing a 1940 German newsreel of French prisoners: soldiers from Morocco, Senegal, Algeria, "a shame for the white race . . . *these* are the guardians of civilization!" We might understand the average Parisian who saw a French newsreel teaching people how to recognize Jews ("cross-bred from Mongols, Negroes, and Aryans"). And the clip from *Jew Süss,* a viciously racist German film that was dubbed and presented as a *French* film in France, demonstrates the way pernicious stereotypes were being fed through the media. The fact that this was one of the most popular films of 1943 is not unrelated to Dr. Lévy's recollection of the French handing groups of victims over in bundles to the Germans: "The Paris police, which carried out the roundup of the Jews with a zeal entirely beyond praise—except from the Germans—arrested the children."

All these fragments point to the need for political awareness in daily life. Elaborating on this theme in *L'Avant-Scène du Cinéma,* Ophuls wrote,

> . . . the terribly bourgeois attitude which consists of believing that you can separate what is conveniently called "politics" from other human activities—like a profession, family life, or love—this popular attitude constitutes the worst evasion imaginable of life, and of the responsibilities of life.[4]

The Sorrow and the Pity demonstrates that the collaborationists were hardly monsters: manipulated by the media and concerned mainly with individual survival and comfort, they took what was often the easy path of unquestioned obedience. Mme. Solange, for instance, reveals her continued blindness when she says, "I was for the Maréchal. I wasn't political, but I was for Pétain." Ophuls asks the collaborationist hairdresser whether it ever occurred to her, when she was held under water by an angry group at the war's end, "that at the time you supported the regime, the same thing was being done to others?"

MME. SOLANGE: Oh, I don't know. I never thought about it.
OPHULS: You are honest enough to say you were for Pétain. . . . Why?
MME. SOLANGE: Maybe it was his ideas.
OPHULS: Which?
MME. SOLANGE: What he wanted to make of France. I thought he was a fine man.
OPHULS: Do you still think so?
MME. SOLANGE: Yes.

(Curiously enough, this is the only woman interviewed in *The Sorrow and the Pity,* and the omission of female Resistance figures seems a distortion.)

Ophuls' questions occasionally betray the degree to which *The Sorrow and the Pity* is a personal film for him. (Jacques Siclier points out in *La France de Pétain et son cinéma* that "André Harris and Alain de Sédouy were the executive producers. They have often been credited, incorrectly, with the direction of the film, which was solely the work of Marcel Ophuls."[5]) The son of director Max Ophuls *(Lola Montès, Letter from an Unknown Woman, The Earrings of Madame de . . .),* he and his Jewish family were forced to leave Germany when Hitler rose to power. They remained in France till 1941 and then fled to America. The younger Ophuls admitted in *L'Avant-Scène,*

Maybe it's because I was uprooted several times in my childhood and grew up in the shadow of a political menace that these watertight compartments they want to erect seem to me absurd, that the tenacious desire to maintain them at whatever cost corresponds to a sickly need to flee, to exonerate oneself, and it explains all the aberrations of contemporary history.

Ophuls would learn that some elements of the French media in 1971 were still unprepared to open the dark chapters of French history. The film was originally conceived for French television (ORTF) but became a co-production of the Norddeutscher Rundfunk (Hamburg), Société Suisse de Radiodiffusion, and Télévision Rencontre (Lausanne). When the film was completed, the ORTF refused to show it—exerting, in Ophuls' words, "a particularly crafty form of censorship, censorship by inertia." It opened theatrically in Paris at the Studio Saint-Séverin, a tiny Left Bank art house that could hardly accommodate the thousands of people who lined up daily. It therefore moved three weeks later to the larger Paramount-Elysées. Finally, in the fall of 1981, *The Sorrow and the Pity* was aired on French television.

Jacques Siclier chronicles the effect of the film in 1971:

The reality of France under the Vichy regime was all there with its ambiguities, shadows, cowardice, moral decomposition, and its authentic part of resistance. The generation that had just made "May '68" discovered a truth that had been masked by imposed certitudes. *The Sorrow and the Pity,* refused by our television, inaugurated a "cinema of awakening."*[6]

The Sorrow and the Pity thus revived and revised ideas about France's role in World War II, and Ophuls' personal quest to comprehend this era became a collage of collective memory. Two of the major "messages" implicit in the methodical juxtapositions are the inadequacy of easy moralizing, and the need for political education and constant reflection. Particularly for an American audience, the final statement of Anthony Eden, former British Prime Minister, is crucial: "If you haven't experienced the horrors of the Occupation, you have no right to judge." And there is a lesson for everyone in the experiences of Mendès-France:

---

*"cinéma d'éveil" also carries the notion of warning.

I learned that when certain tendencies or demagogies are nourished and whipped up, they revive, and we must always prepare young people against this propaganda; we have to talk to them about it, maybe more than we did one or two generations ago.

Ophuls extends this line of reasoning into *The Memory of Justice* (1976), a 4-hour, 40-minute exploration of war crimes within the context of the Nuremberg Trials. Divided into two parts—"Nuremberg and the Germans" and "Nuremberg and Other Places"—this ambitious documentary builds into its very fabric the identity of the filmmaker. It is not simply that we see him interviewing the subjects or feel his presence through intrusive editing; but Ophuls includes personal scenes with his German wife, his film students at Princeton, and even his grappling with cutting and arranging the overwhelming material. *The Memory of Justice* is consequently less a finished product than an active process. The director explained in 1981,

> I try to be autobiographical in *The Memory of Justice* because of my wife's childhood and my childhood—my reaction against what we feel has been misunderstood. I felt a very great misunderstanding concerning *The Sorrow and the Pity* (the movie of my life, like Conan Doyle and *Sherlock Holmes*—I try to get rid of it, but it won't go away): there is no such thing as objectivity! *The Sorrow and the Pity* is a biased film—in the right direction, I'd like to think—as biased as a Western with good guys and bad guys. But I try to show that choosing the good guy is not quite as simple as anti-Nazi movies with Alan Ladd made in 1943.[7]

The intimate tone of this mammoth documentary—which Ophuls prefers to call "non-fiction"—begins at the outset of Part I, where he asks his wife how she feels about it. She admits that although her father was not a Nazi, he was no exception to other people. (Subsequently, she confesses that she was in the Hitler Youth Movement; an older Jewish woman softens the announcement by adding that as a child, even she had wanted to be in the Hitler Youth Group because of their pretty jackets.) Ophuls' daughter complains that her mother doesn't want her to see films of the concentration camps, and it becomes apparent that this engaging woman is not very happy with her husband's obsessive burrowing into the past. When she says she would prefer him to make "a Lubitsch film or *My Fair Lady,*" he inserts a poster of an appropriate film—*The Band Wagon.* The soundtrack complies as we hear "New Sun in the Sky" from this film. The music continues into the next scene—Ophuls' car moving through a snowy landscape—where the songs "That's Entertainment" and finally "I Guess I'll Have To Change My Plan" grow contrapuntal. The place is Schleswig-Holstein, and the director-investigator is searching for Hertha Oberheuser, a former Nazi doctor who was sentenced to twenty years before she began practicing in the region. *The Band Wagon* soundtrack might appease his wife and lighten the film's tone, but Ophuls is clearly bound to his quest—beyond entertainment—for justice.

The truly ambitious or controversial aspect of *The Memory of Justice* is that Ophuls is concerned as much with the present as the past, as much with the recent experiences of Vietnam and Algeria as with the more devastating but more distant horrors of Nazism. The juxtapositions of the pre-credit sequence establish his insistently connective issue:

Mrs. Marcel Ophuls in *The Memory of Justice*. HAMILTON FISH
Telford Taylor, Chief U.S. Prosecutor, Nuremberg Trials, in *The Memory of Justice*. HAMILTON FISH

1) a plea of "Not Guilty" offered in Nuremberg on November 20, 1945;

2) violinist Yehudi Menuhin in Berlin in 1973 saying that every human being is guilty;

3) Vietnam War coverage from NBC News;

4) expressions of remorse by Noel Favrelière, a French paratrooper who deserted in Algeria;

5) Colonel Anthony Hecht, an American decorated for service in Korea, explaining that he respects both those who fought in Vietnam and those who were morally opposed;

6) Eddie Sowder, a Vietnam War deserter (who is also interviewed in Peter Davis' *Hearts and Minds*);

7) Telford Taylor, Chief Prosecution Counsel at the Nuremberg Trials;

8) a German visiting the Dachau Museum in 1973;

9) Marie-Claude Vaillant-Couturier, a French senator and concentration camp survivor;

10) a title of the quotation from Plato—that people are guided by a vague memory and ideal of justice.

These fragments are elaborated in the course of the film as Ophuls proposes that Auschwitz, Dresden, and My Lai belong within the same frame of inquiry. Terrence Des Pres's masterful review of the film in *Harper's* points out,

It can be argued that the film minimizes the evil of the Hitler years, that it obscures the nihilistic nature of that war and undermines the uniqueness of the Holocaust by comparing these enormities with the lesser atrocities of Algeria, Vietnam, Kent State, and so on. . . . But as [Ophuls] himself has said, to compare is not to equate. On the contrary, comparison can function to dramatize distinctions.[8]

For example, Dr. Mitscherlich brings up America's slaughter of the Indians, but makes the important distinction that Indians were an alien people while the Jews were neighbors. Similarly, Edgar Fauré, former Nuremberg prosecutor and then-president of the French National Assembly, warns against lumping Algeria with World War II: he claims that it's completely different for a country to try to keep a colony than to invade neighboring countries. Significantly enough, this is placed after Favrelière's interview and the acknowledgement of torture in Algeria: the paratrooper says he felt like an SS man in his French army uniform and "deserted so as not to kill." He joined the Algerians.

If Ophuls offers a point of view, it is that each view is partial. His technique of the cut often constitutes an undercut, as he tends to counterpoint a statement with testimony or footage to the contrary.[9] Albert Speer says he assumed for economic reasons that conditions in the concentration camps were better than they proved; Ophuls inserts harrowing archival footage of three skeletal prisoners. Hans Kehrl, Speer's planner, complains that Nuremberg was worse than the camps when there were no rations; shots of the concentration camps mock his claim. A young German denies that the Holocaust ever happened and proposes that the Americans built ovens in Dachau; the next scene juxtaposes Joan Baez singing "Where Have All the Flowers Gone?" in German with footage of the transports. German propaganda films coexist with American propaganda (a *March of Time* newsreel that delights in America's capacity

Defendants at the Nuremberg Trials in *The Memory of Justice*. HAMILTON FISH

to bomb Dresden twice); the mother of Nazi hunter Serge Klarsfeld tells how her husband was arrested by the Nazis and killed at Auschwitz, between shots of Frau Kuenzel (mother of Beate Klarsfeld, Serge's wife) saying that the Germans could not ask the SS what they were doing. As in *The Sorrow and the Pity,* the simultaneous voice-over translations in English are remarkably consistent with the tones of the speakers: a different voice is used for each subject, thereby personalizing his or her address. And as in the previous film, there is a fairness of presentation, since almost all the subjects are treated "objectively" by the camera—the same medium close-up is used for both Nazis and Jews—and each individual is seen in his own expressive home or office décor.

For instance, two contrasting attitudes to the Vietnam War are embodied by the homes and family styles of dead war heroes. First there is Barbara Keating,

a woman whose pride and pleasure in the fact that her husband died a War Hero is evident not only in her crisp words, not only in her expensive dress and finely styled hair, but also in her substantial suburban house, in the special cabinet where she displays her husband's war medals, and finally in the fact that Ophuls, throughout the interview, stands on the stairs with Mrs. Keating at some distance above him on the landing.[10]

Marine music is audible in the background, and Ophuls often cuts to her American flags. The widow is also crosscut with Louise and Robert Ransom, for whom the death of their son was a meaningless sacrifice. They sit with

Ophuls around a modest kitchen table, speaking simply and with visible pain about their loss. Just as these people were free to present themselves and their surroundings as they wished, the viewer is free to make his own conclusions about the viability of either response. Those with prowar sentiments will probably approve of Mrs. Keating; those opposed to the Vietnam War will probably side with the Ransoms. Nevertheless, the totality of *The Memory of Justice* implies a condemnation of the Vietnam War, particularly when Lord Shawcross (prosecutor for the British at Nuremberg) observes that you can't compare Germany with Vietnam, where the government asked for help, even if the methods of napalm bombing were comparable. The inclusion of the compelling Daniel Ellsberg, footage of Kent State, and articulate army deserters makes it difficult to regard Mrs. Keating's smugness without some discomfort.

It is within the frame of Nuremberg that she—and all the other elements of *The Memory of Justice*—must be considered; this context implies that personal conscience overrides government dictum, and therefore the state and those who represent it can and must be held accountable for moral atrocities. Ophuls' crosscutting refuses to let the matter rest with the conviction of Nazi war criminals; in Des Pres's words, "Ophuls endeavors to change our awareness of Nuremberg, from a piece of history to an internalized image of our struggle for a clarity of moral vision which has not yet risen, and may never rise, to its conclusion." The film's very title suggests that justice is absent from

The Nuremberg Trials in *The Memory of Justice*. HAMILTON FISH

Serge and Beate Klarsfeld, Nazi hunters, in
The Memory of Justice. HAMILTON FISH

the present, while its format shapes newsreel footage, photographs, and interviews into a quasi-narrative of continuing guilt and continuing responsibility.
The problem is not simply Beate Klarsfeld's contention that former Nazis are
living in West Germany or a stage manager's ironic claim that he must have
been at Nazi rallies alone because everyone else says they weren't there; it is
also in Telford Taylor's observation that *The Diary of Anne Frank* was popular
in Germany because Germans never saw themselves as evil in the book. There
are countless possibilities for evasion, and Ophuls continues to struggle against
them—even if it's with the humorous intercut of a "Do Not Disturb" sign on
a Howard Johnson hotel room door: Americans are hardly exempt from the
charges of indifference.

The Memory of Justice ends with three crucial images: footage from the
Nuremberg Trials in which a young Marie-Claude Vaillant-Couturier gives
testimony about Auschwitz (one night she heard screams, and learned subsequently that because of a gas shortage, children were being thrown into the
ovens alive). As she leaves the stand, this woman who would become a French
senator looks at the defendants in the dock; Ophuls freezes the image, intensi-
fying the confrontation for which she waited so long. We then see Yehudi
Menuhin playing with the Berlin Philharmonic—a unification of Germans and
Jew, and a transcendence through art. The violinist insists, "I'm not the judge.
Judgment should ideally come from the one who committed the crime, or

suffered by it." Although the last word is given to the artist who refuses to judge, the last image is the famous Warsaw Ghetto photograph that includes a little boy with his hands raised in surrender. The camera moves in to this still image, stopping at the child's lifted arms. The return to this raw material insists upon Nazi persecution as the root of Nuremberg and thus of the entire film: the Holocaust remains an uneasy shadow. Moreover, the movement of the camera constitutes an act of selection and investigation. Like Resnais's active camera in the equally personal documentary, *Night and Fog,* Ophuls' last shot expresses the burden of filmmaker and viewer alike—a refusal to be still in the face of inhumanity.

In conclusion, *Night and Fog* and *The Memory of Justice* tower above other films because of an intimacy with (and commitment to) the cinematic medium as well as the historical facts. They avoid the cheap packaging of "Hollywood" motion pictures—manipulative music, melodramatic clichés, literal violence— in favor of a rich and original structure: cinematic language is pushed and prodded into expressing complex truths, disorienting, stinging, and enlightening the viewer. They preserve the reality of the past while provoking the necessary questions of the present. This is not to say that stories like *Holocaust* should be condemned or even ignored; in these times, *any* film that tackles this subject with visibly good intentions is brave, if not commendable.

Rather, the most noteworthy cinematic attempts have been in the direction of either spareness or stylization. Either the "no-ketchup" *Boat Is Full* or the "salami-hurling" *Seven Beauties* has more value than a nice soap opera about Nazis. In between the sober record and the grotesque tableau, things get diluted, processed, and tamed. Along with the documentaries, films such as *The Pawnbroker, Passenger, The Fiancée, The Last Stop,* and *Mephisto* succeed best in illuminating the Holocaust: they keep it visible and render it meaningful. Although these images—captured or created on celluloid—are cast by an event that grows dimmer with the passage of time, they are indelible shadows.

NOTES

Preface and Introduction

1. Elie Wiesel, *A Jew Today,* trans. Marion Wiesel (New York: Random House, Vintage Books, 1978), p. 234.
2. The omission of Czech films such as *Transport from Paradise, The Fifth Horseman Is Fear,* and *Diamonds of the Night* is due not to disrespect but to limitations of space, language, and print accessibility. See Dan Isaac, "Film and the Holocaust," in *Centerpoint*'s special issue, "The Holocaust" (Vol. 4, No. 1, Issue 13), Fall 1980, for more on the Czech contribution.*
3. This and the quotes that follow are from Siegfried Kracauer, *Theory of Film: The Redemption of Physical Reality* (New York: Oxford University Press, 1960), p. 305.
4. Arthur Schlesinger, Jr., "Filmed in New York," *American Heritage* XXXIII, 1 (December, 1981).
5. Jacobo Timerman, *Prisoner without a Name, Cell without a Number,* trans. Toby Talbot (New York: Knopf, 1981), p. 130.

1 The Hollywood Version of the Holocaust

1. Alex Ward, "A Producer of the Provocative: Herbert Brodkin," New York *Times* (Arts and Leisure, Sunday, November 15, 1981), p. 44.
2. "An Interview with Paddy Chayefsky," *American Film* VII, 3 (December 1981), p. 63. Excerpted from John Brady, *The Craft of the Screenwriter* (New York: Simon and Schuster, 1981).
3. Ellen Fine, "Dialogue with Elie Wiesel," *Centerpoint* IV, 1, Issue 13 "The Holocaust" (Fall 1980), p. 19.
4. Ward, p. 39.
5. Jean-Paul Bier, "The Holocaust and West Germany: Strategies of Oblivion 1947–1979," *New German Critique* 19, Special Issue: "Germans and Jews" (Winter 1980), p. 29.
6. Andrei S. Markovits and Rebecca S. Hayden, "*Holocaust* before and after the event: Reactions in West Germany and Austria," *New German Critique,* p. 58.
7. Ibid., p. 60.
8. Sylvie Pierre, "Le Four Banal," *Cahiers du Cinéma* 301 (June 1979). According to "NBC Reports," a poll conducted in West Germany after the telecast showed that 30 percent found Nazism to be "a basically good idea" that was carried out wrong.
9. Author's interview with Peter Lilienthal, New York, July–August 1981. This view is corroborated by Dieter Prokop's research, "*Holocaust* and the Effects of Violence on Television," *International Journal of Political Education* IV, 1/2 (May 1981), p. 59.

*Forthcoming Holocaust-related films include *Lest Innocent Blood Be Shed,* directed by Carl Foreman, based on Philip P. Hallie's book about French resistance in Le Chambon, and *The Survivor,* based on Jack Eisner's autobiographical novel. For further information on *Lest Innocent Blood Be Shed,* see Chris Chase, "A Village That Saved Its Jews," New York *Times* (Friday, July 9, 1982).

10. John J. O'Connor, "Diverse Views of Nazi Germany," New York *Times* (Arts and Leisure, Sunday, September 9, 1979), p. 41.

11. One does not have to look far for the source of Lawson's indignant speeches: when I heard Abby Mann, the screenwriter of *Judgment at Nuremberg,* speak at a meeting of the Holocaust Survivors Memorial Foundation in 1980, his half-shouted, half-cried address was vividly reminiscent of Lawson's pitch.

12. This is also in line with Hans-Jürgen Syberberg's view of the Führer, as presented in *Our Hitler.* In the director's words, "Hitler was the greatest filmmaker of all times. He made the Second World War, like Nuremberg for Leni Riefenstahl, in order to view the rushes privately every evening for himself. . . . It is very interesting that the only objects that remain of the Third Reich are fragments of celluloid." Quoted by Steve Wasserman, "Filmmaker as Pariah," *Village Voice* (January 14, 1980), p. 29.

13. Pauline Kael, *When the Lights Go Down* (New York: Holt, Rinehart and Winston, 1980), p. 454.

14. See Dan Yakir, "Bad Guys Never Looked So Good," New York *Post* (August 6, 1981), p. 31, on the "honorable" Nazi of *Victory, Lili Marleen, Raiders of the Lost Ark,* and *Eye of the Needle.*

15. Peter Demetz's point, made in hosting a series of German films on public television, is applicable to these Hollywood products: "Melodrama does not advance our understanding of history. . . . The question is how the fictions of the cinema illuminate the realities of war, slavery and resistance." Quoted in O'Connor, "Diverse Views of Nazi Germany," p. 41.

16. Terrence Des Pres, *The Survivor: An Anatomy of Life in the Death Camps* (New York: Pocket Books, 1977), p. 160.

17. Jack Kroll, "The Activist Actress," *Newsweek* (September 29, 1980). See also Howard Rosenberg, " 'Playing for Time' Unveiled by CBS," Los Angeles *Times* (September 8, 1980), for an informative interview with executive producer Linda Yellen.

18. James Atlas, "The Creative Journey of Arthur Miller," New York *Times* (Arts and Leisure, Sunday, September 28, 1980).

19. In *The War Against the Jews,* historian Lucy Dawidowicz explains that the functions "assigned to the Jewish councils, though few, were onerous beyond the capacity of any nongovernmental agency: they were charged with the responsibility for carrying out the evacuation of the Jews from the countryside, for providing food supplies en route and housing in the cities of concentration . . ." (New York: Holt, Rinehart and Winston, 1975), p. 117.

20. John Toland, "Can TV Dramas Convey the Horrors of the Holocaust?" *TV Guide* (February 13, 1982), p. 10.

2 Meaningful Montage

1. François Truffaut, *The Films in My Life,* trans. Leonard Mayhew (New York: Simon and Schuster, 1978), p. 303.

2. This and the following quotation from *Nuit et Brouillard* are taken from the complete text to be found in *L'Avant-Scène* 1 (February 15, 1961), pp. 51–54.

3 Styles of Tension

1. The scene brings to mind George Steiner's *In Bluebeard's Castle,* where he discusses Elias Canetti's "intriguing suggestion that the ease of the holocaust relates to the collapse of currency in the 1920s. Large numbers lost all but a vaguely sinister, unreal meaning. Having seen a hundred thousand, then a million, then a billion Mark needed to buy bread or pay for bus tickets, ordinary men lost all

perception of concrete enormity. The same large numbers tainted with unreality the disappearance and liquidation of peoples." (George Steiner, "A Season in Hell," *In Bluebeard's Castle: Some Notes Towards the Redefinition of Culture* [New Haven: Yale University Press, 1971], p. 51.)

2. George Steiner, *Language and Silence* (New York: Atheneum, 1966), p. 123. Corroboration for the existence of these mobile gas chambers can be found in the Belgian documentary, *As If It Were Yesterday,* where a priest recalls "the Nazi vans."

3. From a conversation with Stefania Beylin, September 18, 1961, published in *Film 41/61* and reprinted in the press book for the 1964 Cannes Film Festival.

4 Black Humor

1. André Bazin and Eric Rohmer, *Charlie Chaplin* (Paris: Les Editions du Cerf, 1972), pp. 28–32.
2. Herman G. Weinberg, *The Lubitsch Touch* (New York: Dover Publications, 1977), p. 247.
3. Ibid., p. 175.
4. James Shelley Hamilton in *The National Board of Review* Magazine, March, 1942.
5. Weinberg, p. 247.
6. Kael, *When the Lights Go Down,* p. 139.
7. Terrence Des Pres, "Black Comedies," *Harper's* (June 1976), pp. 26–27. Bettelheim vilified Des Pres's book as well as *Seven Beauties* (both of which did not conform to his own experience of the Holocaust and were therefore suspect); in *Surviving and Other Essays* (New York: Knopf, 1979), he inveighs against *The Survivor* by using images from the film. Bettelheim's claim that Pasqualino is "made to stand for the archetypal survivor, the image of us all" (p. 275) stimulated Des Pres into responding with an impeccably documented critique in *Social Research,* "The Bettelheim Problem" (Winter 1979). Here he perceives how Bettelheim "plainly puts no stock in the idea of art as *criticism of life,* but rather clings to the Romantic notion that the protagonist, simply by virtue of occupying center stage, carries the endorsement of the artist and audience . . ." (p. 636). Des Pres points instead to "Wertmüller's use of parody and displacement" as keys to understanding *Seven Beauties.*
8. Quoted in Martin Esslin, *The Theatre of the Absurd* (New York: Anchor Books, 1961), p. 133.

5 The Jew as Child

1. Judith Doneson, "The Jew as a Female Figure in Holocaust Film," *Shoah* I, 1, p. 11.
2. Robert Paxton and Michael Marrus, *Vichy France and the Jews* (New York: Basic Books, 1981). See "Quand Vichy déportait ses juifs," *Le Nouvel Observateur* (June 1, 1981), pp. 112–128.
3. See, for example, the pernicious reportage by Robert de Beauplan in *L'Illustration* (September 30, 1941), pp. 59–60. It was also pointed out to me by the French critic Claude Gauteur that the most popular film in 1943 France was the viciously anti-Semitic *Jew Süss.*
4. Doneson, pp. 12–13.
5. This and other Truffaut quotations are from François Truffaut, *The Films in My Life,* pp. 331–333.
6. *A Bag of Marbles* (*Un Sac de Billes,* 1975), on the other hand, consists of two Jewish children who must move from Paris to southern France. Directed by

Jacques Doillon, it is really the story of Joseph (Richard Constantini), tracing his development from incapacitating fear to first love and courageous action. His brother Maurice is more visibly heroic, insisting on helping other Jews cross the border once he is safely over. As in Doillon's subsequent film with children, *La Drôlesse* (1979), the use of nonprofessional actors is effective. For instance, the father—who dies in Auschwitz—is played by Joseph Goldenberg, owner of a famous restaurant in Paris' Jewish district. Unfortunately, this film never received American distribution.

7. Annette Insdorf, "A Passion for Social Justice," *Cineaste* XI, 4 (Winter, 1982), p. 37.
8. Carlos Clarens, "The Dark Ages," *Soho Weekly News* (January 19, 1982), p. 39.
9. Annette Insdorf, "*David:* A German-Jewish Film About the Holocaust," *Martyrdom and Resistance* VIII, 2 (March–April, 1982), p. 4.
10. Insdorf, "A Passion for Social Justice," p. 37.
11. Robert Liebman, "Two Survivors: Lilienthal and His Film *David,*" *Long Island Jewish World* (October 30–November 5, 1981), p. 21.
12. Ibid., p. 20.

6 In Hiding/On Stage

1. Annette Insdorf, "How Truffaut's 'Last Metro' Reflects Occupied Paris," New York *Times* (Arts and Leisure, Sunday, February 8, 1981), p. 21.
2. See Stuart Byron, "Truffaut and Gays," *Village Voice* (October 29–November 4, 1980), p. 64, which applauds the director's "unworried acceptance of homosexuals" as "evidence of the supreme humanism of François Truffaut."
3. Insdorf, op. cit.
4. Throughout the film, Lucas is rarely in the light. "There is no sunshine in the film," Truffaut added. "Visually, Nestor Almendros [the cinematographer] and I made a great effort not to have day scenes until fifty minutes into the film. You feel more in the period when it's nocturnal." (Interview with the author, New York, October, 1980.)
5. Peter Pappas, "The Last Metro," *Cineaste* X, 4 (Fall 1980), p. 11.
6. Annette Insdorf, "A Swiss Film Bares Another Chapter of the Holocaust," New York *Times* (Arts and Leisure, Sunday, October 18, 1981), p. 1.
7. Ibid., p. 15.
8. Excerpted in program notes, Museum of Modern Art, New York, April 25, 1981.
9. Insdorf, "A Swiss Film . . . ," loc. cit.

7 Beautiful Evasions?

1. Giorgio Bassani, *The Garden of the Finzi-Continis,* trans. William Weaver (New York: Harcourt Brace Jovanovich, 1977), p. 16.
2. When I interviewed Dominique Sanda in 1981 and asked how she felt about playing the Jewess, the actress confessed, "I was eighteen and rather carefree. The gravity of the film and subject probably didn't touch me as deeply as it should have. I threw myself into it without asking too many questions or analyzing too much. I was proud to be that character and De Sica was exquisite."
3. Bassani, p. 22.
4. Pauline Kael, *Reeling* (Boston: Little, Brown, 1976), p. 421.
5. Author's interview with Bernard Henri-Lévy, Paris, June 3, 1981.
6. John Hughes, "*The Tin Drum:* Volker Schlöndorff's 'Dream of Childhood,' " *Film Quarterly* (Spring 1981), p. 6.

8 The Condemned and Doomed

1. New York *Times* (October 27, 1963).
2. Annette Insdorf, "Making Comedies of Character," New York *Times* (Arts and Leisure, Sunday, July 14, 1981), p. 13.
3. Sigmund Freud, *Group Psychology and the Analysis of the Ego,* trans. James Strachey (New York: Bantam Books, 1971), pp. 17, 76.

9 Political Resistance

1. It is certain that the predominance of Polish films about World War II is a reflection of the devastation undergone by this country. As François Chevassu wrote in his analysis of Polish cinema, "Six million dead, the Warsaw Ghetto (200 survivors out of 500,000 persons), the Warsaw Rising (300,000 dead), and the total destruction of the capital with its one million inhabitants. It is therefore understandable that the war is the major theme of Polish cinema, and one needs no ideological references to explain it. Finally, one has to add that two forces direct this country: the Communist Party and the Catholic Church." "Naissance du cinéma polonais," *L'Avant-Scène* 47 (Spécial Polonais, April 1, 1965), p. 6.
2. *The Survivor,* p. 181.
3. Lucy Dawidowicz, "Visualizing the Warsaw Ghetto: Nazi Images of the Jews Refiltered by the BBC," *Shoah* I, 1, p. 5.
4. Ibid., p. 6.
5. Exceptions can be found in *L'Chaim—To Life!* (Harold Mayer, 1973), a documentary that contains archival material about Jewish schools in the Ghetto.
6. Dawidowicz, p. 6.
7. A doctor imprisoned in Buchenwald reported that "one hundred percent of the female prisoners ceased to menstruate at the very beginning of their term of captivity; the function did not reappear until months after their liberation" (Eugene Weinstock, *Beyond the Last Path,* trans. Clara Ryan [New York: Boni and Gaer, 1947], p. 235); and female survivors of Auschwitz claim that the Nazis put something in the soup to stop their periods.
8. Significant research has been undertaken in this regard by Joan Ringelheim at the Institute for Research in History: "Women and the Holocaust" includes a projected television documentary.
9. Eugen Kogon provides corroboration in *The Theory and Practice of Hell:* "In every concentration camp where the political prisoners attained any degree of ascendancy, they turned the prisoner hospital, scene of fearful SS horrors that it was, into a rescue station for countless prisoners. Not only were patients actually cured wherever possible; healthy prisoners, in danger of being killed or shipped to a death camp, were smuggled on the sick list to put them beyond the clutches of the SS" (trans. Heinz Norden [New York: Farrar, Straus, 1953], p. 141).
10. *The Wajda Trilogy* (London: Lorrimer, 1973), p. 9.
11. Ibid., p. 24.

10 The Ambiguity of Identity

1. This and the following quotation are from George Steiner, *In Bluebeard's Castle,* pp. 45–46.
2. Following Gründgens' death (a possible suicide) in 1963, another attempt was made to publish *Mephisto.* This time, distribution was obstructed by Peter Gorski, Gründgens' adopted son, on the grounds that the book dishonored the memory of his father. The German courts complied with Gorski's request, and although

published, *Mephisto* was banned again in 1971. The courts stated that the German reading public was not interested in a "false picture" of theatrical life after 1933 "from the perspective of an expatriate." Today the book is available in Germany; and, thanks to the film, has even become a best seller.

3. Author's interview with István Szabó, New York, March, 1982.
4. Annette Insdorf, "Oscar Treatment of Art in the Nazi State," *Newsday* (Sunday, April 4, 1982), pp. 7–8.
5. Ibid., p. 8.
6. Robert Chazal, "Un classique de demain," *L'Avant-Scène* 175 (November 1, 1976), p. 5.
7. Pauline Kael, *When the Lights Go Down,* p. 396.
8. Dr. Claude Lévy, one of the key people interviewed in *The Sorrow and the Pity,* served as adviser on "historical documentation" for *Mr. Klein.* Nevertheless, we learn from a note that accompanied the published script of the film that Losey had no pretensions to historical accuracy: "The entire film is indeed centered on the ambiguity of Klein's personality. This is one of the reasons why the narrative unfolds in winter (while the roundup of Vel' d'Hiv took place in July), that Klein gets from Paris to Strasbourg easily. . . . The historical consultant was really supposed to indicate more precisely the spirit, the mentality, and not to remove the eventual anachronisms . . . which mattered little to the director." (Jacques-G. Perret, *L'Avant-Scène* 175, p. 8.)
9. Losey's notes about the characters specify that Janine too undergoes a transformation: "A simple object of pleasure at the outset, she becomes completely different by the end. . . . Her compassion for the victims of the roundup brings out our own compassion. She achieves a degree of maturity that permits her to observe Klein with a critical eye, while still loving him." (*L'Avant-Scène* 175, p. 7.)

11   The New German Guilt

1. Annette Insdorf, "Von Trotta: By Sisters Obsessed," New York *Times* (Arts and Leisure, Sunday, January 31, 1982), p. 22.
2. Author's interview with Jeanine Meerapfel, April 1982.
3. A possible consequence of children inculcated with Nazi doctrine is explored in *Kassbach* (1979), an example of the "new Viennese cinema" by Peter Patzak. This contemporary portrait of a middle-aged, neo-Nazi grocer and the right-wing organization to which he belongs proposes that the dangers of xenophobic racism have not disappeared. Their present target is foreign workers, but Patzak connects this to the Nazi past in a number of ways: the credits include a still of naked women running in a concentration camp; the grocer Kassbach revels in the memory of giving a Nazi speech in July 1943; the thugs—one of whom says, "We need a Hitler"—beat up a "Jewboy." These violent sexists are shrugged off by a TV commentator at the end who labels them "extreme-right . . . on the fringe . . . and of no danger to the general public." Nevertheless, the film insists on the ever-present menace—to everyone—of latent fascism.
4. John Hughes, *Film Quarterly,* p. 2. (See note 6 for Chapter 7.)
5. Ibid., p. 5.
6. Ibid.
7. Lawrence Van Gelder, "A German Filmmaker Looks at Adolf Hitler," New York *Times* (Arts and Leisure, Sunday, January 13, 1980), p. 1.
8. Susan Sontag, "Eye of the Storm," *New York Review of Books* XXVII, 2 (February 21, 1980).
9. J. Hoberman, "The Führer Furor," *Village Voice* (January 14, 1980), p. 28.

10. Jack Kroll, "The Hitler Within Us," *Newsweek* (January 28, 1980).
11. Steve Wasserman, "Filmmaker as Pariah," *Village Voice* (January 14, 1980), p. 29.
12. David Denby, " 'Whoever Controls Film Controls History,' " *New York* (January 28, 1980).
13. Wasserman, *Village Voice,* p. 31.
14. Sontag, *New York Review of Books.*

12 The Personal Documentary

1. André Bazin, *What Is Cinema?,* Vol. I, trans. Hugh Gray (Berkeley: University of California, 1967), p. 13.
2. James Agee, *Let Us Now Praise Famous Men* (New York: Ballantine Books, 1972), p. xiv.
3. The importance of the optical printer was suggested by one of my Yale students, Jeremy Epstein.
4. This and other quotations are from author's interview with Alain Resnais, Paris, May 1980.
5. Author's interview with Laurence Jarvik, New York, December 1981.
6. It should be mentioned that the case of American Jewish response to the Holocaust is not as clear-cut as the film suggests. Historian Lucy Dawidowicz undercuts Jarvik's findings with a minutely chronicled account of attempts in the U.S. to save European Jews ("American Jews and the Holocaust," New York *Times* Magazine, Sunday, April 18, 1982). Her conclusions are that "the European Jews were not rescued, not because American Jews were passive but because American Jews lacked the resources to rescue them" (p. 48), that Bergson had come to the U.S. "to raise money for the Irgun Zvai Leumi, a terrorist military organization in Palestine" (p. 48), and that there had been "deliberate obstruction and suppression of the continuing flow of information about the murder of the European Jews. . . . A handful of men in the State Department had managed to sabotage even the limited possibilities of rescue available" (p. 112). She locates the blame firmly within the State Department, especially Assistant Secretary of State Breckinridge Long.
7. Elie Wiesel, *A Jew Today,* pp. 225–226.
8. Ibid., p. 227.
9. This and other Jarvik quotations are from Annette Insdorf, " 'Who Will Live?' Explodes Myths of Holocaust," Los Angeles *Times* (Calendar section, January 14, 1982), p. 7.
10. The questions raised by Jarvik's film have been treated in a number of books, including Arthur Morse's *While Six Million Died,* Walter Laqueur's *The Terrible Secret,* and Yehuda Bauer's *American Jewry and the Holocaust.* In September 1981, a commission of leading American Jews was formed to inquire formally into the role of the U.S. government and the American Jewish community during the Holocaust (see New York *Times,* Sunday, September 27, 1981, pp. 1 and 40).
11. This and following quotations are from Annette Insdorf, "Heroism amid the Holocaust," *Newsday* (May 18, 1982), p. 21.
12. Ibid. The novice directors are even more gratified that audiences are sensing connections between the film and contemporary problems. "Among people who have seen *As If It Were Yesterday* at festivals," Abramowicz recalled, "there was one woman from Buenos Aires, for example. She said, 'This is what is happening with us now in Argentina. We have to hide our friends, to organize, to falsify documents.' We hope the film shows reactions on a human level, using the Holo-

caust as a backdrop. Jews died because they were Jews, because of what they represented in society. But ultimately, people are beckoned every day, everywhere, for whatever reason, to combat persecution."

13 From Judgment to Illumination

1. This and other quotations are from author's interview with Peter Morley, London, November 1980.

2. Curiously, it is never mentioned in the film that Kitty is Jewish. When I asked the director why, he said, "Kitty doesn't particularly identify herself as being Jewish. I didn't want to nail it to the bannerhead at the very beginning. I felt this film should be a new way of perceiving Auschwitz, and there were more non-Jews than Jews killed. I didn't want this to be another thing about Jews and the Holocaust, but about people who were incarcerated and incinerated there."

3. John Toland, "Can TV Dramas Convey the Horrors of the Holocaust?" *TV Guide* (February 13, 1982).

4. This and other Ophuls quotations, as well as quotations by Mme. Solange, Anthony Eden, and Pierre Mendès-France, are from *L'Avant-Scène du Cinéma* 127/128 (July–September, 1972), pp. 10, 14, and 65.

5. Jacques Siclier, *La France de Pétain et son cinéma* (Paris: Henri Veyrier, 1981), p. 251.

6. Ibid. Another complex and absorbing portrait of France under the Occupation is presented by Edgardo Cozarinsky's *One Man's War* ("La Guerre d'un seul homme"). Shown at the 1982 New York Film Festival, this poetic documentary juxtaposes French newsreels from the war with a voice-over narration taken from the Paris Diaries of Ernst Jünger, a German writer and career army officer who was stationed there. The newsreels depict a nation of collaborators with images of daily accommodation to the Nazis: these jolt and disturb the contemporary viewer with their complacency. The contrapuntal soundtrack adds another level of "deception," as the voice of Jünger (spoken by Niels Arestrup) reflects on his identity as a German in a non-German land. The result is a moving exploration of public and private lies—and of newsreels as sheer propaganda.

7. Author's interview with Marcel Ophuls, Paris, June 1981.

8. Terrence Des Pres, "War Crimes," *Harper's* (January 1977), p. 88.

9. Ophuls was nevertheless adamant when I suggested that the film is more illuminating than judgmental: "There has to be judgment. There's nothing more shitty than the term 'non-judgmental.' What would be the use of trying to communicate the difficulty of reaching judgment, if the working hypothesis is that there is no necessity for it?"

10. This and later quotations are from Des Pres, "War Crimes," p. 89.

FILMOGRAPHY

The list of films presented below is by no means complete, but all these movies deal with the Holocaust, some directly, others indirectly. Titles are all in English, with (whenever possible) the original foreign-language title following it as well. As one quickly learns when researching a film in various reference books, the release dates are not always to be relied on, although every effort has been made here to be correct. Each film is given its director (D) and, whenever possible, its screenwriter (S) as well. Producers were omitted, as this would have unnecessarily burdened the listing, especially since many of the more recent films were co-productions often involving two or more companies.

For those wishing to rent copies of films listed, a rental source (R) is given whenever such is available in the U.S. Addresses of rental sources (generally 16-mm. prints) are given at the end of the filmography.

THE AFFAIR BLUM *(Affäre Blum)*. East Germany, 1948. D: Erich Engel. S: Robert Stemmle. R: FI.

AGUIRRE, THE WRATH OF GOD *(Aguirre, der Zorn Gottes)*. West Germany, 1973. D and S: Werner Herzog. R: NYF.

THE ALIEN'S PLACE *(De Plaats van de Vreemdeling)*. Holland, 1979. D: Rudolph van den Berg. R: ICARUS.

ALL IN ORDER *(Ordnung)*. West Germany, 1980. D: Sohrab Shahid Saless. No U.S. rental source.

AMBULANCE. Poland, 1962. D: Janusz Morgenstern. S: Tadeusz Lomnicki. R: A-DL.

AND NOW, MY LOVE *(Toute une Vie)*. French, 1974. D and S: Claude Lelouch. No U.S. rental source.

ARMY OF SHADOWS *(L'Armée des Ombres)*. France, 1969. D and S: Jean-Pierre Melville, from novel by Joseph Kessel. No U.S. rental source.

AS IF IT WERE YESTERDAY *(Comme Si C'Était Hier)*. Belgium, 1980. D: Myriam Abramowicz and Esther Hoffenberg. R: C5.

ASHES AND DIAMONDS *(Popiol i Diament)*. Poland, 1958. D: Andrzej Wajda. S: Jerzy Andrzejewski and Wajda, from novel by Andrzejewski. R: FI.

AUSCHWITZ STREET *(Lagerstrasse Auschwitz)*. West Germany, 1979. TV documentary. D and S: Ebbo Demant. No U.S. rental source.

THE AVENUE OF THE JUST. U.S., 1978. D: Samuel Elfert. S: Arnold Forster. R: A-DL.

A BAG OF MARBLES *(Un Sac de Billes)*. France, 1975. D: Jacques Doillon. S: Doillon and Denis Ferraris, from novel by Joseph Joffo. No U.S. rental source.

THE BIG RED ONE. U.S., 1980. D and S: Samuel Fuller. No U.S. rental source.

BIRTH CERTIFICATE. Poland, 1961. D: Stanislaw Rózewicz. No U.S. rental source.

BLACK THURSDAY *(Les Guichets du Louvre)*. France, 1974. D: Michel Mitrani. S: Albert Cossery and Mitrani from the book by Roger Boussinot. R: FI.

THE BOAT IS FULL *(Das Boot Is Voll)*. Switzerland/West Germany/Austria, 1981. D and S: Markus Imhoof. R: FI.

BORDER STREET *(Ulica Graniczna)*. Poland, 1948. D and S: Aleksander Ford. R: FI.

THE BOYS FROM BRAZIL. U.S., 1978. D: Franklin J. Schaffner. S: Heywood Gould, based on novel by Ira Levin. R: FI.

BRUSSELS-TRANSIT *(Bruxelles-Transit)*. Belgium, 1980. D and S: Samy Szlingerbaum. No U.S. rental source.

CABARET. U.S., 1972. D: Bob Fosse. S: Jay Presson Allen. R: HUR.

CALIFORNIA REICH. U.S., 1975. R: RBC Films, 933 N. La Brea Ave., Los Angeles, Calif. 90038.

CHARLOTTE. Holland/West Germany, 1981. D: Franz Weisz. S: Judith Herzberg. No U.S. rental source.

CHILD OF OUR TIME. U.S., 1959. CBS-TV (CBS Playhouse). D: George Roy Hill. No U.S. rental source.

THE CHILDREN FROM NUMBER 67 *(Die Kinder aus N<u>o</u> 67)*. West Germany, 1979. D and S: Usch Barthelmess-Weller and Werner Meyer. No U.S. rental source.

CHILDREN IN THE HOLOCAUST. U.S., 1981. ABC-TV. D: Joseph S. Kutrzeba. Narrated by Liv Ullmann. No U.S. rental source.

COLLECTIVE SCENE WITH THE SAINT. Poland, 1974. D: Mariusz Walter, with Andrzej Wajda playing a director trying to reconstruct an incident at Auschwitz. No U.S. rental source.

THE CONDEMNED OF ALTONA *(I Sequestrati di Altona)*. U.S./Italy, 1962. D: Vittorio De Sica. S: Abby Mann and Cesare Zavattini from the play by Jean-Paul Sartre. R: FI.

THE CONFESSIONS OF WINIFRED WAGNER *(Winifred Wagner und die Geschichte des Hauses Wahnfried 1914–1975)*. West Germany, 1975. D and S: Hans-Jürgen Syberberg. No U.S. rental source.

CONFIDENCE *(Bizalom)*. Hungary, 1980. D and S: István Szabó. R: NYF.

THE CONFRONTATION *(Konfrontation)*. Switzerland, 1975. D: Rolf Lyssy. S: Georg Janett and Lyssy. R: NYF.

CONSPIRACY OF HEARTS. Great Britain, 1960. D: Ralph Thomas. S: Robert Presnell, Jr., R: FI. (Also a U.S. TV drama, 1956: Alcoa/Goodyear Theater, directed by Robert Mulligan.)

THE DAMNED *(La Caduta degli Dei)*. Italy, 1969. D: Luchino Visconti. S: Nicola Badalucco, Enrico Medioli, and Visconti. R: FI.

DAVID. West Germany, 1979. D: Peter Lilienthal. S: Lilienthal, Jurek Becker, and Ulla Zieman, from the autobiographical novel by Joel König. R: KINO.

DEATH IS CALLED ENGELCHEN. Czechoslovakia, 1963. D: Jan Kadár and Elmar Klos. No U.S. rental source.

DEATH IS MY TRADE *(Aus Einem Deutschen Leben)*. West Germany, 1976. D and S: Theodor Kotulla, based on the novel by Robert Merle. No U.S. rental source.

DIAMONDS OF THE NIGHT. Czechoslovakia, 1964. D: Jan Nemec. S: Arnost Lustig and Nemec from Lusting's novel. R: ICARUS.

THE DIARY OF ANNE FRANK. U.S., 1959. D: George Stevens. S: Frances Goodrich and Albert Hackett, from their own play. R: FI.

THE DISTANT JOURNEY *(Ghetto Terezin)*. Czechoslovakia, 1949. D and S: Alfréd Radok. No U.S. rental source.

THE EIGHTY-FIRST BLOW. Israel, 1975. R: Alden Films, 7820 20 Ave., Brooklyn, N.Y. 11214.

THE ENCLOSURE *(L'Enclos)*. France/Yugoslavia, 1962. D: Armand Gatti. S: Gatti and Pierre Joffroy. No U.S. rental source.

THE END OF THE WORLD *(Koniec Naszego Swiata)*. Poland, 1964. D: Wanda Jakubowska. (Sequel to *The Last Stop*.) No U.S. rental source.

ERA NOTTE A ROMA. See *It Was Night in Rome* below.

EROICA. Poland, 1957. D: Andrzej Munk. S: Jerzy S. Stawinski from his novels. No U.S. rental source.

THE EVACUEES. Great Britain, 1975. BBC-TV. D: Alan Parker. No U.S. rental source.

EXODUS. U.S., 1960. D: Otto Preminger. S: Dalton Trumbo from the novel by Leon Uris. R: UA.

FEAR NOT, JACOB! West Germany, 1981. D: Radu Gabrea. S: Meir Dohnal, Frieder Schuller, and Gabrea. No U.S. rental source.

THE FIANCÉE *(Die Verlobte)*. East Germany, 1980. D: Günter Reisch and Gunther Rücker. S: Rücker, from three autobiographical novels by Eva Lippold. No U.S. rental source.

THE FIFTH HORSEMAN IS FEAR. Czechoslovakia, 1964. D and S: Zbynek Brynych, based on a story by Jana Belehradska. R: FI.

FIVE MINUTES OF PARADISE. Yugoslavia, 1959. D: Igor Pretnar. No U.S. rental source.

FOREVER YESTERDAY. U.S., 1980. TV documentary, WNEW-TV with the Holocaust Survivors Film Project. R: WNEW-TV, 250 E. 67th St., New York, N.Y. 10021.

THE GARDEN OF THE FINZI-CONTINIS *(Il Giardino dei Finzi-Contini)*. Italy, 1970. D: Vittorio De Sica. S: Cesare Zavattini, Vittorio Bonicelli, and Ugo Pirro, based on the novel by Giorgio Bassani. R: C5.

THE GATHERING. Great Britain, 1981. Produced by Rex Bloomstein, BBC. R: WNET-TV, New York, 250 E. 67th St., New York, N.Y. 10021.

GENERAL DELLA ROVERE *(Il Generale della Rovere)*. Italy, 1959. D: Roberto Rossellini. S: Sergio Amidei, Diego Fabbri, Indro Montanelli, and Rossellini. R: IMAGES.

A GENERATION *(Pokolenie)*. Poland, 1955. D: Andrzej Wajda. S: Bohdan Czeszko. R: FI.

GENOCIDE. Great Britain, 1975. Thames-TV for *World at War* series. D: Michael Darlow. S: Charles Bloomberg. Narrated by Sir Laurence Olivier. R: A-DL.

GENOCIDE. U.S., 1981. D: Arnold Schwartzman. S: Martin Gilbert and Rabbi Marvin Hier. R: Simon Wiesenthal Center, 9760 West Pico Blvd., Los Angeles, Calif. 90035.

GERMANY, PALE MOTHER *(Deutschland, Bleiche Mütter)*. West Germany, 1980. D: Helma Sanders-Brahms. No U.S. rental source.

THE GOLD OF ROME *(L'Oro di Roma)*. Italy, 1961. D: Carlo Lizzani. S: Lucio Battistrada, Giuliani de Negri, Alberto Lecco, and Lizzani. R: FI.

GRAND ILLUSION *(La Grande Illusion)*. France, 1937. D: Jean Renoir. S: Charles Spaak and Renoir. R: IMAGES.

THE GREAT DICTATOR. U.S., 1940. D and S: Charles Chaplin. R: FI.

HIGH STREET *(Rue Haute)*. Belgium, 1976. D: André Ernotte. S: Elliot Tiber and Ernotte. No U.S. rental source.

HOLOCAUST. U.S., 1978. NBC-TV production. D: Marvin Chomsky. S: Gerald Green. R: LCA.

HOLOCAUST—THE SURVIVORS GATHER: A LOOK BACK. U.S., 1981. D: Joel Levitch. R: Public Broadcasting Service.

HOW TO BE LOVED *(Jak być Kochana)*. Poland, 1963. D: Wojciech Has. S: Kazimierz Brandys. No U.S. rental source.

I SURVIVED CERTAIN DEATH. Czechoslovakia, 1960. D: Vójtech Jasný. No U.S. rental source.

I WAS A KAPO *(Bylem Kapo)*. Poland, 1964. D: Tadeusz Jaworski. No U.S. rental source.

IMAGE BEFORE MY EYES. U.S., 1980. D: Josh Waletzky. S: Jerome Badanes. R: C5.

IN DARK PLACES. U.S., 1978. D: Gina Blumenfeld. R: PHOENIX.

IN THE COUNTRY OF MY PARENTS. West Germany, 1982. D: Jeanine Meerapfel. No U.S. rental source.

IN THE NAME OF THE FÜHRER *(Au Nom du Führer)*. Belgium, 1977. D: Lydia Chagoll. No U.S. rental source.

IN THE PRESENCE OF MINE ENEMIES. U.S., 1960. CBS-TV (Playhouse 90). D: Fielder Cook. S: Rod Serling. With Charles Laughton and Robert Redford. No U.S. rental source.

IT WAS NIGHT IN ROME *(Era Notte a Roma)*. Italy, 1960. D: Roberto Rossellini. S: Sergio Amidei, Diego Fabbri, Brunello Rondi, and Rossellini. R: FI.

JACOB, THE LIAR *(Jacob, der Lügner)*. East Germany, 1978. D: Frank Beyer. S: Jurek Becker, from his novel. R: FI.

JUD SÜSS. Germany, 1940. D: Viet Harlan. No U.S. rental source.

JUDGMENT AT NUREMBERG. U.S., 1961. D: Stanley Kramer. S: Abby Mann. R: UA. (Also done in 1959 on CBS-TV, Playhouse 90, directed by George Roy Hill, with Claude Rains in the Spencer Tracy film role and Maximilian Schell playing same role in both versions.)

JULIA. U.S., 1977. D: Fred Zinnemann. S: Alvin Sargent, based on Lillian Hellman's *Pentimento*. R: FI.

JUST A GIGOLO. Great Britain, 1979. D: David Hemmings. S: Joshua Sinclair. R: UA.

KANAL. Poland, 1957. D: Andrzej Wajda. S: Jerzy S. Stawinski. R: FI.

KAPO. Italy, 1960. D: Gillo Pontecorvo. S: Franco Solinas and Pontecorvo. R: FI.

KASSBACH. Austria, 1979. D: Peter Patzak. No U.S. rental source.

KITTY: RETURN TO AUSCHWITZ. Great Britain, 1980. TV (Yorkshire Television). D: Peter Morley. R: Public Broadcasting Service.

LACOMBE, LUCIEN. France, 1974. D: Louis Malle. S: Patrick Modiano and Malle. R: FI.

LANDSCAPE AFTER BATTLE *(Krajobraz Po Bitwe)*. Poland, 1970. D: Andrzej Wajda. S: Andrzej Brzozowski and Wajda, based on stories by Tadeusz Borowski. R: NYF.

THE LAST CHANCE *(Die letzte Chance)*. Switzerland, 1945. D: Leopold Lindtberg. No U.S. rental source.

THE LAST METRO *(Le Dernier Métro)*. France, 1980. D: François Truffaut. S: Suzanne Schiffman, Jean-Claude Grumberg, and Truffaut. R: UA.

THE LAST STOP *(Ostatni Etap)*. Poland, 1948. D: Wanda Jakubowska. S: Gerda Schneider and Jakubowska. (There is one print at the Museum of Modern Art in New York City.)

L'CHAIM—TO LIFE! U.S., 1973. D: Harold Mayer. R: Harold Mayer Productions, 50 Ferriss Estate, New Milford, Conn. 06776.

THE LEGACY: CHILDREN OF HOLOCAUST SURVIVORS. U.S., 1980. D: Miriam Strilky Rosenbush. R: Viewfinders, P.O. Box 1665, Evanston, Ill. 60204.

LILI MARLEEN. West Germany, 1981. D: Rainer Werner Fassbinder. S: Manfred Purzer and Joshua Sinclair from Lale Andersen's autobiography. R: UA.

LISSY. East Germany, 1957. D: Konrad Wolf. S: Alex Wedding and Wolf, from a novel by F.C. Weiskopf. R: FI.

LUCKY STAR. Canada, 1980. D: Max Fisher. No U.S. rental source.

MALOU. West Germany, 1982. D and S: Jeanine Meerapfel. R: Quartet Films, 60 E. 42nd St., New York, N.Y. 10016.

THE MAN IN THE GLASS BOOTH. U.S., 1975. American Film Theatre. D: Arthur Hiller. S: Edward Anhalt, from the play by Robert Shaw. R: PAR.

THE MARATHON MAN. U.S., 1976. D: John Schlesinger. S: William Goldman, from his novel. R: FI, PAR.

MARIANNE AND JULIANE *(Die Bleierne Zeit)*. West Germany, 1981. D: Margarethe von Trotta, based on the book by Christiane Ensslin. R: NYF.

THE MARRIAGE OF MARIA BRAUN *(Die Ehe der Maria Braun)*. West Germany, 1978. D: Rainer Werner Fassbinder. S: Peter Märthesheimer and Pia Fröhlich. R: NYF.

MEIN KAMPF. Sweden, 1960. D: Erwin Leiser. No U.S. rental source.

MEMORANDUM. Canada, 1965. D: Donald Brittain and John Spotten. R: A-DL, IMAGES.

THE MEMORY OF JUSTICE. U.S., 1976. D: Marcel Ophuls. R: PAR.

MEPHISTO. Hungary, 1981. D: István Szabó. S: Peter Dobai and Szabó, based on the novel by Klaus Mann. No U.S. rental source.

MR. KLEIN. France, 1976. D: Joseph Losey. S: Franco Solinas. R: FI.

THE MORTAL STORM. U.S., 1940. D: Frank Borzage. S: Claudine West, George Froeschel, and Andersen Ellis, based on the novel by Phyllis Bottome. R: FI.

MURDERERS ARE AMONG US *(Die Mörder Sind unter Uns)*. East Germany, 1946. D and S: Wolfgang Staudte. R: FI.

MUSIC OF AUSCHWITZ. U.S., 1978. CBS-TV (*60 Minutes* "On Fania Fenelon"). R: A-DL.

MY NAME IS IVAN *(Ivanovo Detstvo)*. U.S.S.R., 1962. D: Andrei Tarkovsky. R: FI.

NIGHT AND FOG *(Nuit et Brouillard)*. France, 1955. D: Alain Resnais. S: Jean Cayrol. R: IMAGES.

THE NIGHT PORTER *(Il Portiere di Notte)*. Italy, 1974. D: Liliana Cavani. S: Italo Moscati and Cavani. No U.S. rental source.

THE NINTH CIRCLE. Yugoslavia, 1960. D: France Stiglic. No U.S. rental source.

NOW . . . AFTER ALL THESE YEARS *(Jetzt . . . nach so viel Jahren)*. West Germany, 1981. TV production. D: Harald Lüders and Pavel Schnabel. R: Arthur Cantor, Inc., 33 West 60th St., New York, N.Y. 10023.

NOW DO YOU GET IT, WHY I AM CRYING? Holland, 1973. D: Louis van Gasteren. No U.S. rental source.

NUREMBERG. U.S., 1946. Compiled by Pare Lorentz and Stuart Schulberg. R: IMAGES.

OBEDIENCE. U.S., 1962. Documentary of the Milgram experiments at Yale University. R: NYU Film Library, 156 Washington Square, New York, N.Y. 10003.

THE OCCUPATION IN 26 PICTURES. Yugoslavia, 1979. D: Lordan Zafranovic. No U.S. rental source.

ONCE UPON A HONEYMOON. U.S., 1942. D: Leo McCarey. S: Sheridan Gibney and McCarey. R: FI.

ONE MAN'S WAR *(La Guerre d'un Seul Homme)*. France, 1981. D and S: Edgardo Cozarinsky, based on Ernst Jünger's Parisian diaries. R: WNET-TV, New York, 250 E. 67th St., New York, N.Y. 10021.

THE ONLY WAY. Denmark, 1967. D: Bent Christiansen. With Jane Seymour. R: JWB Lecture Bureau.

OPEN CITY *(Roma, Città Aperta)*. Italy, 1945. D: Roberto Rossellini. S: Sergio Amidei, Federico Fellini, and Rossellini. R: IMAGES.

ORDINARY FASCISM. U.S.S.R., 1967. D and S: Mikhael Romm. No U.S. rental source.

OUR HITLER, A FILM FROM GERMANY *(Hitler, ein Film aus Deutschland)*. West Germany, 1978. D: Hans-Jürgen Syberberg. No U.S. rental source, but released in U.S. by Zoetrope Studios.

PASSENGER *(Pasażerka)*. Poland, 1962. D: Andrzej Munk (film completed by Witold Lesiewicz). S: Zofia Posmysz and Munk, based on novel by Posmysz. R: FI.

THE PAWNBROKER. U.S., 1965. D: Sidney Lumet. S: Morton Fine and David Friedkin, from the novel by Edward Lewis Wallant. R: FI.

PLAYING FOR TIME. U.S., 1980. CBS-TV drama. D: Daniel Mann. S: Arthur Miller, from Fania Fenelon's autobiographical account. No U.S. rental source.

THE PRODUCERS. U.S., 1967. D and S: Mel Brooks. R: IMAGES.

PROFESSOR MAMLOCK. U.S.S.R., 1937. D: Adolph Minkin and Herbert Rappaport. S: Friedrich Wolf, from his play. No U.S. rental source.

RAINDROPS *(Regentropfen).* West Germany, 1982. D and S: Michael Hoffmann and Harry Raymon. No U.S. rental source.

THE RAVEN *(Le Corbeau).* France, 1943. D: Henri-Georges Clouzot. S: Louis Chavance. R: FI, BUD.

RETURN FROM THE ASHES. Great Britain, 1965. D: J. Lee Thompson. S: Julius J. Epstein, from novel by Hubert Monteilhet. R: UA.

RETURN TO POLAND. U.S., 1981. TV film. D and S: Marian Marzynski. R: WGBH, 125 Western Ave., Boston, Mass. 02134.

REUNION *(Le Retour).* U.S., 1946. D: Henri-Cartier Bresson, for U.S. Information Service. No U.S. rental source.

ROADS IN THE NIGHT *(Wege in der Nacht).* West Germany, 1980. D: Krzysztof Zanussi. R: Teleculture.

SAMSON. Poland, 1961. D: Andrzej Wajda. S: Kazimierz Brandys and Wajda. R: FI.

SANDRA *(Vaghe Stelle dell'Orsa).* Italy, 1965. D: Luchino Visconti. S: Suso Cecchi d'Amico, Enrico Medioli, and Visconti. R: COR.

THE SERPENT'S EGG. U.S./West Germany, 1977. D and S: Ingmar Bergman. R: PAR.

SEVEN BEAUTIES *(Pasqualino Settebelezze).* Italy, 1975. D and S: Lina Wertmüller. R: C5.

SHADOW OF DOUBT *(Een schijn van twijfel).* Holland, 1975. D: Rolf Orthel. R: NYF.

SHIP OF FOOLS. U.S., 1965. D: Stanley Kramer. S: Abby Mann, based on the novel by Katherine Anne Porter. R: FI.

THE SHOP ON MAIN STREET *(Obchod na Korze).* Czechoslovakia, 1965. D: Jan Kadár and Elmar Klos. S: Ladislav Grosman. R: FI.

THE SICK MEN WHO GOVERN US *(Ces Malades Qui Nous Gouvernent).* France, 1980. D: Claude Vajda. S: Vajda, based on the book by Pierre Accoce and Pierre Rentchnick. No U.S. rental source.

SIGHET, SIGHET. U.S., 1964. D: Harold Becker. S: Elie Wiesel. R: IMAGES.

SKOKIE. U.S., 1981. CBS-TV drama. D: Herbert Wise. S: Ernest Kinoy. No U.S. rental source.

SOMEWHERE IN EUROPE *(Valahol Europaban).* Hungary, 1947. D: Geza von Radvànyi. No U.S. rental source.

SOPHIE'S CHOICE. U.S., 1982. D and S: Alan Pakula, from the novel by William Styron. No U.S. rental source as yet.

THE SORROW AND THE PITY *(Le Chagrin et la Pitié).* France, 1970. (Produced for Switzerland's Lausanne Télévision Rencontre.) D: Marcel Ophuls. R: C5.

SPECIAL SECTION *(Section Spéciale).* France, 1975. D: Costa-Gavras. S: Jorge Semprun and Costa-Gavras, based on the book by Hervé Villeré. R: UNIV.

STARS *(Sterne).* East Germany, 1958. D: Konrad Wolf and Rangel Vulchanov. S: Anzhel Vagenstein and Christa Wernicke. R: FI.

SWEET LIGHT IN A DARK ROOM *(Romeo, Julie a Tma).* Czechoslovakia, 1959. D: Jiri Weiss. S: Jan Otcenasek. R: FI.

TEAR IN THE OCEAN *(Une Larme dans l'Océan).* France, 1971. D: Henri Glaeser. S: Glaeser, based on the novel by Manès Sperber. No U.S. rental source.

TEMPORARY PARADISE *(Ideiglenes Paradicsom).* Hungary, 1981. D and S: Andras Kovacs. With André Dussollier. No U.S. rental source.

THE TIN DRUM *(Die Blechtrommel).* West Germany, 1979. D: Volker Schlöndorff. S: Jean-Claude Carrière, Franz Seitz, and Schlöndorff, from the novel by Günter Grass. R: FI.

TO BE OR NOT TO BE. U.S., 1942. D: Ernst Lubitsch. S: Edwin Justus Mayer. R: IMAGES.

TOP SECRET—THE HISTORY OF THE GERMAN RESISTANCE AGAINST HITLER *(Geheime Reichssache).* West Germany, 1979. D: Jochen Bauer. S: Karl-Heinz Janszen. No U.S. rental source.

TRANSPORT FROM PARADISE. Czechoslovakia, 1962. D: Zbynek Brynych. S: Brynych, based on book by Arnost Lustig. R: ICARUS.

TRIUMPH OF THE WILL *(Triumph des Willens)*. Germany, 1935. D: Leni Rienfenstahl. R: IMAGES.

25 FIREMAN'S STREET. Hungary, 1973. D: István Szabó. R: FI.

THE TWO OF US *(Le Vieil Homme et l'Enfant)*. France, 1966. D and S: Claude Berri. R: COR.

VICTORY. U.S., 1981. D: John Huston. S: Evan Jones and Yabo Yablonsky. R: PAR.

LES VIOLONS DU BAL (American as well as French release title). France, 1973. D and S: Michel Drach. R: FI.

VOYAGE OF THE DAMNED. Great Britain, 1976. D: Stuart Rosenberg. S: Steve Shagan and David Butler. R: FI.

THE WALL. U.S., 1982. CBS-TV. D: Robert Markowitz. S: Millard Lampell, from the novel by John Hersey. No U.S. rental source.

THE WARSAW GHETTO. Great Britain, 1968. BBC-TV. R: IMAGES.

THE WAVE. U.S., 1981. ABC-TV. D: Alex Grasshoff. S: Johnny Dawkins, from autobiographical story by Ron Jones.

WE WERE GERMAN JEWS. U.S./West Germany, 1981. D: Michael Blackwood. R: Blackwood Productions, N.Y.

WHO SHALL LIVE AND WHO SHALL DIE? U.S., 1981. D: Laurence Jarvik. R: KINO.

THE WITNESSES *(Le Temps du Ghetto)*. France, 1962. D: Frédéric Rossif. R: FI.

Rental Sources

A-DL: Anti-Defamation League of B'nai B'rith, 823 UN Plaza, New York, N.Y. 10017.

BUD: Budget Films, 4590 Santa Monica Blvd., L.A., Calif. 90029.

C5: Almi-Cinema 5, 1500 Broadway, N.Y., N.Y. 10036.

COR: Corinth Films, 410 E. 62 St., N.Y., N.Y. 10021.

FI: Films, Incorporated. 440 Park Avenue South, N.Y., N.Y. 10016.

HUR: Hurlock Cine-World, 13 Arcadia Rd., Old Greenwich, Ct. 06870.

ICARUS: Icarus Films, 200 Park Ave. South, N.Y., N.Y. 10003.

IMAGES: Images Film Archive, 300 Phillips Park Rd., Mamaroneck, N.Y. 10543.

JWB: Jewish Welfare Board/Jewish Media Service, 15 E. 26 St., N.Y., N.Y. 10010.

KINO: Kino International, 250 W. 57 St., New York, N.Y. 10019.

LCA: Learning Corporation of America, 1350 Ave. of the Americas, N.Y., N.Y. 10019.

NYF: New Yorker Films, 16 W. 61 St., N.Y., N.Y. 10023.

PAR: Paramount Non-Theatrical, 5451 Marathon St., Hollywood, Cal. 90038.

PHOENIX: Phoenix Films, 470 Park Ave. South, N.Y., N.Y. 10016.

UA: United Artists 16, 729 Seventh Ave., N.Y., N.Y. 10019.

UNIV: Universal 16, 445 Park Ave., N.Y., N.Y. 10022.

Note: There is a growing collection at the National Center for Jewish Film. Contact Sharon Pucker Rivo, Film Curator, Lown Building/102, Brandeis University, Waltham, Mass. 02254.

BIBLIOGRAPHY

Books

Agee, James. *Let Us Now Praise Famous Men.* New York: Ballantine Books, 1972.

Ainsztein, Reuben. *Jewish Resistance in Nazi-Occupied Eastern Europe.* New York: Barnes and Noble, 1975.

Ainsztein, Reuben. *The Warsaw Ghetto Revolt.* New York: The Holocaust Library, 1978.

Alexander, Edward. *The Resonance of Dust: Essays on Holocaust Literature and Jewish Fate.* Ohio State University Press, 1979.

Arendt, Hannah. *The Origins of Totalitarianism.* New York: Harcourt, Brace, 1951.

The Auschwitz Album, text by Peter Hellman. New York: Random House, 1981.

Barnouw, Erik. *Documentary: A History of the Non-Fiction Film.* New York: Oxford University Press, 1974.

Bassani, Giorgio. *The Garden of the Finzi-Continis.* Trans. William Weaver. New York: Harcourt Brace Jovanovich, 1977.

Bauer, Yehuda. *American Jewry and the Holocaust.* Detroit: Wayne State University Press, 1981.

Bazin, André and Eric Rohmer. *Charlie Chaplin.* Paris: Les Editions du Cerf, 1972.

Bazin, André. *What Is Cinema?* Vol. I. Trans. Hugh Gray. Berkeley: University of California Press, 1967.

Bettelheim, Bruno. *The Informed Heart.* London: Thames and Hudson, 1961.

Bettelheim, Bruno. *Surviving and Other Essays.* New York: Knopf, 1979.

Borowski, Tadeusz. *This Way to the Gas, Ladies and Gentlemen.* New York: Viking, 1976.

Brady, John. *The Craft of the Screenwriter.* New York: Simon and Schuster, 1981.

Demetz, Hana. *The House on Prague Street.* New York: St. Martin's Press, 1980.

Dawidowicz, Lucy. *The Jewish Presence: Essays on Identity and History.* New York: Holt, Rinehart and Winston, 1977.

Dawidowicz, Lucy. *The War Against the Jews, 1933–1945.* New York: Holt, Rinehart and Winston, 1975.

Des Pres, Terrence. *The Survivor: An Anatomy of Life in the Death Camps.* New York: Pocket Books, 1977.

Donat, Alexander (ed.). *The Death Camp Treblinka.* New York: Schocken Books, 1979.

Donat, Alexander. *The Holocaust Kingdom.* New York: Schocken Books, 1978.

Eisner, Jack. *The Survivor.* New York: William Morrow, 1980.

Esslin, Martin. *The Theatre of the Absurd.* New York: Anchor Books, 1961.

Ezrahi, Sidra DeKoven. *By Words Alone: The Holocaust in Literature.* University of Chicago Press, 1980.

Feingold, Henry. *The Politics of Rescue.* New York: The Holocaust Library, 1980.

Fenelon, Fania. *The Musicians of Auschwitz.* With Marcelle Routier. Trans. Judith Landry. London: Joseph, 1977.

Fine, Ellen. *Legacies of Night: The Literary Universe of Elie Wiesel.* New York: State University of New York Press, 1982.

Frank, Anne. *The Diary of a Young Girl.* New York: Pocket Books, 1952.

Freud, Sigmund. *Group Psychology and the Analysis of the Ego.* Trans. James Strachey. New York: Bantam Books, 1971.

Friedlander, Albert. (ed.) *Out of the Whirlwind: A Reader of Holocaust Literature.* New York: Doubleday, 1968.

Friedlander, Saul. *When Memory Comes.* Trans. Helen R. Lane. New York: Farrar, Straus, Giroux, 1979.

Friedman, Lester. *Hollywood's Image of the Jew.* New York: Frederick Ungar, 1982.

Friedman, Philip. *Their Brothers' Keepers.* New York: The Holocaust Library, 1978.

Garlinski, Jozef. *Fighting Auschwitz.* New York: Fawcett Crest, 1975.

Gordon, Thomas and Max Morgan Witts. *Voyage of the Damned.* New York: Stein and Day, 1974.

Green, Gerald. *Holocaust.* New York: Bantam Books, 1978.

Hallie, Philip P. *Lest Innocent Blood Be Shed.* New York: Harper and Row, 1979.

Hart, Kitty. *I Am Alive.* London and New York: Abelard-Schuman, 1962.

Hellman, Peter. *Avenue of the Righteous.* New York: Atheneum, 1980.

Henri-Lévy, Bernard. *Le Testament de Dieu.* Paris: Grasset, 1979.

Hersey, John. *The Wall.* New York: Knopf, 1950.

Hilberg, Raul. *The Destruction of the European Jews.* New York: Octagon Books, 1978.

The Holocaust. Compiled from material originally published in the *Encyclopedia Judaica.* Jerusalem: Keter Books, 1974.

Hull, David Stewart. *Film in the Third Reich.* New York: Simon and Schuster, 1973.

Kael, Pauline. *Reeling.* Boston: Little, Brown, 1976.

Kael, Pauline. *When the Lights Go Down.* New York: Holt, Rinehart and Winston, 1980.

Kaplan, Chaim A. *The Warsaw Diary of Chaim Kaplan.* Trans. Abraham Katoh. New York: Collier, 1973.

Kogon, Eugen. *The Theory and Practice of Hell.* Trans. Heinz Norden. New York: Farrar, Straus, 1953.

Korczak, Janusz. *Ghetto Diary.* New York: Schocken Books, 1978.

Kracauer, Siegfried. *From Caligari to Hitler: A Psychological History of the German Film.* Princeton University Press, 1974.

Kracauer, Siegfried. *Theory of Film: The Redemption of Physical Reality.* New York: Oxford University Press, 1960.

Kraus, Ota and Erich Kulka. *The Death Factory: Document on Auschwitz.* Trans. Stephen Jolly. Oxford: Pergamon, 1966.

Kurzman, Dan. *The Bravest Battle: The Twenty-Eight Days of the Warsaw Ghetto Uprising.* New York: Putnam's, 1976.

Langer, Lawrence. *The Holocaust and the Literary Imagination.* New Haven: Yale University Press, 1975.

Langer, Lawrence. *Versions of Survival: The Holocaust and the Human Spirit.* New York: State University of New York Press, 1982.

Lanzmann, Claude. *The Bird Has No Wings.* New York: St. Martin's Press, 1976.

Laqueur, Walter. *The Terrible Secret: The Suppression of Information About Hitler's Final Solution.* Boston: Little, Brown, 1981.

Leitner, Isabella. *Fragments of Isabella.* New York: Crowell, 1978.

Levi, Primo. *Survival in Auschwitz.* Trans. Stuart Woof. New York: Collier, 1969.

Levy, Claude. *La Grande Rafle du Vel' d'hiv.* Paris: Laffont, 1967.

Lustig, Arnost. *Darkness Casts No Shadow.* Trans. Jeanne Nemcova. Washington: Inscape, 1976. (Basis for *Diamonds of the Night.*)

Lustig, Arnost. *Night and Hope.* Trans. George Theiner. Iowa City: University of Iowa Press, 1972.

Lustig, Arnost. *A Prayer for Katerina Horovitzova.* Trans. Jeanne Nemcova. New York: Harper and Row, 1973.

Marrus, Michael and Robert Paxton. *Vichy France and the Jews.* New York: Basic Books, 1981.

Michalek, Boleslaw. *The Cinema of Andrzej Wajda.* Trans. Edward Rothert. London: The Tantivy Press, 1973.

Milosz, Czeslaw. *Native Realm.* Trans. Catherine S. Leach. New York: Doubleday, 1981.

Monaco, James. *How To Read A Film.* New York: Oxford University Press, 1981.

Morse, Arthur. *While Six Million Died: A Chronicle of American Apathy.* New York: Random House, 1968.

Novich, Miriam. *Sobibor: Martyrdom and Revolt.* New York: The Holocaust Library, 1980.

Ophuls, Marcel. *The Sorrow and the Pity.* Trans. Mireille Johnston. New York: Outerbridge and Lazard, 1972. (Distributed by E.P. Dutton and Co.)

Pisar, Samuel. *Of Blood and Hope.* Boston: Little, Brown, 1980.

Poliakov, Léon. *Harvest of Hate.* New York: The Holocaust Library, 1978.

Rabinowitz, Dorothy. *New Lives: Survivors of the Holocaust Living in America.* New York: Knopf, 1976.

Ringelblum, Emmanuel. *Notes from the Warsaw Ghetto.* Trans. Jacob Sloan. New York: McGraw-Hill, 1958.

Rosenfeld, Alvin. H. and Irving Greenberg. *Confronting the Holocaust: The Impact of Elie Wiesel.* University of Indiana Press, 1978.

Rosenfeld, Alvin. H. *A Double Dying: Reflection on Holocaust Literature.* University of Indiana Press, 1980.

Semprun, Jorge. *The Long Voyage.* Trans. Richard Seaver. New York: Grove, 1964.

Shirer, William. *The Rise and Fall of the Third Reich.* New York: Simon and Schuster, 1960.

Siclier, Jacques. *La France de Pétain et son cinéma.* Paris: Henri Veyrier, 1981.

Sontag, Susan. *Under the Sign of Saturn.* New York: Vintage, 1981.

Steiner, George. *In Bluebeard's Castle: Some Notes Towards the Redefinition of Culture.* New Haven: Yale University Press, 1971.

Steiner, George. *Language and Silence.* New York: Atheneum, 1966.

Styron, William. *Sophie's Choice.* New York: Random House, 1979.

Suhl, Yuri. *They Fought Back: The Story of the Jewish Resistance in Nazi Europe.* New York: Schocken Books, 1975.

Sypher, Wylie (ed.). *Comedy.* New York: Doubleday, 1956.

Timerman, Jacobo. *Prisoner without a Name, Cell without a Number.* Trans. Toby Talbot. New York: Knopf, 1981.

Truffaut, François. *The Films in My Life.* Trans. Leonard Mayhew. New York: Simon and Schuster, 1978.

Vogel, Amos. *Film As A Subversive Art.* New York: Random House, 1974.

The Wajda Trilogy. London: Lorrimer Publishing, 1973.

Wallant, Edward Lewis. *The Pawnbroker.* New York: Harcourt Brace and World, 1961.

Weinberg, Herman G. *The Lubitsch Touch.* New York: Dover Publications, 1977.

Weinstock, Eugene. *Beyond the Last Path.* Trans. Clara Ryan. New York: Boni and Gaer, 1947.

Wiesel, Elie. *A Jew Today.* Trans. Marion Wiesel. New York: Random House, Vintage, 1978.

Wiesel, Elie. *Night.* Trans. Stella Rodway. New York: Avon Books, 1969.

Articles

Alter, Robert. "Deformations of the Holocaust," *Commentary,* February 1981.

Atlas, James. "The Creative Journey of Arthur Miller," *The New York Times* (Arts and Leisure), Sunday, September 28, 1980.

Byron, Stuart. "Truffaut and Gays," *The Village Voice,* October 29–November 4, 1980.

Chase, Chris. "A Village That Saved Its Jews," *The New York Times,* Friday, July 19, 1982.

Clarens, Carlos. "The Dark Ages," *The Soho Weekly News,* Jan. 19, 1982.

Dawidowicz, Lucy. "American Jews and the Holocaust," *The New York Times* (Magazine), Sunday, April 18, 1982.

Dawidowicz, Lucy. "Visualizing the Warsaw Ghetto: Nazi Images of the Jews Refiltered by the BBC," *Shoah* 1, 1.

Denby, David. " 'Whoever Controls Film Controls History,' " *New York,* January 28, 1980.

Des Pres, Terrence. "The Bettelheim Problem," *Social Research,* Winter 1979.

Des Pres, Terrence. "Black Comedies," *Harper's,* June 1976.

Des Pres, Terrence. "War Crimes," *Harper's,* January 1977.

Doneson, Judith. "The Jew as a Female Figure in Holocaust Film," *Shoah* 1, 1.

Fine, Ellen. "Dialogue with Elie Wiesel," *Centerpoint* IV, 1, Issue 13 "The Holocaust," Fall 1980.

Goldstein, Richard. "Whose Holocaust?", *The Village Voice,* December 10, 1979.

Hoberman, J. "The Führer Furor," *The Village Voice,* January 14, 1980.

Hughes, John. *"The Tin Drum:* Volker Schlöndorff's 'Dream of Childhood,' " *Film Quarterly,* Spring 1981.

Insdorf, Annette. *"David:* A German-Jewish Film About the Holocaust," *Martyrdom and Resistance* 8, 2, March-April, 1982.

Insdorf, Annette. "Heroism amid the Holocaust," *Newsday,* Sunday, May 18, 1982.

Insdorf, Annette. "How Truffaut's 'Last Metro' Reflects Occupied Paris," *The New York Times* (Arts and Leisure), Sunday, February 8, 1981.

Insdorf, Annette. "Oscar Treatment of Art in the Nazi State," *Newsday,* Sunday, April 4, 1982.

Insdorf, Annette. "A Passion for Social Justice," *Cineaste* XI, 4, Winter 1982.

Insdorf, Annette. "A Swiss Film Bares Another Chapter of the Holocaust," *The New York Times* (Arts and Leisure), Sunday, October 18, 1981.

Insdorf, Annette. "Von Trotta: By Sisters Obsessed," *The New York Times* (Arts and Leisure), Sunday, January 31, 1982.

Insdorf, Annette. " 'Who Will Live?' Explodes Myths of Holocaust," *The Los Angeles Times* (Calendar Section), January 14, 1982.

Isaac, Dan. "Film and the Holocaust," *Centerpoint* IV, 1, Issue 13, Fall 1980.

Kroll, Jack. "The Activist Actress," *Newsweek,* Sept. 29, 1980.

Kroll, Jack. "The Hitler Within Us," *Newsweek,* January 28, 1980.

Liebman, Robert L. "Two Survivors: Lilienthal and His Film *David,* " *Long Island Jewish World,* Oct. 30–Nov. 5, 1981.

Maslin, Janet. "Bringing 'Sophie's Choice' to the Screen," *The New York Times* (Arts and Leisure), Sunday, May 9, 1982.

Middleton, Drew. "Why TV Is Fascinated with the Hitler Era," *The New York Times* (Arts and Leisure), Sunday, Nov. 16, 1980.

O'Connor, John J. "Diverse Views of Nazi Germany," *The New York Times* (Arts and Leisure), Sunday, September 9, 1979.

Pappas, Peter. *"The Last Metro,"* *Cineaste* X,4, Fall 1980.

Ryan, Desmond. "Remembrances: Three Movies on the Holocaust," *The Philadelphia Inquirer,* Sunday, April 18, 1982. (On *David, Transport from Paradise,* and *Now . . . After All These Years.*)

Schiff, Ellen. "Plays About the Holocaust—Ashes into Art," *The New York Times* (Arts and Leisure), Sunday, Dec. 2, 1979.

Schlesinger, Arthur, Jr. "Filmed in New York," *American Heritage* 33,1, December 1981.

Sontag, Susan. "Eye of the Storm," *The New York Review of Books,* XXVII,2, February 21, 1980. Reprinted in *Under the Sign of Saturn.*

Toland, John. "Can TV Dramas Convey the Horrors of the Holocaust?", *TV Guide* 30, 7, February 13, 1982.

Van Gelder, Lawrence. "A German Filmmaker Looks at Adolf Hitler," *The New York Times* (Arts and Leisure), Sunday, January 13, 1980.

Ward, Alex. "A Producer of the Provocative: Herbert Brodkin," *The New York Times* (Arts and Leisure), Sunday, November 15, 1981.

Wasserman, Steve. "Filmmaker as Pariah," *The Village Voice,* January 14, 1980.

Yakir, Dan. "Bad Guys Never Looked So Good," *The New York Post,* August 6, 1981.

Foreign and Other Periodicals

L'Avant-Scène du Cinéma 1, février 1961: screenplay of *Night and Fog.* (English version in *Film: Book 2, Films of Peace and War,* ed. Robert Hughes, New York: Grove Press, 1962, pp. 234–255.)

L'Avant-Scène du Cinéma 47, avril 1965: "Spécial Polonais," including the screenplays of *Passenger* and *Ashes and Diamonds.*

L'Avant-Scène du Cinéma 127/128, juillet–septembre 1972: screenplay and assorted documents concerning *The Sorrow and the Pity.*

L'Avant-Scène du Cinéma 175, novembre 1976: screenplay of *Mr. Klein.*

Cahiers du Cinéma 301, juin 1979: article on *Holocaust,* "Le Four Banal," by Sylvie Pierre.

Centerpoint IV, 1, Issue 13, Fall 1980. Entire issue devoted to "The Holocaust" with various articles cited in Notes.

L'Illustration, 30 septembre 1941: reportage by Robert de Beauplan.

Impact: Revue du Cinéma Direct 10/11, 1979 (France).

International Journal of Political Education IV, ½, May 1981 (Netherlands): Dieter Prokop's research, *"Holocaust* and the Effects of Violence on Television."

New German Critique 19, Winter 1980: Special Issue, "Germans and Jews."

Le Nouvel Observateur, 1 juin 1981: article, "Quand Vichy déportait ses juifs."

INDEX

ABOUT THE AUTHOR

ANNETTE INSDORF was born in Paris, France. She
received her B.A. (summa cum laude) from Queens
College, and her M.A. and Ph.D. from Yale
University, where she was a Danforth Fellow. Dr.
Insdorf is Associate Professor of English and
American Studies at Yale University, where she has
been teaching film history and criticism since 1975.
She also teaches film at Columbia University.

Annette Insdorf is a frequent contributor to the
New York *Times* (Arts & Leisure) and her articles
have appeared in *American Film, Film Comment,*
the Los Angeles *Times, Cineaste* and *Newsday.* Her
previous book is the widely acclaimed *François
Truffaut,* the definitive study of the works of the
French director. A popular lecturer, translator,
panel moderator and T.V. personality, Dr. Insdorf
hosts "TéléFrance CinéClub," a national cable-TV
program, and "Years of Darkness," films about the
World War II experience shown by WNET in New
York. She also does a lecture series at the 92nd
Street "Y" in New York entitled "Understanding
the Holocaust through Film."